INTERTEXTU

INTERTEXTUALITY

:

debates and contexts

Mary Orr

polity

First published in 2003 by Polity Press in association with Blackwell Publishing Ltd

Editorial office:
Polity Press
65 Bridge Street
Cambridge CB2 1UR, UK

Marketing and production:
Blackwell Publishing Ltd
108 Cowley Road
Oxford OX4 1JF, UK

Distributed in the USA by
Blackwell Publishing Inc.
350 Main Street
Malden, MA 02148, USA

A catalogue record for this book is available from the British Library.

Library of Congress Cataloging-in-Publication Data
Orr, Mary, 1960–
Intertextuality : debates and contexts / Mary Orr.
p. cm.
Includes bibliographical references and index.
ISBN 0-7456-0621-0 – ISBN 0-7456-3121-5 (pbk.)
1. Intertextuality. I. Title.
PN98.158 O88 2003
809 – dc21

                                        2002154586

Typeset in 10.5 on 12 pt Plantin
by SNP Best-set Typesetter Ltd., Hong Kong
Printed and bound in Great Britain by MPG Books Limited, Bodmin, Cornwall

For further information on Polity, visit our website: www.polity.co.uk

Contents

Acknowledgements

This book could not have been written and completed without the following support. My particular thanks go to:

the University of Exeter, for granting research leave for the winter semester 2000–1, and my colleagues in the School of Modern Languages for shouldering my teaching and administration;

the AHRB, for a Research Leave Scheme Award for the summer semester 2001, and to my referees, Professor Michael Worton and Dr Graham Allan, for supporting the project;

Dr John Thompson and colleagues at Polity Press, for their patience and continued enthusiasm for the project;

Leslie Gray, for her careful reading and comments on the draft, and Dr Ian Johnson, for his insightful comments on chapter 4.

Last, but not least, thank you Neil for sharing in the journey of this book.

Prologue

A Palinode to 'Deconstruction'

Supercaligramma-listic hypertextulosis,
Even though the sound of it is something quite precocious. . . .

Meta-para-palimpsestic-intertextualitis
Even though the sound of it is medically frightening. . . .

Mary Poppins coined the word which kids can say like lightning,
Yet intertextual as term will never r-hym(n)e with writing.

$\star$ $\star$ $\star$

LEAR: Nothing will come of nothing: speak again.

King Lear, 1. i. 92

Serious studies of intertextuality do not normally begin with non-sense verse, or a parody of it. This is because, in high and popular culture, 'intertextuality' is the very non-frivolous name given by critical theory to inter- and intracultural dynamics and their operations. While there are differences of approach and application, books about intertextuality are unanimous about the etymology of the word: it was coined in the late 1960s by Julia Kristeva and enjoyed immediate and resounding success. Not least, as critical term and catchphrase, intertextuality captured the mood of May 1968 in its spearheading of extensive cultural reappraisal.[1] Non-hierarchical and democratically inclusive notions of text in a vast mosaic of other texts could now be prioritized. Such notions directly questioned and challenged pre-1968 ideologies. Among these were the concept of (1) a unified self (especially a male subject position in hierarchical structures of knowledge and power); (2) the pre-eminence of high-cultural expression (as essentially white, male and European); and (3) direct referential connections between language and the world (whether mimetic, semantic, symbolic or metaphysical). It was the model of Saussurian linguistics which was pivotal. It has only two terms, an arbitrarily connected signifier and signified, whereas other linguistics models include a third term of reference to the world outside language. Texts and intertextuality as complex linguistic systems therefore heralded for the late twentieth century an infinity of new cultural possibility through the endless connectivity of a world as 'super-text' or its later deconstruction.

Nonsense, however, uncovers some of the presuppositions and problems within Saussurian linguistics and hence intertextuality. As a non-language calqued onto dictionary language grammars and vocabularies, nonsense immediately questions how arbitrary the connections are in fact between signifier and signified. Even in the most arbitrarily assigned of sign systems, speakers nevertheless assume that communication will occur and recur because there is sufficient stability and consensus. Otherwise, interlocutors with varying levels of competency and linguistic sophistication could not be included, and the language system itself would only collapse into randomness or secret code. Because nonsense is not totally anarchic yet is quintessentially a non-utilitarian linguistic form, it then puts pressure on how such linguistic purposes can be distinguished within the Saussurian system. Trial and error cannot explain how speakers distinguish an utterance that is 'factual' from one that is mocking, jesting, ironic or poetic. By creating understandable 'words', nonsense presses the Saussurian model on a further issue. How can a system respond to new concepts? If it incorporates 'foreign' words or forges new words or neologisms from within a given linguistic rootstock, how are these also arbitrary?

Nonsense verse or prose therefore has serious disruptive and re-evaluative roles. It provides a position whereby serious critical discourse, or seriously ludic mockery of received ideas and unquestioned patterns, can be distinguished from the circulation of glib, faddish jargon, which may ultimately prove rather meaningless, or a private language. Even as early as 1978, and in the introduction to one of the first studies of intertextuality, Jeanine Parisier Plottel questioned the authenticity of this buzzword:

> Intertextuality is a fashionable word in academic literary circles. This is to be expected when we consider that the word implies a subtle sensation of a very special learnedness and pomposity! Such characteristics are the leading assets of most literary terms that come to be in vogue. Another shorter term would surely be more desirable, but none has yet been devised to convey the message of intertextuality.[2]

Is intertextuality then merely inventive, or is it also analytically critical? Is it, and will it continue to provide, a viable theoretical tool, or is intertextuality (with deconstruction) like the story of 'The emperor's new clothes', nonsense parading as grand theory? Clearly these questions are central to this book. It took only the naïve child in Andersen's story to ask the obvious question to unmask the serious pretentiousness of the adult world for what it was.

While children obviously have a lot to tell serious criticism about what makes a text captivating, worth retelling and fun, the more adult realms of nonsense poetry, nursery rhyme and *Alice in Wonderland* logic provide a clear answer to the question 'What is intertextuality?' at its most obvious. Rather than heading immediately for corpora or other theories as complement of the 'what?', the route that most readers, guides and applied studies of intertextuality have taken,[3] there is a simpler answer to the question. Intertextuality (as indeed also deconstruction and *différance*) is unequivocally a neologism. This kind of rhetorical coinage serves to fill a specific gap in pre-existing vocabularies, whether a whole concept or a nuance. Because neologisms enter a specific language in a particular historical context, they can be plotted and dated as regards their success. As grafts of other longer-established words, they either beat off competitor terminologies or become dated, if not obsolete, longer term. Translation often further extends, rejuvenates or kills such neologisms. The closer a neologism therefore is to major Indo-European roots, the more likely it is to survive translingually, its successful circulation then bound up with the affinities of its coinage in related languages. Kristeva's 'intertextualité' ('Intertextualität', 'intertextuality', etc.) operates supremely well in this respect, but can it fend off Derrida's related, and equally successful, neologisms to maintain its distinctive relevance, even difference from *différance*? And, more crucially, can it fare well in the open marketplace of common usage where, as neologism and not ordinary word, it may become a pejorative term?

If intertextuality's lasting significance is challenged from within literary and critical theory by deconstruction's neologisms, its future status and survival is no less under threat from rivals and newcomers on its borders. Late twentieth- and early twenty-first-century electronic media and text-messaging developments pose interesting questions about the status of printed book or paper-bounded theories. Is intertextuality (and indeed deconstruction) a last gasp expression of such bricolages or mosaics of (print) text, which multimedia theories and possibilities will inevitably replace? Will 'interdiscursivity', 'hypertextuality' and 'interdisciplinarity' then take precedence over intertextuality, or is the latter specific enough to withstand onslaughts from these newer terms? Has intertextuality a flexibility to expand its remit even beyond its first disciplinary contexts and successful involvements into adjacent areas as diverse as classics, biblical studies, film and media studies? Or has its former drive towards decentring centres and demarginalizing margins ossified into a new variant, or even more pernicious version, of the very orthodoxies it sought to replace?

In the history of cultural recycling of which intertextuality is but a twentieth-century manifestation, what has not previously been given serious critical attention offers a good potential site for new investigation to test intertextuality's remits and qualities. The realm of children's literature is one such relatively uncharted field, while the arts of nonsense, scribbling or improvisation could constitute mainly untried approaches to socio-criticism and histories of cultural production. An important twentieth-century critical legacy was just such a prioritization of what was absent, whether theorized as lack (by Freudian or Lacanian psychoanalysis), aporia (by deconstruction), positive blanks and silences (by proponents of *écriture feminine*) or revisioning of negatively ascribed notions such as *négritude*. The contributions of feminist, gay and postcolonial cultures and criticism about how to theorize and recuperate the so-called marginal in order to fill in the lacunae of official or mainstream culture and criticism have also been vital. Indeed, intertextuality has often been harnessed as description of such alternative linguistic turns. Yet retrievals of lost voices, or reversals of previous cultural trends and hierarchies which focus on other corpora, do not necessarily reveal the intrinsic dynamics of intertextuality, or demarcate its specific role within critical theory. Its detractors have already labelled it a meaningless catch-all, a 'Passepartoutbegriff', conflating with the word 'postmodern'.[4] If, in fact, intertextuality is interchangeable with, or collapses into, the word 'postmodern' or 'deconstruction' via the outworkings of deferral such as ambiguity, indetermination or equivocation, it is already doomed to redundancy. But so, too, are intertextuality's replacements, and, in turn, their replacement neologisms. Is intertextuality's 'newness', like the emperor's new clothes, non-existent? Or is it a commentator on fashion's motor of eternal return, where cast-offs are recycled as the latest retro-gear? Clearly, unless and until the particular parameters of intertextuality have been ascertained, its applications (both as theory and practice) can only remain various, contradictory, limited or vague.

However, if 'nothing only comes of nothing', goes endlessly round and round or empties out, how can intertextuality's parameters be ascertained? The epigraph above from *King Lear* provides a most serious reply. Rather than defining intertextuality by what it is not, for example, against nonsense (the *via negativa*), or, indeed, by a double negative (a deconstruction of deconstruction), this study, like Lear, will press it further for what it is. Lear's personal tragedy in so doing, however, also constitutes a warning. From the outset, his error was to take at face value the wordy reformulations of 'love' of his elder daughters Goneril and Regan, whereas it was his youngest daughter Cordelia's more profound silence that spoke the more. His failure to discern between her 'nothing' as no response, and nothing as something infinitely more than was expressible, is the ultimate tragedy of the play and a timely reminder to debates grounded in linguistics. Terms such as 'love' or 'intertextuality' can be nothing without the qualifiers and contexts in which they can speak again.

Prologues, like prologomena, and formal introductions of strangers to one another, are prefatory remarks, preliminary events or acts, and set forth or summarize the main action of a work. In like manner, the main debates and open questions of this book concerning the potential and future of intertextuality as term are now set out. But prologues also remind us that there may be contexts and speaking prior to (pro-logos) what the subject may say it is about. The primary question 'What is intertextuality?' now requires specific contexts the better to frame it, and to allow it to speak again in reply. As Cordelia knew to her cost, a third or more of the cultural and critical kingdom depends keenly upon the answer.

Introduction

As its most focused studies take as read, intertextuality's definition and specific parameters are grounded in the French intellectual scene of the late 1960s.[1] Almost without exception, both theoretical and applied surveys delimit intertextuality within the contexts of Saussurian linguistics, semiotics, post-structuralism, and the *Tel Quel* group of intellectuals.[2] Those unfamiliar with any of these movements need not even look to general works on critical theory for elucidation. Recent glosses and guides to intertextuality, such as Graham Allen's *Intertextuality* (2000) and Tiphane Samoyault's *Intertextualité: mémoire de la littérature* (2001), give clear expositions of these conceptual contexts, and potted versions of the main theories. Allen even provides the uninitiated reader with a glossary of critical terms, and a tour round critical theory more widely, including feminist theory, post-colonial criticism and multimedia, using intertextuality as a vehicle. Common to these recent guides and to older applied and theoretical studies, however, is a surprising consistency: intertextuality remains singular in their titles.[3] There is also an agreed canon of its theorists and theories. While inevitable variation comes by extension of the core list, applied and theoretical studies nevertheless reiterate, endorse and reinforce the roles of the central players. Starting with Kristeva's coinage of intertextuality with reference to Bakhtin as important staging post, the main discussion focuses on the contribution of Barthes, not least his (in)famous death of the author. Kristeva's too overarching term is then further clarified by Riffaterre's emphasis on the reader and Genette's more nuanced taxonomies. Harold Bloom's 'anxiety of influence' is universally the stalking-horse.

While these reiterations certainly clarify and refine various aspects of intertextuality, they also tacitly exclude alternative theories or positions that might challenge (their own) pre-given dispositions of viewpoint, appraisal and methodological approach. What follows in this book is such a challenge to the received canon of what 'intertextuality' is, and how this canon has been formulated, especially in critical guides. Consequently, the formula of further gloss or anthology inherent in critical 'readers', or overtly reformist promotion of an alternative list and gloss of theories or theorists, will be eschewed. Instead, this book seeks first and foremost to question afresh the 'canon' of French theorists of intertextuality – the coiner Kristeva, Barthes, Genette and Riffaterre – and how they fit together, but without the baggage of accepted critical accretion to let them speak again in context. This reverbalization (rather than reiteration) is therefore the main objective of the first chapter, but is foundational for the parameters of the remainder of the book. Such a revisionary route will reveal the received version of 'intertextuality' as much more diverse and partial, especially when the historical and ideological contexts of late 1960s and 1970s France are reconsidered. Within critical theory, intertextuality may then appear less 'French' and less 'postmodern' than has previously been claimed.[4] This may prove a distinct advantage in intertextuality's favour when it is compared, in the remainder of chapter 1, to other globalizing and rival terms for cultural recycling such as 'interdiscursivity', 'interdisciplinarity' and 'hypertext'.

To prepare the ground for this first chapter, and for the remainder of the book, several unexamined assumptions that undergird critical theory readers and guides to intertextuality, and more sophisticated applied studies, need first to be verbalized. These comments also constitute en route a brief overview of other important contributions to the critical story of intertextuality to date, which have been previously sidelined or silenced. Their recuperation here provides a shortcut to certain ideas in later chapters of this study. By highlighting unvoiced modes of intertextual work in other guises – paraphrase, formulaic expression, variant, recontextualization, translation – various tacit critical agendas behind intertextuality's representations become visible. Among intertextuality's most practical functions is (re-)evaluation by means of comparison, counter-position and contrast. These operations openly inform the ensuing study and its method throughout.

Of foremost concern, however, is the question how and why certain players in the story of intertextuality have come to be canonized. Circulation of their works by constant repetition and critical gloss is obviously essential, but this would not be possible without readily available copy and aids to rapid assimilation. To this end, accessible bibliographies as vehicles of 'required' reading lists have been hugely significant disseminators. Indeed, many major guides to intertextuality have seen the provision of such bibliographies as a major service to their readers.[5] Obviously, for non-initiates, works or theorists not catalogued do not exist. Such lacunae, if filled, would make for a more comprehensive survey of available information, but may in fact have little to do with unrepresented fields of expertise or narrowness of disciplinary range. The *language(s)* of bibliographies count(s) as much in dissemination of information as contents. Although the first bibliography of bibliographies, Udo Hebel's *Intertextuality, Allusion and Quotation: an International Bibliography of Critical Studies* (1989), was in English, its coverage is primarily of works in other European languages, because English was but the third or fourth in his own portfolio. In stark contrast is the monolingualism of recent readers, such as Allen and Samoyault, epitomized by their bibliographies. There is no reference to any work that is not in English or English translation in Allen, so that in effect 'French' theory is already tantamount to a gloss. In Samoyault, there is equal bias, but towards works only in French; she subordinates 'foreign' matter through second-hand citation and tokenist appraisal relegated to footnotes. Popularizing anthologies and guides dependent largely on translations may not in fact be serving intertextuality well, as we will discover in various contexts throughout this study. Thus, the multilingual bibliography test underscores how critical (in many senses) is the availability of key texts, and, if in translation, that they follow rapidly on the heels of their language of first publication. Where a theorist, or his/her whole corpus, is not translated, material simply disappears from reading lists, bibliographies and, more important, cultural and critical circulation.

It is for the simple reason that it has not been translated from German into either English or French that the groundbreaking essays in Broich and Pfister (1985) are rarely cited. The extensive annotated bibliography categorizing intertextuality under other guises such as allusion, adaptation, quotation and parody is also largely undiscovered, although it is the likely model for the very similar format in Hebel (1989). As also a Germanist, Hebel fully acknowledges the contribution of this volume, one of his top two with Stierle and Warning (1984). Even in the early 1980s, these critics were challenging intertextuality as a monolithic, blanket term in ways that non-German-speaking critics are only now beginning to suggest.[6] Moreover, the contributors in Broich and Pfister (1985) were examining intertextuality as theories and practices (plural), well before Worton and Still (1990) adopted a similar format, and across various critical traditions, of which two are cause for particular reflection. First, in accord with Broich and Pfister's subtitle, works of English (and American) literature, and from the Renaissance to postmodernism, constitute the 'case studies' for the 'forms' and 'functions' of intertextuality in practice throughout. The historical breadth and choice of this corpus doubly challenges what is perceived as 'cutting edge' literary theory and reading practice. If it is not in effect French,[7] it must then inhabit English departments in the United States or Britain, where work on related continental (usually French) critical theory is undertaken mainly through English translation. However, Gisela Ecker's essay 'A map for re-reading: Intertextualität aus der Perspektive einer feministischen Literaturwissenschaft' (Broich and Pfister, 1985) makes Allen's foray into feminist approaches in 2000 extremely belated, even arguably derivative. Similarly, Joseph Schöpp's 'Endmeshed in endtanglements: Intertextualtität in Donald Barthelmes *The Dead Father*' pre-empts much of what is taken as definitive work on intertextuality and postmodern practices such as Waugh (1984) or Hutcheon (1988 and 1989), even if their treatments are more extensive.

While work on practices is vital to the extension of intertextuality's definitions, the more important contribution that Broich and Pfister's volume makes is to its theories, both across several linguistic traditions (German, French, English) and across traditions of linguistics. Thus, French semiotic theories, such as Kristeva's, are integral to the debate, but in counter-distinction to developments in structuralist poetics, such as the more formalist Jenny (1976), or post-structuralist Genette of *Palimpsestes* (1982). These French theories are, however, of equal significance to the rich, German contribution to Central European and Slavist theories of 'intertextuality'. These issue from Russian Formalism and the Bakhtin circle, where socio-critical dimensions and considerations are paramount. The world is not a text, but a referent to which texts can point and are affiliated. Broich and Pfister (1985) highlight the particular importance of work by Renate Lachmann (1982), who was also a key contributor to Stierle and Warning (1984). Her work epitomized landmark research in a similar vein to contributors in Schmid and Stempel (1983), prioritizing not Kristevan intertextuality, but development of Bakhtin's work on dialogism and speech genres, as the very titles and series of these collections underscore.[8] Again, because Lachmann's work is unavailable in French or English, more recent reappraisals of intertextuality from precisely such viewpoints, such as Bruce (1995), lay claim to such ideas as new departures, developing similar, but French, socio-criticism, such as Angenot (1983a). Interestingly, Angenot's essay and much of his later work is equally unavailable in English. Only critics with wider linguisitic access can therefore tell whether the provenance of ideas is really as new as is claimed. Thus, Broich and Pfister (1985) remain a veritable gold-mine for intertextuality's theories and practices. In its range and depth, it also outstrips subsequent work by its individual contributors in English, such as Plett (1991). He, like Hebel (1989), while multilingual, and a promoter of multilingual practices, opts for inter-textuality under not a socio-critical but largely a semiotic and post-modern umbrella, since the late 1980s and 1990s were more alive to such ideas via Derrida and Lyotard. Referentiality is then inter-referentiality of text to text, not text to referent outside it.

Greater diversity or linguistic range may not, however, be the only panacea to intertextuality's misrepresentations. As Broich and Pfister (1985) demonstrate, a parallel prerequisite is openness to a number of theoretical angles, often coupled with pre-postmodern viewpoints on practices to provide counterchecks to 'the new', or the latest, as the only sites worthy of consideration. Openness of approach is not unsurprisingly found in the earliest, albeit largely monolingual, responses to intertextuality of the 1970s. The overtly pluralized special number of *Poétique* (1976), *Intertextualités*, interestingly, has no editorial résumé. Rather, it revels in the free plurality and strate-gies of its form, but not as limitless play, as Jenny's essay therein indicates.[9] Already critical of Kristevan intertextuality as both too broad and too narrow a term within semiotics, Jenny's famous 'lead-ership du sens' advocates text cognizant of its material contexts.[10] Only then may it offer 'meaning' as a centring position for critical evaluations. Hence, other epochs have equally enjoyed 'intertextual-ity', whether in the medieval rhétoriqueurs (Zumthor, 1976), post-structuralist *mise en abyme* (Dällenbach, 1976),[11] the Renaissance of Dante (Contini, 1976) or the modernism of Joyce (Topia, 1976). The final essay by Leyla Perrone-Moisés, underlining the intertextual status of criticism not as para- but 'pariah-literary',[12] will find par-ticular resonance in the second chapter below. There is much to prove if one is a latecomer writer or, indeed, poet-critic or critical theorist, which may be why critical readers endorse largely *one* view of inter-textuality at the expense of others. As Germaine Brée put it in 1978, 'Intertextuality, in *one* interpretation (Julia Kristeva's) of the much used term, is the power of the written text to impose a reorganiza-tion of the corpus of texts that preceded its appearance, creating a modification in the manner in which they are read.'[13] Fixity (critical canonization) is the endpoint in the largely unvoiced, and undocu-mented, process of such impositions, which begins from much more critically diverse, eclectic, or even iconoclastic, positions. These are exemplified in the collection edited by Plottel and Charney (1978), in the preface of which Plottel openly states that it will make no attempt 'to define or establish an orthodoxy'.[14] Rather:

> [i]ntertextuality is the recognition of a frame, a context that allows the reader to make sense out of what he or she might otherwise perceive as senseless. This seems quite obvious when dealing with the corpus of an unfamiliar culture [. . .] Such is, of course, Lévi-Strauss's method, in his study of myth. When dealing with works that belong to a familiar tradition, we may not be quite as aware of the lenses with which we read. [. . .] Interpretation is shaped by a complex of relations between the text, the reader, reading, writing, printing, publishing and history: the history that is inscribed in the language of the text and in the history that is carried in the reader's reading. Such a history has been given a name: intertextuality.[15]

Multifariousness, we are reminded, was what the theory of intertextuality hailed, yet such practices are sidelined when critical rigour is prioritized, such as in the agenda of Riffaterre. As intertextuality is thus 'refined', it becomes (purer) semiotics, (post-)structuralist poetics, socio-criticism, deconstruction, depending where referentiality is pinned; to itself, language, a system or the world. Plottel and Charney (1978) none the less remind critics of what actually happens in practice: theory is never 'pure', but a 'pick and mix'. In what can only be described as their 'cocktail' rather than formulaic approach to intertextuality, where theory is as often derived from practices, the seriously experimental *and* fun can be returned to definitions of intertextuality. However, given the intervening plethora of studies on and about intertextuality since Hebel (1989), how can the term avoid becoming one uniform mélange of all cultures, languages and media, or an even more impossibly vague and overly large cultural and critical *Gesamtkunstwerk*?

The major principles and lessons drawn from the above short survey round others' and other versions of the story of intertextuality inform and pertain to the working methods in this book. First, unlike monolingual readers or critical guides, no theory represented here is relayed second-hand through translations or unquestioned recycling of the work or bibliographies of other critics. This book assumes a rather different first premise, that readers' curiosity and interest extend beyond one cultural tradition, language and critical school, and that no card-carrying cultural critic, especially in a global twenty-first-century culture, can be resolutely monolingual. Because it draws mainly on French, German and Anglo-American theories of intertextuality, but includes comparisons with among others Russian, Chinese or Japanese traditions where strategic, the question of intertextuality more broadly, as translation, interlingual communication, or new word overlapping with precursor terms, is constantly in view. To these ends, and following Broich and Pfister (1985), this book provides two indices of the critical vocabularies and alternative terms that 'intertextuality' as catch-all word encounters, or has ingested. Such tools will then allow readers to think laterally about related critical terms, to cross-reference a keyword where it occurs in a variety of different contexts, or to demonstrate the unsuitability or compatibility of certain concepts then applied in practice.

A related issue, also faced differently by Broich and Pfister (1985), Hebel (1989) and Plett (1991), is the choice of English as 'main' language. Rather than seeing it as the *lingua franca*, this book challenges such monolingualism by reintroducing those theories or critics which have been particularly badly served by lack or inadequate provision of translations. Such 'foreign' material is not secondary in my own translations, but fully equal through reference in the notes, bibliography and index to the original. Clearly because certain texts in the original fall outside my linguistic competency – the theories of the Bakhtin circle, for example, are not represented in depth – Bakhtin's work is given coverage in the first chapter with respect to its reception in France. Similarly, Russian Formalism as 'science' of signs is discussed with reference to theories of rhetoric and poetics, not least those of Genette, in chapter 3. The invitation is then for Russianists and specialists in other languages and cultures to follow through the ideas opened up.

Contrary to the wonderful diversity of application that are the essays in *Poétique* (1976) or Plottel and Charney (1978), or the more nationally focused exemplifications of theory in practice in Broich and Pfister (1985) or Worton and Still (1990), this book is not about specific practices, or how these extend theories of intertextuality. By also breaking with previous practices of guides on intertextuality, this book attempts to uncover some of the basic principles underlying various theories of intertextuality, so that this term or its cognates may be used to better critical advantage. Hence, the aim is to provide readers with a well-stocked critical toolbox to describe intertextuality for the range of jobs it does. A major advantage of this is that applications are left entirely to the reader's own spectrum of theoretical interests regarding intertextuality, or questions of its specific cultural and historical manifestations. The corollary of this is that the close readings of the texts of one national literature, genre or epoch, or of one race, class, sex or creed, will not predominate or occlude discussion of the mechanisms of intertextuality, or its related or affiliated terms. Slippage into simple oppositions or their reversals will equally be avoided. Concentration on 'popular' cultural forms as opposed to 'high' cultural ones, or priority of say music over photography, does not necessarily enhance understanding of how intertextuality operates across media. New readers from a wide variety of media backgrounds can then be drawn into the critical community, and one where 'mainstream' and 'marginal' cease to be divisive. Thus, where sparing reference is made en route to aid theoretical understanding, this is to something interculturally familiar so that the viability of this book can be maximized by others' application of key terms to a multiplicity of contexts, epochs, media or genres. The literary, cultural or critical knowledge of one person could never encompass all possible examples or theories, let alone attempt exhaustive codification. Indeed, where the reader finds that the principles discussed throughout this study cannot be applied to a certain corpus or tradition, this should stimulate and enlarge critical debate about intertextuality itself.

With this rather different practical methodology now in place, a further requirement is a sharper yet more diverse *theoretical* method and comparative framework than are offered by previous guides which gloss the 'canonical' theorists of intertextuality. Provision of alternative lists of theories, media, aesthetic value systems or comparative geographies may only provide more of the same. It is the very ubiquity of intertextuality that gives the lead. Inhabiting not just the context of 1960s France, semiotics and postmodernism, but prior contexts, its atemporality has been the visible running thread in many practice-orientated studies of intertextuality, which treat older forms and genres alongside recent ones.[16] From the 1990s on, critics such as Worton and Still (1990) and Piégay-Gros (1996),[17] followed by Limat-Letellier and Miguet-Ollgnier (1998) and Samoyault (2001), are more specific and expansive about the longer history of intertextuality in France, its theoretical background prior to Kristeva.[18] Clearly, as some commentators have noted, a wider cultural history of the term, its manifestations and contexts beyond France, would be desirable.[19] Such a task has not been tackled probably because it would represent a mammoth undertaking on two counts. It would need first to encompass comparative investigations between modes and media of cultural production – *inter alia* music, painting, literature, sculpture, architecture, photography, film, television, video, and computer-generated forms – as well as investigate their historical importance or evolution in one or several national heritages. A related remit would entail plotting the evolution of intertextuality as a critical term in Western and non-Western cultures. Yet, not to undertake such a cultural history of intertextuality potentially isolates or overdetermines its aegis within late twentieth-century cultural contexts. Intertextuality is not independent of modernism or its heritage in Romanticism, just as the 'post' in post-modern, post-feminist, post-colonial, etc., may be closer to modernism, feminism and colonialism than first imagined. To assure continuity rather than discontinuity, questions need to be asked of intertextuality as label for operations which are in fact far from new, and still going strong in different guises.

To assure intertextuality an ongoing place beyond its specific contexts, this book rises to the second challenge, the mapping of its evolutions, but responds from within the Western critical condition and its traditions. While there is nothing new under the sun, this has never prevented humanity from engaging in artistic or critical reinventions. At the very least, such a platform allows this book to elucidate how the term intertextuality differs and is similar to older forms of very much the same thing, since the interplay of such manifestations will undoubtedly find analogues in the cultural future. In best Renaissance tradition, this book also recognizes the foundational work and previous insights of other critics, for they make possible the space for my version of the story of intertextuality. This book thus steps into the gap ascertained by Richard Schoek: 'Intertextuality has its own literary history, although it is not yet written',[20] but first as a direct question to its 1960s context. What was the semantic vacuum that the neologism, intertextuality, duly filled? And why were perfectly valid terms that had been in circulation to describe the referential processes between and within works, and between works and the material world, no longer appropriate? Since the word intertextuality is a graft, what other alternatives were available at the same time? Which did intertextuality reinforce, and which did it silence?

Examination of what has been downplayed or dismissed everywhere constitutes the main mode of reconsideration in the following chapters. The assumption underlying this book is that there exist what I call 'shadowland' terms to intertextuality such that, like the tip of an iceberg, it is but a part of a greater whole. These shadowlands have been closed to view in order to prioritize or valorize another term, and invent a lineage to support its importance. This process trades under names such as ideology, power, or simply cultural criticism. By re-examining this lineage, but with a firm eye on its shadow and an ear to the echo of its voice, this book does not, however, set out to discover territories which have not been included in the mainstream. Instead, the shadowlands of concern here are as much the most tried and tested forms of cultural recycling, such as quotation and imitation and the former mainstream of previous epochs (canonical authors, rhetoric, genres), as the works of so-called marginal writers. Indeed, by underlining the concept of shadowlands, the labels 'mainstream' or 'marginal' cease to play a key role in determining a hierarchy or value system of literary or cultural production and its rejuvenations. Heritage can then be investigated more broadly, and understood in a variety of ways that may also set out paths for intertextuality's development within, and beyond, the currently perceived crisis of postmodernism.[21]

It is the interaction of intertextuality with its shadowlands – related and rival terms to describe the processes of cultural rejuvenation – that structures this book and its four main chapters. Intertextuality (as cultural form of Saussurian linguistics, celebrating the arbitrariness and relativity of signifiers to signifieds, and later developed into deconstruction and postmodernism) claims to break with the old sureties, especially about meaning as mythical and metaphysical or atheistic, agnostic, or anti-metaphysical. The first chapter examines the shadowlands to such a notion of intertextuality as (clean) break or disconnection with the past, to examine what it might also have recuperated. Intertextuality can then be more sharply assessed in the light of its two kinds of competitor. First, there are its close relations. Kristeva's coinage is not necessarily Barthes's or Riffaterre's version of intertextuality. Second, to intertextuality in all its versions, there are rival terms, especially regarding its alleged inclusiveness. Concepts such as interdiscursivity and interdisciplinarity manifest the same ability to colonize cultural space. To conclude this chapter, some of the same possibilities and problems experienced by postmodernism – cultural fusion, information storage, retrieval and verification – and encapsulated in electronic hypertext and the internet, find parallels in third-century AD Alexandria. Cultural expansion on one level was the negotiation of an increasingly elitist high culture of the polymath on another. In their differences and similarities, Alexandrianism and postmodernity may be much less polarized when surface appearance is peeled back.

Intertextuality may then also discover that it has less leverage than the ingrained concepts it 'radically' overturned or sought to dispose of. The second chapter focuses on intertextuality's most blatant shadowland, its arch-enemy. The term it reacted to most violently, and desired to replace and displace, was influence, with all its baggage of critical source-hunting and authorial intention. Previous criticism on intertextuality has consistently named Harold Bloom's 'anxiety of influence' as stalking-horse theory.[22] By re-examining Bloom's ideas also for their shadowlands, the second chapter will reveal their surprising similarities with deconstruction and intertextuality. Although their surface vocabularies are so different, Bloom may in fact be talking the same language as Derrida, and even deconstructing deconstruction in so doing. Does Bloom then equally consign influence to the dustbin of literary history, or to its recycling plant? The questions the remainder of the chapter asks are how and why influence came to have such negative and pejorative implications in the 1970s. Can influence be put in a more positive light by shadow-land theories that were circulating in parallel, especially those examining and, more important, recognizing tradition, canon and the reader? One of the key issues chapter 2 highlights is how cultural value and its revaluation are imparted, not least by critics. At the very least, Harold Bloom spearheads the insertion of the critic-'poet' into the holy trinities of text, writer and reader, or work, author and world. The influence of the critic as arbiter and disseminator presses into the open some very undeconstructed terms at the heart of the decon-structive turn itself.

The positive value and mediation of influence in the Enlighten-ment or Romanticism to express individuality (of poets, critics, or works, etc.), suggests this hid its own shadowland scapegoat. At work on very similar questions concerning models and anti-models, the antagonist term to recover in chapter 3 is imitation. Rather than be-ing tantamount to a stifling precursor or dull copy, imitation's posi-tive and creative implications emerge. The essential role of iteration for inspiration within the Renaissance and seventeenth-century clas-sicism, for example, reopens debates about mimicry and models, copy and cornucopia, plagiarism and parody. Postmodernity's simulacrum, virtual reality, electronic copy-cut-and-paste, or mod-ernism's bricolage and collage techniques, make of imitation not intertextuality's distant double-remove, but double. Genette's theo-ries of the palimpsest are first compared to Kristeva's intertextual-ity as imitation, the better to surpass her coinage. His earlier *Mimologiques* (1976), however, further illustrate Genette's imitations of the strongest precursors when it comes to Western mimesis and representation, Plato and Aristotle. Mimesis and anti-mimesis thus form a configuration that is found to be central to cultural genera-tion and individuation in domains other than art such as zoology and psychology. Chapter 3 examines theories in these domains, and, at seemingly polar opposites, Richard Dawkins's evolutionary 'meme' theory and René Girard's anthropology of the scapegoat. Both have much to say about principles of cultural survival and change, which inspired the mimetic or anti-mimetic function of art itself not least as ritual. Drama is thus singled out for particular consideration in the final part of the chapter. As the imitative form *par excellence*, it challenges the status of the novel as the primary dialogic genre. Is it then the mimetic bond itself that intertextuality tried, but failed, to break? Is distinctiveness always relative to, and imitative of, previous models?

How, then, do norms, models, paradigms or genomes come about? The fourth chapter looks not to a further encapsulating concept such as intertextuality, influence or imitation to find out, but to the micro-level of intercommunication, quotation. As kind of linguistic imitation, quotation has a focusing and crystallizing function, where part is often also the whole. As utterance that verifies, authorizes, transports and redefines meanings across time and national boundary, quotation and its accomplice, allusion, name borrowing practices for very specific ends, whether authentication of or separation and autonomy from authorities. Indeed, quotation and allusion fully contend with intertextuality regarding utterances such as saws, proverbs, anonymous or multi-authored words, ballads, orally transmitted lore that have no identifiable first user or historical context.

When also doubled by translingual equivalent, quotations have an even more far-reaching and potent revivifying role. This is demonstrated in what are usually viewed as starkly contrasting epochs. Where the Renaissance with its vernacular imitations sought distance from authority texts and the authoritative languages of Hebrew, Greek and Latin, the Middle Ages negotiated the same problems from the position of creative deference. Commentary, translation, exegesis, all return pre-modern views on interpretation and interpreting references and authority texts, including the Bible, to the postmodern world of texts and intertextuality. Running threads throughout the preceding chapters on imitation and influence also converge on the issue of translation as form of copy that interprets and creates afresh. Its vibrancy in its inter- as well as intralingual and metaphorical senses offers a different way of combining the transitional, transactional and transformational aspects of intertextuality, influence and imitation, from the angle of quotation as reinterpretation. The saying again of the same or similar words has at least two concomitant senses, past and present, literal and figurative, factual and ironic, serious and joking, poetic and prosaic, semantic and semiotic. Affecting one or more cultural heritages, moments or contexts, this constant overlayering of language to speak with forked or double tongue represents the problems of communication since time immemorial: fidelity or fickleness, authority or fakery, truth(s) or deception(s), utility or art. Is language then merely an infinite system or network of unmarked quotations, or is it dependent on textual quotation of its oral diversity for its regeneration? Does postmodern emphasis on audiovisual media then revivify or further distance oral and popular forms? And will inter*text*uality be made redundant when the printed text no longer rules?

By linking the shadowlands together, the fourth chapter then puts intertextuality back in the balances to assess whether it has, first, the durability to outlast its strategic place in the evolution of critical ideas and, second, the specificity sufficient to prevent it from becoming too overarching, nebulous or dépassé in the longer term. Unlike all good tragedies, comedies, epics, novels, fairy stories and romances, there is no happy, tragic, or even postmodern, suspended, ending to this book. Yet, as with all fourth acts of classical dramas, we can have intuitions about the fifth, knowing that it will ultimately be about inheritance, conflict, death, future succession, love, and hope of continuity. These may come about by a tragi-comic twist, a supernatural turn of events, an unmasking of what was hidden in the logic of the plot. Combination and new combination is all. Thus, ideas of cultural sedimentation, stultification and weightiness of the past which postmodernity has nurtured as crisis to undergird deconstruction, and that intertextuality has fostered as mosaic of fragments, may not, after all, be the end of the cultural story or its critical retellings.

The debates and contexts of the four chapters of this book are now in place. To begin with intertextuality so as to uncover influence, behind which is imitation, with quotation as a final layer of an onion-like conceptualization of literary and cultural reference, could, however, merely replicate old-fashioned nostalgia for a greater cultural past. For those readers and critics who remain sceptical about literary-historical studies and hence the presumed foundation and approach of this book, it also openly eschews such a retrospective, nostalgic evaluation. Furthermore, the important work of deconstruction to challenge binary taxonomies or dialectics no longer allows such a (naïve) move. However, to challenge deconstruction also to examine its own limits, and what deferral of meaning implies for national history, gender, race, or aesthetic or moral judgements, a theory, of literature, rather than literary theory, is required, as Antoine Compagnon rightly notes.[23] 'Theory', like intertextuality, influence, imitation and quotation, has its own history and desire for distinctiveness. Thus, contrary to the mainly chronological and linear exposition of standard literary histories, this book looks at evolution as also simultaneous development. Instead of simply rewinding the spool of time, or imagining a retrospective 'progress' towards some original or root term for intertextuality, each chapter highlights theories and theorists from its same contexts, late 1960s and 1970s France. While tenets found in Romanticism (chapter 2), in Renaissance modes of revisionism (chapter 3) and medieval micro-macrocosmic structures (chapter 4) are revisited, these ideas are anchored firmly in those of the 1970s. The clear advantages of this are that debates common to all historical periods, and cutting across national or linguistic cultural boundaries, remain uppermost. Redefinition and reordering here also break with the standard recipe of previous readers and guides. Finally, the multiple contexts of the 1970s and its contributions to the 'crisis in postmodernism' may find unexpected enlightenment by rediscovery of parallels with former epochs. The way will then be open for future studies to examine the many theories that intertextuality (and deconstruction) may have eclipsed initially, but whose lasting significance may be ascertained only as these pass away.

Recent media in fact provide a much more integrated model than the image of concentric nesting onion skins, for the working method of this book and a metaphor for its space in late twentieth- and early twenty-first-century cultural criticism. Our four chapters can better be envisaged as a set of open electronic windows, with intertextuality first and, by virtue of its position to hide and reveal the contents of the other chapter windows, last. Once all four windows are open, questions can then be asked of them together, about patterns and procedures, precedents and replications, which otherwise could be hidden. The ultimate issue is then the collective overcoming of all four, of survival beyond the fourth act. In other words, what role does intertextuality play now for its own future and the future of art in contradistinction to the *opus* of science, philosophy, history, religion? Do we need to expand, delimit or replace it? Are there better alternatives such as citation, or cultural recycling in an electronic age? Fast-forwarding to 'end' to find out would spoil this retelling of the story, so let us now illuminate the first and most familiar screen, intertextuality, to let it 'speak again'.

1

Intertextuality

If Kristeva is openly acknowledged for coining the term intertextuality in the late 1960s, this recognition is surprisingly fleeting and dismissive.[1] However supportive critics may be of its semiotics contexts, they glide rapidly over Kristeva's term, to concentrate on its more illustrious theorists such as Barthes.[2] Indeed it was he, not Kristeva, who wrote the definition for intertextuality in the *Encyclopédie universalis* in 1973. In arenas outside semiotics, critics of intertextuality also relegate Kristeva's contribution and its French contexts, but as derivative of the work of Bakhtin and the Bakhtin circle.[3] A notable exception is provided by Worton and Still (1990), who focus extensively in their introduction on Kristeva's part in a French high-cultural, avant-garde and intellectual tradition that combined experimental writing, literary theory, Saussurian linguistics and left-wing politics. By placing Kristeva firmly within the French critical and intellectual elite of *Tel Quel*, however, they separate her brand of intertextuality, as specifically highbrow, from similar modes of cultural borrowing practised by popular culture. Film and popular music had quickly adopted recycling and sampling in distinctly non-French, and non-theoretical, ways.[4] While these critical snapshots of Kristevan intertextuality focus on very different issues, they have all contributed to one outcome, marginalization of Kristeva's contributions to the 'real' work and texts on intertextuality:

> Kristeva's first published work in France is on Mikhail Bakhtin's literary writings, Roland Barthes' seminar is the place where this first substantial part of the Kristevan *oeuvre* would be presented. Roland

Barthes is not there in the writing, but he is, in part, its precondition. Or perhaps it is more accurate to say that Barthes is there, but only in a displaced form. [. . .] Kristeva will not take up Barthes' theories as such in her work, but it was Barthes' writings from *Le Degré zéro de l'écriture* (1953) onward, which opened up the whole terrain for studies in semiotics. Roland Barthes, then, is Kristeva's Parisian mother, as it were; there is nothing Oedipal here.[5]

There is, however, some sinister transference at work. Why has Kristeva's version of intertextuality been sidelined, even actively discredited, whereas Barthes's among others has not? Is such discrediting of Kristeva as coiner and theorist of intertextuality deliberate, or justifiable? This chapter seeks to answer these questions as central to the wider importance of intertextuality's ongoing justification as term, especially in view of its rivals. These are not only the rival French theories of intertextuality proffered by Barthes, Riffaterre or Genette. Newer contenders, such as 'interdiscursivity', 'interdisciplinarity' and 'hypertext', provide possible replacements of intertextuality as concept. In the twenty-first century, are these not better, less elitist and more inclusive ways of describing cultural recycling than intertextuality in whatever French guise?

Kristeva's term in context

By default, Anglo-American as well as French critics of intertextuality base their understanding of it on Kristeva's essay 'Word, dialogue, novel', the fourth chapter of *Semeiotikè*, published in Paris in 1969, but not translated into English until 1980.[6] The classic definition, enshrined in critical readers in English and French, is taken from a sentence early in the essay: intertextuality is 'a mosaic of quotations; any text is the absorption and transformation of another. The notion of *intertextuality* replaces that of intersubjectivity, and poetic language is read as at least double.'[7] While reappraisals of intertextuality as critical term in English, French and German highlight the imprecision or overgeneralizations generated by this 'definition',[8] these may have less to do with the 'theory' itself than with the practical circumstances and parameters of its reception and circulation. In non-French-speaking intellectual circles, particularly Anglo-American academe, the early production of translations of 'French' critical theory has been crucial to its inclusion in key debates, and its dissemination via conferences, publications and university curricula. Barthes's *oeuvre*, particularly the early texts pertinent to intertextuality and semiotics, was immediately accessible in translation, whereas Kristeva's work was very belatedly, and often only partially, translated.[9] Obviously, by 1980, Kristeva's ideas then appeared very similar to those of the already familiar Barthes and Derrida. From this alone, it is unsurprising that 'intertextuality' rapidly elided with the Barthesian notion of the 'death of the author', adapted readily as another version of (Derridean) deferral of text, or was subsumed by the larger theoretical framework of postmodernism and deconstruction. 'Intertextuality', then, was the linguistic Big Bang, the deconstruction of 'Text' into texts and intertexts where these two terms ultimately become synonymous. On every count, Kristeva's coinage was but a pre-semiotic moment in the ensuing deferrals of (inter)text in semiotic space.

While the problems and influences of translations will be the subject of the fourth chapter, the relevant and central point here is that translation, or the lack of it, has created a 'Kristeva' of Anglo-American critical theory that we will discover is not the Kristeva of *Semeiotikè*.[10] If the reader has remained crucial as a 'clearinghouse' outside the text and intertext for Kristeva's French-speaking critics,[11] whether fellow theorists such as Barthes and Riffaterre or German and Canadian bi- or trilingual critics, reception of 'Kristeva' in translation and in the critical reader industry has never been questioned. No doubt is ever cast on the authority of her 'text' as other than a completely reliable and transparent cultural transfer. Since the original essay in French is never compared, any distortions, misappropriations or blatant misrepresentations of 'Kristeva's' theory of intertextuality in translation remain invisible.[12] Moreover, since *Semeiotikè* is in fact still inaccessible in its entirety to all but French speakers, no one has ever questioned whether 'Word, dialogue, novel' is in fact 'the intertextuality essay', let alone whether Kristeva's work in *Semeiotikè* as a whole might inform it or, indeed, pre-empt and outstrip ideas found later in deconstruction. Even more radically, Kristeva's wider *Semeiotikè* as other prefiguration of deconstruction has received no critical re-evaluation as a whole, not even in France or within French-speaking critical communities, such that it might then also offer a solution to thinking various ways out of its impasses and the so-called crisis in postmodernism.

If inaccessibility to the French language or to *Semeiotikè* as a whole provides some excuse as to why Kristeva's intertextuality has been marginalized in Anglo-American critical theory, more puzzling is why her term has fared equally badly in France. French critical guides to intertextuality seem unanimous, and surprisingly consistent with the Anglo-American version of the story. Kristeva is again seen as coiner, but, as the quotation from Lechte above endorses, this time her term becomes tantamount to a recuperation or a French version of

Bakhtin's 'dialogism'. Hence, because the more concerted theorization of intertextuality by a Barthes, Riffaterre or Genette brought the critical rigour her original work was deemed to lack, French critical guides eclipse Kristeva's version and concentrate on theirs. Consequently, French guides to intertextuality, like their English counterparts, once again ignore *Semeiotikè* as a collection of supporting essays to the fourth, 'Bakhtin', chapter. Within France, critical guides then only reinforce a French intellectual hierarchy and critical canon of 'intertextuality' which allows no voice, least of all a female one, to question such constructs.

Marginalization of Kristeva in France extends beyond her theory of intertextuality, however. Although she was part of the *Tel Quel* intellectual establishment alongside Sollers, Derrida and Lyotard, her enormous contribution (*via Semeiotikè*) to intertextuality's wider theoretical contexts in linguistics, poetics, psychoanalysis, comparative religion and philosophy of language has always been perceived derivatively, and differently, to theirs. In France, because the philosophical tradition is ingrained – it has been integral to the curriculum in boys' lycées, and only recently taught to girls – tacit demarcations about its status and seriousness obtain. Thus, Derrida is obviously a philosopher, and stratospherically so, whereas women thinkers, without a lineage of philosopher foremothers behind them, rank in the arena only of ideas about emotions such as psychoanalysis, not of pure thinking. Kristeva cannot then be a philosopher in French intellectual terms (or league), whether with or without the 'feminist' qualification that her work (in translation) after *Semeiotikè* enjoys in some Anglo-American academic feminist and critical theory circles. If these have recuperated Kristeva's importance as postmodern thinker, and widened access to her work through monograph studies and readers, they have unwittingly downplayed her primary contributions to the philosophy of language. This is because her work in linguistics and intertextuality is severed from her later work within psychoanalysis and poetics.[13] In France, critical occlusion of Kristeva is further compounded by her approach, epitomized in fact by *Semeiotikè*, which we would now name interdisciplinary, but which was clearly and strikingly at odds with the 'pure' research pursued by her male *Tel Quel* contemporaries in the late 1960s. At the very least what follows will rescue Kristeva's *oeuvre* as symbiosis, not suture into 'periods' or shifts of disciplinary loyalty, to allow her most recent work to be read in the light of *Semeiotikè*.

If 'Kristevan' and Kristevan intertextuality are not to be doomed to an honorable mention in literary and critical history, rereading *Semeiotikè* is of paramount importance in the recuperation of a major figure in its double sense: for Kristeva's intertextuality in literary and

cultural theory, and for Kristeva as woman intellectual. Full rereading of *Semeiotikè* is a study in its own right, but this chapter can offer
no better beginning than to elucidate what Kristeva's intertextuality
is. How *Semeiotikè* attempted to navigate it between the Scylla of the
death of the unified subject and the Charybdis of the non-existence
of any outside of the text will be elucidated. Returning to *Semeiotikè*
as a whole can then reopen two key questions. The first reconsiders
Kristeva's role in transposing Bakhtin's work on dialogism and the
polyphonic novel. The second concerns her theorization of the
dynamics of intertextual production. The way will then be cleared to
reassess those sections of *Semeiotikè* that have not seen the critical
light of day for want of translations or critical consideration, but
which also bear enormously on translation as model for intertextual
work.

Kristeva's intertextuality and *Semeiotikè*

If there is one word to sum up Kristeva's striking interdisciplinarity
of approach, both regarding intertextuality and its encompassing
Semeiotikè and since, it is interconnection of ideas where previously
none existed. The roots of all Kristeva's interests can be found in her
doctoral thesis (1966) in linguistics from an at least double tradition.
As a linguist and translator, Kristeva brought hitherto unknown work
in Russian to bear on French intellectual inquiry into linguistics and
language as meta-system. What was original about Kristeva's doctoral work was her combinatory exploration of Russian Formalist and
structuralist ideas (not least Bakhtin's), and the grafting of these
within Saussurian linguistics and the Barthes/*Tel Quel* politics of post-
Marxist materialism to envisage a theory of intersubjectivity as text.
While Todorov is usually credited with launching Bakhtin's European
and thence American reception, Kristeva's much earlier part in
Semeiotikè has yet to be fully mapped.[14] She has too often been
assumed as 'French' in French and Anglo-American criticism, and
her rich Eastern European heritage has mainly been sidelined,
although it was clearly noted as early as 1978 by Plottel and Charney:

> Cultural historians might trace the concept of intertextuality in
> [Kristeva's] work to the Eastern European formalist tradition of the
> early twentieth century. Although Kristeva's present audience is
> primarily an audience steeped in the most recent developments of the
> critical model emerging through Franco-American transatlantic
> commuting, the issues that she tackles appear also in many pages of
> Soviet semioticians, especially Iouri Lotman, for whom intertextuality
> is the public domain of culture itself.[15]

'Word, dialogue, text', therefore, may be less Kristeva's manifesto for 'intertextuality' than her advocacy of various aspects of Bakhtin's extensive *oeuvre* within Russian semiotics channelled specifically towards a range of similar questions that were current in intellectual circles in France.[16] In other words, Kristeva's essay is primarily a 'translation' of Bakhtin as informed transposition. Source- and target-text traverse a space that is mediated by a translator-interpreter of two languages, and expert in two frames of reference in linguistics. Credit has therefore rarely been given to Kristeva's legitimate and transparent reworking, even 'proselytizing', of Bakhtin.[17] One reason may be because the translation is particularly 'unfaithful' to Kristeva's original essay on this very subject.

The original essay in *Semeiotikè*, written in 1966, appends to the end of its title an all-important footnote. This directly acknowledges that Kristeva's ensuing study is based on, and emerges from, Bakhtin's two recent literary studies, on Dostoyevsky (Moscow, 1963) and Rabelais (Moscow, 1965). Furthermore, Kristeva notes how Bakhtin visibly influenced Soviet theoreticians of language and literature of the 1930s (Voloshinov and Medvedev), and announces that Bakhtin is working on a study of genres of discourse. Kristeva can only have had access to this material in the original Russian. This footnote is transposed in the translation to the end of the first sentence (where it is of tangential relevance). It is also pared down to a bald reference to the *translations* of *Rabelais and his World* (translated in 1965) and *Problems of Dostoyevsky's Poetics* (translated in 1973). The translation then crowns this first note not with the additional information on Bakhtin's influence, but with a reference to his death in 1975 and to the publication (Todorov's) of some of his essays in French in 1978. Elsewhere, the translation elides often partial renditions of the notes in Kristeva's original essay with glosses for an Anglo-American readership. While it may seem a point of pedantry, such improper referencing and acknowledgement in the first footnote of the Bakhtinian context in its rich multiplicity has led to unjustifiable assessments of Kristeva's essay. Its import has been reduced either by suggesting that, retrospectively, it is tantamount to a plagiarism of Bakhtin,[18] or, inversely, that Kristeva's reworking of intertextuality falls painfully short of the precisions in 'Bakhtin's' original work.[19]

By contrast, and from its outset, Kristeva's original essay signals how *belated* the French intellectual scene in linguistics is when compared to work already well developed in the 1930s in Russia. Secondly, Bakhtin's double place in the transformation of issues to do solely with linguistics derives from his role in and outside Formalism, and his calling into question of science as meta-structural term. Kristeva's scrupulousness (unlike Barthes or Derrida for example) in citing or referencing ideas gleaned from elsewhere, because unrecorded, or unnoticed in French-speaking circles, has in fact played against her work being seen as highly informed transformation. What ensues in her 'Word, dialogue, text' essay is the planting out of Bakhtin's various concepts, such as dialogism, carnival, poetic language, as various seedlings in the French seedbed of Saussurian linguistics. At each planting out, Kristeva begins overtly with reference to Bakhtin, such that her own contribution can then also be inserted. Bakhtin is in fact mentioned seven times in the first six pages of Kristeva's essay, as well as indirectly through his works. Most significantly for our analysis, the famous 'definition' of 'intertextuality' is the second half of a longer sentence prefaced by a reference to Bakhtin as originator: 'Yet what appears as a lack of rigour is in fact an insight first introduced into literary theory by Bakhtin: any text etc.' The mosaic of quotations phrase is then a *gloss* and transposition of Bakhtin's thought. This is doubly obvious in that this sentence is itself appositional and expands a prior idea also fully attributed to Bakhtin. It is worth quoting it in full: 'In Bakhtin's work, these two axes, which he calls *dialogue* and *ambivalence*, are not clearly distinguished.'[20] The two axes in question are horizontal (subject-addressee) and vertical (text-context). It goes without saying that subjects, addressees and exterior texts are all very alive in Kristeva's Bakhtin, which she renders faithfully, and in Kristeva's intertextuality developed from these Bakhtinian co-ordinates in the *following* paragraph. Indeed, both Bakhtin and Kristeva honour the author as funnel, so that textuality enters into dialogue with other determining elements. Together, these produce in the novel its polyphony. Neither Bakhtin nor Kristeva, therefore, posits the reader as pivot of interpretability within or outside the text. It is on the question of mediation, however, that Kristeva opens up space for her own concept of intertextuality:

> The word as minimal textual unit thus turns out to occupy the status of *mediator*, linking structural models of cultural (historical) environment, as well as that of *regulator*, controlling mutations from diachrony to synchrony, i.e., to literary structure. The word is spatialized: through the very notion of status, it functions in three dimensions (subject-addressee-context) as a set of *dialogical*, semic elements or as a set of *ambivalent* elements. Consequently the task of literary semiotics is to discover other formalisms corresponding to different modalities of word-joining (sequences) within the dialogical space of texts.[21]

For Kristeva, the novel exteriorizes this linguistic dialogue and is at the same time the expansion of the horizontal and vertical axes above through two interconnected operations of the 'translinguistic'. This is the spatialization of both the condensation of words transmitted in a language (as 'langue' and 'discours') and the elaboration of language within generic formalizations which ever renew and transform socially marked instances of words (dialogism and carnival). The remainder of Kristeva's essay reads Bakhtin to rewrite it into *French*, not as 'translation' of 'langues', but as translinguistic dialogue between two intercultural situations. Combining gloss, interpretation, résumé or elaboration of *Bakhtin's* key terms – the ensuing and clearly designated subsections of Kristeva's essay make this again abundantly clear – Kristeva is precisely this *mediator-regulator* of textual dialogue. Moreover, French cultural heritage is returned via the 'strangeness' of reading it proleptically through Bakhtin's *Rabelais* (carnival, the grotesque). It is from such (Bakhtinian) 'double-voiced' critical dialogue that Kristeva's essay takes its cue so that her own translingual project can be integrated within the French intellectual climate of left-wing *Tel Quel* and structural (post-Formalist) notions of morphology. What is therefore so stunningly new in Kristeva's work here is the advancing of a theory of *translinguistics*, and the transformative operations at work in any cultural transfer, whether intra- or interlingually. It is but a short step from this to notions of transference and counter-transference and the realm of the pre-linguistic and pre-semiotic in her later 'psychoanalytic' works.

This leaves us with a problem, however. If much of 'Word, dialogue, novel' is a revision of Bakhtin for the rather different French context of Saussurian linguistics, what, in short, is Kristeva's intertextuality? Within *Semeiotikè* as a whole, the term is first mentioned in the preceding essay, 'Le Texte clos' ('The closed text', 1966–7):

> The text is therefore *productivity*, meaning that (1) its relation to the language in which it is sited is redistributive (destructive-constructive) and consequently it can be approached by means of logical categories other than purely linguistic ones; (2) it is a permutation of texts, an intertextuality: in the space of a text, many utterances taken from other texts intersect with one another and neutralize one another.[22]

While the full significance of this definition will be made even more apparent in the next part of the chapter, the key phrase is 'a permutation of texts, an intertextuality', but in apposition to the text's quality as 'productivity'. Text is the translinguistic arena of language (as 'langue', 'parole', and their logical reformations in writing and other cultural productions) in active and constant redistribution. Intertextuality thus names this interactive, permutational production of text, its constant intersecting and neutralizing processes. While the final verbs might best be rendered in the passive in English, their reflexive form in French ('se croisent et se neutralisent') underlines the dynamic mode of such 'productivity' in language. Reflexivity is indeed the essential motor of language itself for its own rejuvenation. Thus, neutralization is not so much a cancelling out as an interactive levelling. Prior text materials lose special status by permutation with others in the intertextual exchange because all intertexts are of equal importance in the intertextual *process*.

Moreover, it is at this point of permutation (intertextuality) that the ideological implications of text (and its various ideologemes) are materialized even as the new text is also transformed by its contexts.[23] Such translinguistic and transformational productions, such as the novel, allow ideologemes on a number of levels, including the extra-textual, to appear. Historical or national referents are one example, but socio-temporal evolutions of language as archaism or dialect are also recoverable. The ideological is thus constantly threading and rethreading the textual fabric, not outside it in hermeneutical or critical analysis. Kristevan intertextuality as permutation, like Bakhtin's 'dialogism' before it, amply allows for socio-historical, 'polyphonic' and 'carnivalesque' ideologemes in order that the status quo will be challenged.[24] There can be no authoritative fixity for interactive, permutational (inter)text. Hence, 'intertextuality' as static, all-encompassing network, with no outside of the text, is not Kristevan.

While admittedly abstract, the remainder of 'Le Texte clos' elaborates the key ideas of its opening paragraphs and also prepares the ground for the sixth essay, 'La Productivité dite texte', where Kristeva does battle with, and brings together, Marxist notions of dialectical materialism and literary notions of verisimilitude.[25] Kristeva ultimately wants to avoid both a science model, where matter and simulacra converge, and a mimetic function for art (whether it imitates nature or the world). We will return to these questions in the context of mimesis in chapter 3. These two concerns (language modelled on science, signifiers potentially eliding with signifieds) are of course central also to debates in Eastern European linguistics and for Bakhtin. I leave specialists in these fields to explore Kristeva's work in 'Le Texte clos' comparatively. At the very least, what needs to be recognized is that the observations of this essay, especially on the polyphonic nature of the translinguistic, reveal it as the hitherto hidden interlocutor with the more famous fourth 'intertextuality' essay. 'Le Texte clos' offers the French half of Kristeva's French–Russian dialogue on translinguistics.

Kristeva's retransplantation of Bakhtin's negotiation of Rabelais (the carnivalesque) for the context of French Saussurian linguistics allows her theory of intertextuality as permutation to avoid the Scylla of the death of the author and the Charybdis of the non-existence of any outside of the text. As appositional to 'productivity', however, intertextuality as permutation still requires some generator to ensure that its redistributive, intersecting and levelling processes continue. Pressure by Barthes and Riffaterre on exactly this *lacuna* in Kristeva's theory, and their various reader response solutions, will be examined below. Kristeva's own theory, however, already tackles the problem and from within the semiotics of *Semeiotikè*. As the quotation above from 'Le Texte clos' intimates, 'logical categories other than purely linguistic ones' are where such productivity occurs. What might these logical categories be?

In the opening paragraph of the first essay in *Semeiotikè*, 'Le Texte et sa science' (The text and its science), Kristeva sets out her thesis for what becomes the amplified subtitle for the volume as a whole, 'recherches pour une sémanalyse' (research towards a seme-analysis), in which intertextuality plays an integral part. This opening paragraph functions rather like the innermost knot of a concentric-ity of ideas which *Semeiotikè* expands outwards. This incipit is arguably also essential to understanding the ensuing development of Kristeva's theoretical work as a whole.

> *To make language an operator* [. . .] at work in the materiality of that which, for society, is a means of contact and understanding, does this not make of it immediately an outsider to language? The so-called lit-erary act, by dint of its not admitting to an *ideal* distance in relation to the *that* which it signifies, introduces radical otherness in relation to what language is claimed to be: a bearer of meanings. Strangely close and intimately foreign to the substance of our discourse and dreams, 'literature' today appears to be the very act which grasps how language works and signals what it has the power tomorrow to transform.[26]

In this dense and allusive passage, there are two clusters of key ideas. Work ('faire', 'travail', 'oeuvrer', 'se faire') is integrally connected to ideas about being outside, foreign, other ('étranger', étrangeté, 'étrangement'). Productivity is the conjunction in language of 'acts' or enactments and their transformations as different from them-selves. A hyphen after the prefix, 'trans-formation', would underpin Kristeva's attempt to describe language form that makes itself foreign to itself, a notion already common currency within Russian Formal-ism, as the 'making strange'. The hyphen also serves to highlight the logical or mathematical relation at work here. This is the relation of 'x and not x', or binary number systems, which should not be con-fused with binary oppositions or Hegelian dialectics. These nodal terms, 'work', 'outsideness' and 'trans-formation', can then be seen as foreshadowings of the terms in the title of the fourth 'intertextuality' essay, 'Word, dialogue, novel'. Neither diachronic (duration) nor synchronic (a point in time), they allow reflexive synergy to flow both ways between them. From its very incipit, *Semeiotikè* thus attempts to uncover the method and process of these terms as seme-analysis, and the role of translinguistic and trans-formative permutation in producing a 'materialist gnoseology'. The theoretical model undergirding this is not science, but a larger model of *text* where science participates alongside sociology, mathematics, psychoanalysis, linguistics and logic. This decentring of science as primary model for all other disciplines also reworks the science/philosophy dichotomy.[27] For Kristeva, text of any kind is not a vehicle of information ('the *that* which it signifies'), but so many forms of reflexive and hence 'poetic' language (including science) in co-operation.

The focus on 'strangeness', 'foreignness', 'being outside' in the introit to *Semeiotikè* meshes with and is expanded in the seventh essay, 'Poésie et négativité' (Poetry and negativity), published later in 1968. Here, particularly in its third section, where there is explicit development of her theory of intertextuality as permutation, 'étranger' is the key word, and, as above, 'négativité' is not oppositional, but appositional levelling. It is in the active translation/transformation in poetic language of discourse that the text's infinite 'anotherness' (an-otherness) can best be glimpsed.[28] The intertextual is the pinpointing of this ontogenetic signifying trail whereby language can question itself in its strangeness and unfamiliarities to itself. Stepping alongside itself ('intimement étranger'), word/text is neither outside itself through a transcendent signifier, nor inside itself as ontological identity.[29] It is always allogamous, disconjoint.[30] Early in 'Le Texte et sa science', Kristeva names this as a 'polyvalency of non-unity', altogether synonymous with her later intertextuality as permutation.[31] As translation studies and Kristeva's later essay on translation, 'L'Autre Langue ou traduire le sensible',[32] endorse, the signified can never be a one-to-one relationship (either as the repetition of a noun in the same language or the equivalent in another). At best, it will be an approximation because context and nuance come with accretions in time, whether intra- or interlingually. This incomplete and uncompletable position for the text is tantamount to the speaker's experience of a self-in-translation where one is the other of the same in another language, or in one's own language from different, adjacent, perspectives.[33] Meaning and subject are therefore never unified, but share the space of insider–outsider to language. For Kristeva, persons contribute to the process, but as unimportant mediators of the text's alterior trans-formations and translations into writing, ideas to which the fourth chapter will return. In other words, trans-formativity in Kristeva's work highlights permutationality as signifying practices not of orders (such as systems or mosaics), but of constant, logical *disordering*. What Kristeva's *Semeiotikè* so richly heralds here, and which her later deliberations on psychoanalysis will theorize, is the interface between translation and the pre-semiotic and their disorders.[34]

The corollary of the alignment of disorders and disordering principles is that Kristeva's theory of language and intertextuality does not envisage chaos, the inchoate or abyssal deferral as negative, but as reconstitutive synergies of text. Her essay 'Le Texte et sa science' is again richly indicative of her later work. It is not a theory of a science of language or an attempt to validate poetic language by scientific or mechanistic/formalistic means. Neither is it a theory of the inchoate *other* of science, whether of madness, psychedelia, psychic or psychotic phenomena, or of avant-garde experimental texts. Rather, through permutations of order, disorder and transformation, Kristeva's is the attempt to theorize another text ('étranger') of science. In the first essay, and as hints throughout *Semeiotikè*, what appears is what I can only call a 'quantum theory of translinguistics' (as opposed to mechanics).[35] In the section of 'Poésie et négativité' (the seventh essay), directly following her cogitation of the strange, the foreign, Kristeva describes texts in intertextual permutations as the observable poetic meaning effects of semes and lexemes in play as unobservable because unfixable particles and waves.[36] It is a short step from here to psychoanalytic free association and stages of psychic development, or its absence, a Brownian movement of internal or external stimuli blending together.[37]

From this rereading of Kristeva, the theories of semiology, deconstruction and 'intertextuality' of Barthes, Derrida and the Anglo-American 'Kristeva' emerge as much less accommodating of the other, as *other*. Strangeness, alienation and foreignness are not the Other, or other, but (an)other of the self, seen in cameo in Kristeva's own experience as translated into her works from *Semeiotikè* on. Clearly, there is then no epistemic 'break' between the two periods of her writing. Her personal positioning as Bulgarian émigrée and the alterity she discovered in her work in and through the medium of French, particularly her contributions to *French* linguistic, pre-linguistic and translinguistic theories, as well as her position *vis-à-vis* Russian Formalism, are what inform her theory, whether intertextuality as permutation, or disorders as reconstitutive of new productivity. Her own subject position as same and another through language that is and is not her own crystallizes the seme-analytical dialogue at work in text in general, whether mono- or multilingual. Similarly, writing as poetic language is a translation and transformation (beside itself) of the negative–positive tow of language as 'langue', 'parole' and other texts. Moreover, *Semeiotikè* as blueprint for a 'materialist gnoseology' challenges science as meta-model for knowledge, by aligning ways of knowing by sojourning, encountering and passing on into text. Kristeva's theory of intertextuality as permutation of texts, as her introduction of Bakhtin into France, is then best summed up as 'strangers to ourselves'.[38] The author is not dead, but *in rememoriam*.[39] Otherwise, as the double erasure of 'Kristeva'/Kristeva through translation or its lack has demonstrated, sexed, gendered and ethnically different bodies are all too easily disinherited by becoming de-unified subjects, or by being denied a signature. Kristevan intertextuality is therefore not a mosaic,[40] or a limitless web of deferred meanings, but a logical relationship of 'X and/or not X', an 'an(d)other'. It is at the point of translinguistic permutability that borders are drawn even as they are crossed, because the trans-formativity of words within and between language(s) cannot but be at work together.[41] Thus, while some of the same problems that have been charged against the intertextuality of 'Kristeva' as 'mosaic of texts' remain, as we will see below, there seems much in *Semeiotikè* that bears more than a second glance, however unpolished or tangential some of the rich fusion and interplay of ideas appear. In the concluding deliberations of the chapter we will weigh up the usefulness of Kristevan intertextuality as critical term now revised by our reading of *Semeiotikè* as a whole rather than as belatedly translated fragment. To do so, however, the 'strangers to herself' need first to be considered.

Barthes

If Kristeva opened intertextuality up to all its borders and permutations, Barthes and Riffaterre directly address its blind spots as theory of text as productivity. As Tilottama Rajan points out, such a conception:

> requires us to posit this reader as an extratextual subject, even in cases where the text consciously inscribes itself as a reading. For such a text can reread the anterior corpus and can situate its own reading, but in order to make this situatedness dialectical, it is necessary that transposition also be conceived as a communicative transfer to a subsequent reader. The positing of a reader [. . .] is also a corollary of Kristeva's failure to negotiate the problem of intention.[42]

How both Barthes and Riffaterre reread and overwrite Kristeva in the 1970s, as Genette will also do later in 1982 (as chapter 3 more fully investigates), brings us to a central issue of intertextuality however it is envisaged, the authority of quotations and citations. It is not only who signs them, but also who circulates them. The example to hand is the major part Kristeva played in Barthes's seminars in the late 1960s, which, like her coinage of intertextuality, is mentioned by critics (as Lechte above) only in passing. What is rarely questioned is her importance for Barthes's theory, rather than the reverse, and why and how hers has been suppressed. Aside from the availability or not of translations as contributory factor, it is the power of a certain authority (even though authors are 'dead' according to Barthes) as cult figure or familiar brand name that is the issue in the ensuing reassessment of Barthes's contribution to 'intertextuality', in both its semiotics and non-semiotics contexts. Some very strange Oedipal rivalries will be seen to be at work, and to play for, in Barthes's treatment of Kristeva.

One of the most 'authoritative' sites for definition and assertion is the dictionary or the encyclopaedia, and it was Barthes, not Kristeva, who provided the entry for 'Texte (théorie du)', in the *Encyclopédie universalis* in 1973. In the following sections taken from it, note the unmistakable echoes and reworkings of Kristeva's phrases, even plagiarisms if one has prior access to *Semeiotikè*:

> The text is a productivity. Not in the sense that it is a product of being worked (as narrative technique or the mastery of style would demand), but as the very theatre of a production where the producer of the text and the reader come together: the text 'works' whenever and however it is taken up; even in written fixed form, the text does not stop working, or undertaking a process of production. The text deconstructs the language of communication, representation or expression [. . .] and reconstructs another language. [. . .] Every text is an intertext; other texts are present within it to varying degrees and in more or less recognisable forms. [. . .] Every text is a new tissue of recycled citations. Fragments of codes, formulae, model rhythms, bits of social discourse pass into the text and are redistributed within it. [. . .] The intertext is a field of anonymous formulae whose origin is rarely recoverable, of unconscious or automatic citations without speech marks.

This definition, with its subversive reworkings of what Barthes would see as 'public' language, offers in cameo 'his' theory of *text*. While it is blatantly similar to Kristeva's intertextuality, it is equally an overtly different graft of it. What results is that Barthes's formulation goes against the grain at precisely those points where direct lifting of Kristeva's words could be seen to occur. Barthes, therefore, subverts 'authority' even as he eschews authors to whom certain words can be attributed. The pressure point here is 'the theatre of production' so that Barthes, as impresario, may rechoreograph the lines of the Kristevan script. That he is cognizant of it is, however, quite clear from his backhanded tribute in the revised foreword to the *Essais critiques* of 1971. The 'defraction' of semiology Barthes notes from 1967 onwards is illustrated in a list beginning with Derrida's writing ('livres'), the action of *Tel Quel* and last (and least?) the work ('travail' not 'livres') of Julia Kristeva.[43] It is against her work as labour that Barthes can derive an intertextuality of play. For those familiar with Kristeva's later *Pouvoirs de l'horreur* (1980), the very Oedipal work here is the 'abjectification' of the mother's body. Only by making this other can the child become separate. Thus, whether as the unrecorded voice from his seminar, or the overwriting of her 'mother' terms in the definition above, Barthes's sleight of hand makes her *work*, as labour in both senses, secondary. Similarly, *Le Plaisir du texte* (also published in 1973) trades her idea of 'writing aloud' as his grain of the voice.[44] It is by the elliptical use of Kristeva's 'phéno-texte' and 'géno-texte' that Barthes diverts her work on the polyphonic into the more performative and libidinous channels of his own. Thus, as theatre of the text of pleasure, *Le Plaisir du texte* (also quickly available in translation in 1975) elucidates inter-textuality as a theory of reading:

> I savour the reign of formulas, the reversing of origins, the offhand manner in which the anterior text is made to come after the ulterior one. [. . .] A bit of Proust is what comes to me, not what I call on; it is not an 'authority', simply a *circular memory*. The inter-text is just that: the impossibility of life outside the infinite text – whether the text is Proust, the daily paper, or what's on TV: the book makes the meaning, the meaning makes life.[45]

To pick up the all-important hyphen in Barthes's inter-textuality, the reader is not the absent mediator-translator as in Kristeva,[46] but body of mediation or medium for the text's effect or, more important for Barthes, affect to come into play. In Barthes, theatrical metaphors and similes abound, and his earliest essays dealt specifically with French theatre (*Sur Racine*, 1963), costume (*Système de la mode*, 1967), the staging of the persona (*S/Z*, 1970).[47] The drama of play in a variety of senses leaves its traces in this passage. Play is not causal or goal related, but impromptu, improper, unexpected pleasure and, on rare occasion, *jouissance*. It is outside the adult world of responsibility and 'authority' with its attendant patriarchal institutions, including the author.[48] It is also mime, dressing up in another's clothes, borrowing or being invaded by the other like a character by an actor. Dialogue is then taken up as the staging, the reiteration of another's words, as one's own in reading. The reader is therefore no passive vehicle, or echo chamber, but the *reagent* of the text. Depending on how arresting, pleasurable, seductive the text is, a whole gamut of potential reactions could then occur, from quixotic, whimsical, perverse, blasphemous, philistine, erudite to bored and distracted like a child. Since there is no authority or intention to regulate this playtime or its responses, the writer becomes impresario, the one who stages in the text the possibility of its pleasure or *jouissance*.[49] As go-between of text and reception in the interval that is the inter-text, the writer remains apparent only by double trace as the spider implied by the web woven by *this* text.[50] Judgement of writing, a writer, or text in whatever form by the Barthesian reader will therefore necessarily be 'fickle', playful towards moral orders, aesthetic systems or ideological application. Only the affect or '*brio*' of a text, and at certain pitches, counts as laudable.[51] Necessarily, such qualifiers put uppermost emotive response, entertainment, the arts of seduction (immediacy, fascination, repetition), and banish critical and impersonal criteria of taste (beauty), morality (the good) or correctness (truth). Barthes thereby neatly circumnavigates the old chestnut whether allusions or quotations in a text are intentional or non-intentional and therefore faithful or unfaithful to the original.[52] This move also releases the reader from the stigma of not spotting either kind. The one-upmanship of successful source-hunting, the search for hidden references to, or influences on, the author's life or context are everywhere anathema and irrelevant for Barthes. Since authorities of any kind are actively disregarded, this theory cannot offer an ethics of reading, whether good or bad. Yet, the intellectual or the culturally highbrow text is then not demoted *per se*. If the reader finds it erotic or libidinous, it may provoke physiological or intellectual pleasure, *jouissance* and epistemophilia.[53]

If Barthes's inter-textuality is then everywhere divergence and diversion, reader satisfaction with the text's seduction and siren call is of paramount importance.[54] Indeed, one of the key terms Barthes employs to describe this state is 'dérive', usually translated as drift (as for ships off course, or continents).[55] Since it also means a diversion of a river, it usefully offers a direct negation of the concept of influence in two ways. First, like a piece of flotsam and jetsam fragmented from some former whole and floating at the limit of its potential undoing, the 'dérive' is lack of fixity and direction. Second, it is a move going directly against the flow. As Bloom's 'anxiety of influence' in the next chapter will also demonstrate, the Barthesian 'dérive' ultimately describes the very pleasure of the text going against the (Kristevan) grain, or writing aloud, with all the incestuous, Oedipal titillations of totem and taboo. What has not been noted, however, is that such phonetic stereophony of articulation is made out of the skins of other texts.[56] While Barthes's move has been read as a kind of sexual politics, bringing what others label as the deviant into a wider 'theory' for all reworking of text, there are distinctly narcissistic and misogynistic undercurrents.[57] Not least, the stereophonic articulations of pleasure, whether of Proust, Bataille, Montaigne, Lyotard and many others, constitute an almost exclusively *male* chorus in *Le Plaisir du texte*. Unlike the use of the palimpsest (particularly by Genette, as we shall see in chapter 3), this scratching on others' 'vellum' is the desire to put one's mark on, and all over, it. Unlike a forger or plagiarist, Barthes is then everywhere a graffiti artist scribbling over the flaunted texts of others.[58] For too long his seductive analyses of advertising, with its affects and semi-aphoristic and fragmentary catchphrases that critics have upheld at face value, have not been applied back to Barthes's own writing as self-advertisement, even exhibitionism. It is not the other that counts but the bruise of the other's skin, which marks where the *self* has passed, invisibly visible.

The Barthesian model of the reader, chasing the pleasure principle through the most deviatory of routes, and playing with other texts in a cavalier or counter-directional manner, cannot therefore offer a paradigm for reader response theory, except perhaps one of reader irresponsibility.[59] Barthes's theory does, however, display the intertext's ludic function at its most performative, entertaining, entrancing, seductive, erotic or gratuitous. As one of art's oldest rationales for storytelling, entertainment including Barthes's spin on it ('plaire') cannot, however, ignore art's other rationale, to instruct ('instruire'). It is precisely this missing heuristic dimension that Riffaterre adopts as his, not least to distinguish his theories of reader response and intertextuality from Barthes's:

> The implicit intertext must therefore be carefully distinguished from R. Barthes's concept of intertext [. . .] which proclaims the reader's freedom to associate texts at random, as dictated by his culture or personal idiosyncracies – a response by definition personal, shared with others only by chance: this is hardly the disciplined reading the text in its structured entirety demands of the reader; it hardly gives the text a physiognomy readers *must* agree on.[60]

With stress here on discipline, concerted channelling of reader attention and coerciveness, is Riffaterre's version the serious unpleasuring and unleisuring of the text and its intertexts? Is his countenancing of textual directives a new didacticism? Or is Riffaterre's theory of textual self-discipline, surveillance and sanction another kind of eroticism of reading?

Riffaterre

Where the seductions and impostures of Barthes's inter-textuality of play have mostly generated positive critical response, Riffaterre's concerted and sober restoration of the (guided) reader to the text, and its intertexts, has elicited only faint praise.[61] Bruce (1995) is among few French-speaking critics to have actively compared Kristeva's and Riffaterre's theories of intertextuality.[62] However, Riffaterre's own bilingualism has gone unnoted, as, too, his very French training in close reading or 'explication de texte'. It is this context which is crucial to understanding Riffaterre's model for the intertext as *syllepsis* (as against Barthesian ellipsis). Syllepsis, the use of a single construction that has two syntactic functions, pinpoints Riffaterre's shared interests with Kristeva concerning the doubling of discourse that is poetic language on the one hand, and, on the other, their mutual regard for Saussure's fascination with anagrams. 'To perceive the text as a transform of an intertext is to perceive it as the ultimate word game, that is, as literary.'[63] While Kristeva takes up Saussure's original term, the paragram in the fifth essay of *Semeiotikè*, Riffaterre transmutes it as hypogram.[64] The main difference is that Riffaterre focuses on the 'perceiver' and language code-breaker (the reader), not on the accretive text. Almost more important, Riffaterre develops a theory of reading that foregrounds the various kinds of textual logic and binary matrices we discovered above in Kristeva's theory of intertextuality as productivity and permutation.

In contradistinction to play to derive pleasure (Barthes), Riffaterre sees game-playing as skilful decoding within complex sets of rules, leading to the delight of recognition, or the victory of successful negotiation of a textual maze.[65] What is so striking about Riffaterre's work is its none the less engaging and provocative qualities that align it much more with storytelling than with didacticism or dry criticism and theory. While Riffaterre's method is altogether that which Barthes most abhors, the Socratic,[66] Riffaterre's particular skill in 'explication de texte' is no less seductive, but intellectually and maieutically so. Reader attention is teasingly controlled so that s/he is led through the textual elements towards the 'plot' that links them differently from their purely grammatical connections.[67] It is primarily to the reading plot of poetry that Riffaterre attends, not narratives reliant on intricate plots and sub-plots, whether the serial realist or naturalist novel, formalist bricolage, postmodern collage, or prose sub-genres of intrigue such as the fairy-tale collection, mystery stories, detective fiction or the campus novel. For Riffaterre, poetry not only remains the most clearly framed genre by its long self-

exclusion from 'ordinary' prose language, it also 'expresses concepts
and things by indirection. To put it simply, a poem says one thing
and means another.'[68] It is 'indirection', the production of meaning
by displacement, that solves Riffaterre's main concern regarding significance, which is not text in endless deferral or literature's mimetic
representations of reality. It is, 'rather, the reader's praxis of transformation, a realization that it is akin to playing, to acting out the
liturgy of a ritual – the experience of a circuitous sequence, a way of
speaking that keeps revolving around a key word or matrix reduced
to a marker.'[69] 'Intertextuality' names these markers, made visible to
the reader of the poem as a whole by various 'ungrammaticalities'
that belie them as a nexus of significations, not single lexical items.
Included are the remodelling of poetic paradigms, conventions of
versification, stock images and epithets (conceits and blasons), or
rhetorical overdeterminations such as paronomasia (the playing out
of meanings of words that sound alike), catachresis (the improper use
of terms in a given context), anaphora (repetition of certain words
in subsequent clauses, extended metaphors), syllepses (words pertinent to two or more registers), hypograms proper (puns, anagrams,
homophones, homonyms) and symbols. In short, poetry is always
'anagrammatical', naming its artifice as 'already a stylistic structure,
hot with intensified connotations, overloaded discourse'.[70]

While thus also circumventing source-hunting or authorial intention as modes of criticism or interpretation, Riffaterre's *Semiotics of
Poetry* (1978) is much more than a virtuoso reader response to some
of the most complex and enigmatic poetry in French, the advocacy
of high-cultural mastery, or example of master-reading.[71] Riffaterre
pinpoints the ambivalence present in Kristeva's intertextuality, that
(all) writing is poetics or the literary translation of language, but foregrounds the adept reader as arbiter of what makes language poetry
and not prose. To clarify both of these, Riffaterre looks not to increasingly hermetic, self-sufficient or self-referential poems, but to a genre
no other theorist has properly tackled, the prose poem. Its interest
for intertextuality is that it has indirection (lack of pre-determined
frame), interpretative chiaroscuro dependent on 'ungrammaticalities'
and readerly praxis; it has communicability yet remains ultimately a
word game. In line with Riffaterre's understanding of significance
above, it is the prose poem's move from prosaic form, representationality and mimetic delivery that openly reveals its anti-mimetic
plot as such because it pushes even harder on its *prosody*.[72] The reader
sees (at least) two things at once, but can also interpret them analo-
gously and with some certainty since the clues relate to the overall
second-level interpretation. All the postmodern and deconstructive
aporias, such as undecidability, irony or ambivalence, are therefore

not part of Riffaterre's theory of intertextuality since they constitute subjective responses. His intertextual syllepsis claims verifiability by intersubjective response: a number of readers will join up the dots and find a similar resulting pattern of *expansion* of meanings, not a limited pre-determination such as satire or allegory.[73] Unlike the postmodern text revelling in black holes and gaps, then, the prose poem opens towards plenitude since it also allows for subsequent and finer-meshed readings.

How can such refinements be evaluated? Rather than providing a solution to the problems in Kristeva's theory of intertextuality as permutation of texts, Riffaterre's theory of reader response is equally problematic. Prior knowledge, whether by readers or texts, remains the nub of a problem for intertextual research in general, and one which Worton and Still (1990) signal as primordial:

> a text is available only through some process of reading; what is produced at the moment of reading is due to the cross-fertilization of the packaged material [. . .] by all the texts which the reader brings to it. A delicate allusion to a work unknown to the reader, which therefore goes unnoticed, will have a dormant existence in that reading. On the other hand, the reader's experience of some practice or theory unknown to the author may lead to a fresh interpretation.[74]

Clearly the reader of the prose poem rather than prose requires a high(er) degree of intertextual experience and micro-attention to indirections and ungrammaticalities. S/he cannot then be some 'ordinary' reader, but a super-sleuth. While endless permutations (Kristevan intertextuality) exist hypothetically, particularization must be at work to overrule certain readings as arbitrary, subjective or nonsensical.[75] Riffaterre's reader is therefore no apprentice or youthful enthusiast, nor even someone highly informed in rhetoric or linguistics,[76] but a well-equipped reader formed in the school of accumulated experience of *reading*. Although Riffaterre calls such reader formation simply 'competence', his version of intertextuality as syllepsis is not merely experience of the *déjà lu*, but quantified and qualified by terms such as 'widely read', 'well-educated', 'erudite'.[77] His 'reader' is then also highly problematic as universal, or some transnational self outside the particularities of gender, race, class, creed.[78] Responsibility for such elements in the pattern arrived at is squarely returned to determinations within the text.[79] Riffaterre thus delimits intertextuality to a heuristic-hermeneutic grid where the reader traces threads in its web to find not a minotaur in the labyrinth of meaning, but resolution of consistent patterns. The last word of his chapter on the prose poem sums this up in true Socratic fashion. His is the theory of intertextuality as riddle, or logogriph.[80]

Riddles and matrices, sieves and grids, however logical or mathematical (scientific) they may be, are not without their own specific
cultural heritage. Riffaterre's method is not universal or singular.
Although it shares much with New Criticism, it remains firmly,
though not explicitly, rooted in a French education in 'explication de
texte' and its application to canonical works. However, Riffaterre is
a bilingual critic between the French and New Critical Schools, and
his theory adds understanding of the role of the reader as transmit-
ter and refiner of cultural transfer. For all its immediate charisma,
Barthes's range by contrast is limited to intertextual play with very
French samplers, even though they are taken from high and low
culture, or appeal to the cultural snobbery of non-French speakers.
Barthes's brilliance is then the choreography of the intertext as
ephemeral and sensate, the white heat of pyrotechnics. Kristeva,
behind this display, already saw the laws of 'translingua-physics', the
particles and waves of the 'Big Bang' of (inter)textuality. Ever her
matching opposite, Riffaterre then takes her to task by explaining the
nucleus, or nexus, the 'text' in intertextuality.[81] Unlike the monolingual Barthes, their bi- or trilingualism opens the 'inter-' and 'text' of
intertextuality to properly translinguistic applications and dimensions. It is in these, however, that lie the shadowlands of communication practice. By looking now at speech and discourse rather than
text and writing, the way will be paved to question in the remainder
of the chapter how cultural hierarchies and their ideological frameworks reinforce fixity and pattern over instance, variation, improvisation and change.

Interdiscursivity

In what was the first of several 'second-wave' responses to theories
of intertextuality in France from the 1960s and 1970s, Marc Angenot
(1983a) offered a critical survey of its theorists and its workability as
term.[82] Not only was he among the first critics to highlight the far-
reaching problems that intertextuality posed for textual criticism
per se. He was also far-sighted in his appraisal of intertextuality's own
critical future, as well as aware of other ideas in circulation concur-
rently with it:

> The idea of intertextuality has come to trouble all sorts of epistemo-
> logical schemas and vectors which connected the author to the work,
> empirical reference to expression in language, source to influence
> undergone, part to whole, code to performance and, in the text,
> to question its linearity and closure. [. . .] To all these models, inter-

textuality opposes a problematics of multiplicity, heterogeneity and
exteriority which is, it seems to me, beyond certain misconceptions
[. . .] the essence of *our* problem for years to come.[83]

While eschewing notions of textual productivity, the fetishism of the
text for itself or as system, and the ambivalence of multiplying and
fragmenting the subject by a text-based revision of the notion of
intersubjectivity, Angenot highlighted the positively oppositional
forces of multiplicity, heterogeneity and exteriority that Kristeva's
version of intertextuality demonstrates. Angenot's 'exteriority', which
he does not in fact explore further, names what we found to be the
'an-otherness' and 'outside-ness' in *Semeiotikè*. Crucially, Angenot
takes this same triad as blueprint for, and watershed between,
Kristevan intertextuality and his own work within socio-criticism, not
least that of J.-P. Faye. Because Angenot's article is not translated,
and is thus rarely cited in Anglo-American criticism, its full force,
and critical development as theory of interdiscursivity (Angenot,
1983b), is little known.[84] Multiplicity, heterogeneity and exterioriza-
tion are here returned to communication with the world, not to
textual interrelationships. Thus, where Kristeva's *Semeiotikè* detached
Bakhtinian dialogism from its communicative context to concentrate
on the polyphony of poetic language, Angenot reattaches Bakhtin's
'heteroglossia' as *social* discourse to interdiscursivity, in order to highlight ideological manifestations and articulations. Ideological transmission is then the key problem for interdiscursivity, one overlapping
with Barthes's interest in the semiotics of popular culture of *Mythologies* (1957), but without the loss of exterior points of reference. As
Peter Nesselroth puts it, 'the framework of the argument has to be
much broader, [. . .] the difference is not between ordinary *language*
and literary *language* but between everyday *communication* and literary *communication*.'[85] Re-emphasis on social discourse automatically
overturns the primacy of writing within deconstructive remodelling
of Kristevan intertextuality to uncover another of its shadowlands,
oral heritage. What distinguishes Angenot from theorists such as
Walter Ong (1982), however, is advocacy of specifically social, rather
than individual, universal or transcendental theorizations of literacy
and orality.

The test of interdiscursivity as more than a variant of discourse
analysis or speech-act theory is its application.[86] Donald Bruce has
been Angenot's most concerted proponent, not least as his student,
but as critic of intertextuality because it cannot accommodate
ideological texts as such. Bruce's main work to date, entitled *De
l'intertextualité à l'interdiscursivité: histoire d'une double émergence*
(1995), overtly borrows key terms from Angenot's seminal article on

intertextuality (Angenot, 1983a). Following Angenot, it demolishes
Kristevan intertextuality and its subsequent reworking by Riffaterre
and Genette, before opening up interdiscursivity as theory and practice in the wake of Bakhtin. The case study is the tracing of the range
of discourses that operate in the ideological, symbolic and socio-
historical strands of Jules Vallès's trilogy set during the Paris
Commune of 1871. Where Bruce diverges from Angenot, however,
is his cavil with intertextuality, which he reads less as Kristevan than
'Kristevan' and postmodern.[87] By negating Angenot's positive evaluations of intertextuality's multiplicity, heterogeneity and exteriority,
Bruce makes these weaknesses, against which the strengths of interdiscursivity are only made more manifest.[88] By emphasizing what
makes discourses specific or performative in their interplay (interdiscursivity) within past and present history and culture, the lived
aspect of change, including ideological counter-movements, can be
countenanced.[89]

Interdiscursivity, in short, recalls the Bakhtinian chronotope from
its intertextual exile. This move, however, would seem to make of
interdiscursivity but another variant (like Kristeva's intertextuality)
of Bakhtin's concept of dialogism, albeit maintained firmly within
socio-criticism. Bruce would then appear to be resorting to exactly
the same revisionist tactics as Kristeva, but in order to reframe the
Bakhtin of the later *Speech Genres* (1986). If this is the case, the
further problem with interdiscursivity is that it seems to replicate
Lachmann's earlier and arguably more sophisticated developments
of Bakhtin in the 1980s in exactly the same directions, all of which
Bruce seems unaware.[90] While Angenot's and Bruce's interdiscursivity then seems to have nothing to redeem or recommend it, let alone
make it a rival term for intertextuality, it is its shift of emphasis that
is all important. Where Bakhtinian dialogism concerns speech genres,
it is mainly the manifestations of these as ideologemes and sociolects
within literary and hence poetic language and text (especially the
polyphonic novel) that is of primary focus.[91] The proper aegis for
interdiscursivity, on the other hand, is not experimental poetic texts,
but communicative and often intersubjective discourses, as recorded
for example in newspapers, tracts, recorded conversations, witness
reports and documentaries. The tracking of ideology is a more
specific task for interdiscursivity than in the work of Bakhtin or
Kristeva. For Bakhtin, every speech-act betrays an *ideology* or ideologies issuing from individual speakers in the ideological context of
a given dialogue. Kristeva revises Bakhtin's 'ideologeme' to see the
production of text through intertexts as the diffusion of the *ideological*. Interdiscursivity is the concerted effort to probe and pinpoint the
ideological dimensions of communication principally in its *inter*sub-

jective interlocutory contexts, to ascertain and separate strands from their interconnections. It is thus concerned with a dynamic of contingent discourses and contexts, not merely contiguous ones. In so doing, interdiscursivity attempts to return cognition, the knowledge acquired by social dialogue and ordinary language as opposed to intellectual or 'book' knowledge, to the forefront of how meanings are conveyed. Interdiscursivity thus permits the separation of 'text' and 'discourse' from their often interchangeable or elided positions within intertextuality, both on the micro-level of individual linguistic samples and on the wider level of speech genres. By recognizing multiple social contexts of enunciation, interdiscursivity also firmly embraces meanings, or the third term, referentiality, that the binarist, Saussurian, linguistic model (and its related theories) actively rejects.[92] Interdiscursivity can then say something about how discourse is actualized and can change, not least as retrospective or prospective possibility, whether as imagination, hypothesis, virtual or historical re-presentation of experience. This is not the infamous and maligned authorial intention, but the intentionality or orientation process of discourse that any grammatical sequence of tenses configures in everyday speech. Moreover, interdiscursivity's embrace of multiple meanings makes it amply able to accommodate explicit and implicit levels of interlocution, not least irony, sarcasm or humour. It can also examine speech-acts and oral traditions that may be prior to, or appropriated into, writing.

If interdiscursivity challenges intertextuality precisely where text replaced intersubjectivity, and can unpack historico-cultural particulars where intertextuality's synchronicity is unable to do this, it cannot, however, provide the same meta-level of interrogation as Kristevan or postmodern intertextuality, which easily accommodates 'ordinary' and 'poetic' language as 'text'. Whereas intertextuality accommodates genres connected to *durée* (myth, ceremonial, ritual, religion, poetry) interdiscursivity can only discuss *temps* (instances of mythic, ceremonial, poetic or other utterance) in specific socio-critical frames. Hence, however capable interdiscursivity is in identifying ideological discourses, it cannot scrutinize hidden prejudice or agendas behind such investigations. To put it simply, how can we know where the interdiscursive critic is situated *ideologically vis-à-vis* the ideologies under scrutiny? For interdiscursivity, then, part and partiality must ever be prioritized over the whole, or meta-critical, stance, a move that seems simply to reverse the allegedly impartial textual operations of postmodern intertextuality. The 'text' versus 'discourse' roots of intertextuality and interdiscursivity both transcend the other's limitations, but fail equally to transcend themselves. The prefix 'inter-' is perhaps the problem that frees and imprisons them both. It is the meta-critical level of ideological scrutiny that is equally a problem for intertextuality (in whatever manifestation), for issues of gender, race, creed or class *prejudice* may go unnoticed not because they are excluded, but because they are always potentially included categories. An example will make the case. A feminist scholar can apply both intertextuality and interdiscursivity as methods to unpack patriarchal paradigms or discourses in a nineteenth-century novel penned by a woman. To speak of patriarchal hegemony, however, is outside the aegis of interdiscursivity, for ideologies and hegemony are indistinguishable concepts, requiring a further critical vantage point to separate them. Intertextuality, in the same vein, cannot distinguish the novel *per se* as feminist or non-feminist.

Interdiscursivity would, however, argue that such overview perspectives have never been its aegis. Rather, it is via interdisciplinarity that such meta-discursive and critical perspectives come into play, precisely to guard against and highlight disciplinary ideological bias, or intertextual misreadings, already caught up within their practices. Gender studies and postcolonial criticism are two powerful and competing interdisciplinary approaches that have found hegemonic theories of text wanting. We will now investigate interdisciplinarity to see if it is up to the task of discriminating between 'bad' or 'good' interdiscursivity, or intertextuality, and thus potentially able to surpass both as derivative and expendable critical terms.

Interdisciplinarity

As rival meta-critical and umbrella configurations, interdisciplinarity and intertextuality both operate by means of comparison, contrast and accumulation to produce new permutations and alignments. The manifestation of the synthesizing drives behind their 'inter-' prefix is of course possible only because of prior, and established, definitions of disciplines or kinds of text respectively. Albeit anti-humanist, postmodernism (as Kristevan intertextuality) shares the same humanist ideological heritage as the supra-humanist interdisciplinarity. Both eschew and reformulate the Enlightenment encyclopaedic, and nineteenth-century positivist, promise of some future universal science by instead stressing heterogeneity and recombination.[93] The world as either the playground of 'science' or anonymous 'text' can then be traced back to the role that nineteenth-century science and industrialization took on as arbiters of criteria for intellectual validation, disciplinary status or subsequent disciplinary subdivisions. Not least, the established orders of knowledge of the eighteenth century were redefined. The faith versus reason categorizations of the eighteenth century, all-important for severing science cleanly from myth, and the devalued 'arts' such as literature, art and music were revalued by nineteenth-century rationalist inquiry. It was concerted investigation of world history, archaelogy and non-European languages that spawned the social sciences, while from the reasoned study of comparative religions it was a short step to the burgeoning of anthropology and ethnography as distinct disciplines. Tocqueville, Gobineau and Freud among others provided a second path for the language of myth to be relabelled as 'sciences'. Psychoanalysis, structuralist linguistics, post-structuralism and deconstruction are but the latest versions of these language-orientated (human) sciences, where *scientia* (as knowledge) elides with the concept of (hard) science and programmed technology. While the next section will take up the importance of computer technology as a further means of removing discipline distinctions in the forms of the internet and hypertext as post-textual rivals of intertextuality, the methodological assumptions behind both intertextuality and interdisciplinarity as synthetic need first to be examined. What leverage does either have to reconfigure orders of knowledge?

The card that intertextuality holds to trump interdisciplinarity is comprehensiveness and inclusivity of constituent texts. As we have seen, intertextuality thus levels hierarchy between scientific and non-scientific, high- or low-cultural text. However, it is none the less the 'text' in intertextuality that largely delimits its methodologies to those of reading words (textuality), such as literature, history, philosophy, however hard it has tried to envisage 'text' as any kind of sign system, including numbers. Consequently there can be no outside of the text if language is its paradigm. Yet how this thinking can be done is problematic, since any such self-reflexive move requires some degree of transcendence of limits or reliance on metaphor where, strictly, any such *a priori* positions should be rejected. The logic of intertextuality certainly breaks down old boundaries concerning taxonomies of items, and can rearrange them, but it can make no value judgements *per se*. It can neither evaluate their efficacy nor assess alternative taxonomies for (positive) change or (more invidious) control. 'Good' intertextuality cannot then readily be determined from 'bad': it is quite simply summative, redistributive and relative.

Interdisciplinarity, on the other hand, has never displaced its humanistic core, only rethought it in the light of the shifting boundaries of individual human disciplines. While interdisciplinarity's bias has been towards the same scientific paradigms that largely determined the disciplines that preceded it, its concerns are less with orders of things than with second-order modes of knowledge, that is the re-examination of how such frames of reference are drawn up in the first place.[94] Interdisciplinarity can then examine itself through its disciplines and also as 'meta-discipline', because its dynamic emerges from combinations not only of fields of knowledge, but of what determining methodologies pertained to prior individual fields. Consequently, any discipline is enabled to consider its methodological blind spots through reference to adjacent disciplines or inter-disciplinary collaboration. By the same token, any discipline or interdisciplinary grouping can redefine how its methods and substance are discrete from others. Indeed, this 'how' may reveal previously hidden agendas within disciplines and their traditions within humanist and Enlightenment endeavour. As Julie Thompson Klein has pointed out, 'Interdisciplinarity and specialization are parallel, mutually reinforcing strategies. The relationship between disciplinarity and interdisciplinarity is not a paradox but a productive tension characterized by complexity and hybridity.'[95] The dynamic is played out between increased disciplinary specialization (greater specific methodological complexity) and increasingly complex integration and combination of methodologies (interdisciplinarity). Ultimately, interdisciplinarity has the potential to combine studies in the science of culture and the culture of science into one mega-discipline and thus to allow all disciplines to enjoy a greater self-validation outside old arts versus sciences dichotomies.

In terms of active promotion of second-order thinking, interdisciplinarity has clearly greater potential leverage than intertextuality to discriminate and arbitrate between practices, as well as evaluate outcomes of its work. As self-evaluative, its second-order thinking allows for self-corrective strategies either inwards to its disciplines or outwards to its interdisciplinarity. However, the very paradox that Klein discounts is extremely apparent here: inclusiveness for some is necessarily exclusiveness for others and cannot work in both directions equally or at once. This is because two second-order modes are confused. For sake of simplicity, let us call them quality and quantity. The theoretical power of both interdisciplinarity and greater discipline distinctiveness is further constrained by pragmatic limits on their power. These are the *institutional* structures that ultimately support and verify such second-order intellectual activity, whether disciplinary or interdisciplinary. The ideological assumptions behind these may be at odds with any changes at second-order level since these institutions are largely the very bodies that originally controlled the encyclopaedic or scientific projects of the eighteenth and nineteenth centuries – universities, academies and societies. Hence, as tertiary-level arbiters, and keepers of certain unquestioned ideological values, these bodies continue to determine the knowledge economy – what is or is not taught and transmitted, and to whom. They also arbitrate in the economics of knowledge by funding and promoting, or demoting, fields of study. Intertextuality as inclusive study of 'all text' therefore presents no marketable field of study for itself and so is reabsorbed in the conventional practices and individual disciplines it sought to overturn. It has unsurprisingly as yet to emerge in the context of the hard sciences from which so much of its rationale is drawn. Interdisciplinarity, because methodologically and economically more robust – it is collaborative, competitive, dynamic, often also highly dependent on computer literacy, innovative, responsive to complex forms of knowledge – fares better, but is none the less delimited because too dangerously collaborative. In its ideal, meta-disciplinary, form, interdisciplinarity also poses too much of a challenge to institutions both financially and conceptually, not least because it questions by its second-order remit their very operational rationale. The economics of institutional power – funding, profitability, marketability of the outcomes of research – thus overrides any 'pure' motivation for interdisciplinarity as principle. Yet as label to enfold newer disciplines that would otherwise remain homeless within the institutional structure, interdisciplinarity provides a ready way of administering such studies so as to window-dress the institution's modernity, while at the same time leaving its (hard) core untouched. Interdisciplinarity is therefore embraced to maximize knowledge production, but is refused support in terms of institutional organization or recruitment.[96] Indeed, for many 'pure' researchers, and not only in the sciences, interdisciplinarity represents a double burden (quality and quantity of specialist expertise), which spells the end not only of individual disciplines, but ultimately of interdisciplinarity as well.[97] Institutions such as the university therefore incorporate interdisciplinarity as paradigm for modern, efficient knowledge production, yet justify and financially underpin their nineteenth-century ideological legacy by continuing to sustain and support a hierarchy of disciplines. 'Chalk and talk' subjects (text) lose out to laboratory-based disciplines (numbers and machines), even though new technologies in mixed (interdisciplinary) fields such as the social sciences, modern languages and, latterly, media and gender studies undermine such neat and old-fashioned teleologies. Contrary to its theoretical aims, interdisciplinarity paradoxically is of greatest use not to second-order knowledge, but to institutions to ground divisive, hierarchical, undemocratic and utilitarian value systems in a market-driven knowledge economy.

Intertextuality and interdisciplinarity both fail, then, to provide a meta-critical frame to discuss connections, not between media ('text') or disciplines, but between these and power. Intertextuality fails first and therefore fails less as tool to disarm hegemony (in whatever form) since it cannot appraise it in the first place. Interdisciplinarity promises and delivers more, but is disarmed because it provides ammunition to the very enemies it would seek to overcome. Where intertextuality denies agency in any form from the outset, interdisciplinarity finds too late that it is a double agent, as potentially revolutionary as it is reactionary, depending on whose hands hold the purse strings.

Initial, optimistic response to intertextuality and interdisciplinarity as salvific, 'postcolonial' terms quickly deflates before economic reality. At best they may both be recognized as localized configurations of late twentieth-century forms of knowledge fledged by postmodernism. At worst, hybridity as value (the 'inter-' prefix) has, like others, a shelf life before it implodes as too vague and catch-all a term (as some deem intertextuality) or becomes the dynamic of a new territorialism.[98] In the final analysis, interdisciplinarity can ask hard questions about discursive practices and determine prejudice or imbalance for interdiscursivity. In examining discipline boundaries, interdisciplinarity can also flush out the occluded economic motives in the gap between theory and practice. What this then spearheads is the necessity to address this gap before various orthodoxies are fuelled, whether economic arguments within institutions or exclusionist, purist rationales within academies. Outside its brief, interdisciplinarity cannot take control over how institutional power can be turned from such outcomes, or legislate against future abuses of such power. '[T]he structures that organize how we know are not eliminated by interdisciplinarity, but relocated.'[99] Is it in what was relocated by the scientific method prior to any reorganization of sciences by interdisciplinarity that the answer lies? Are the shadowlands to both of these post-Enlightenment forms so-called esoteric domains of knowledge – astrology, alchemy, wisdom literature – precisely because their modes of understanding (prophetic vision, revelation, inspiration) challenge the empiricism of the Enlightenment project and its university? By its necessary inclusiveness, intertextuality can at least put texts from 'aberrant' fields back on the map. Can the wizardry of digitalization then recall them, as ethnography did religious rite, so that structural anthropology could become a forerunner of intertextuality itself? The final part of this chapter turns to the 'magic' of computer-generated text as 'pure' *techne* to find out, and to assess how intertextuality as term then fares alongside hypertext and the web as allies or rivals.

Internet and hypertext

There is no doubt that new computer technologies have revolution-
ized knowledge transfer and its textual and disciplinary categories.
Digital media, as postmodern intertextuality, are inclusive of all
forms of 'text', encouraging free play and maximum circulation.
Indeed, this mobilization has permitted popular forms not only to be
fully inserted into cultural production, but to enjoy equal status with
the highbrow. Similarly, new technologies have spearheaded interdisciplinary activity to an unprecedented degree. It could even be
argued that, under the auspices of information technology, the
previously polarized arts and (hard) sciences are but part of one
mega-discipline, the social sciences. The worldwide web also
circumnavigates institutional control and censorship at local levels
due to global access to electronic materials and internationally available means to explore them. Gone, too, is elitist ownership of knowledge by only the rich or the educated. Does this elitist ownership
in fact include intertextuality and interdisciplinarity, so that their
electronic versions will replace them?

As powerful research tool and metaphor, the internet has often
been compared to intertextuality as tissue of texts (Barthes) because
of their similarly connective structures.[100] Yet electronic inclusiveness
and facility with textual manipulation makes both postmodern intertextuality and Kristevan intertextuality as permutation pale by comparison. Automatically, microchip makes 'translatable' every branch
of human understanding and its textual productions since the interstices and interface between domains of knowledge are no longer
relevant concepts. In terms of information range, speed of access and
ease of update, electronic media outstrip the reach of print forms.
Such democratic and instantaneous production, reproduction, dissemination and reception thus make potentially for global dialogue,
and for expansion of knowledge both quantitatively and qualitatively.
Indeed, as Caxton with his printing press before him, Tim Berners-
Lee set up the worldwide web specifically as a democratic way of
maximizing knowledge by linking people, cultures, information, data,
without the need for specialized education. In short, he envisaged an
electronic extension to the summa of all dictionaries, encyclopaedias
and specialist studies by means of a gadget with small financial and
learning cost and spanning the whole gamut from ordinary to extra-
ordinary users, from the computer as pastime or research tool.

As with any instrument, its test is its practicality as well as usefulness. With microchip facilitation of programming and information
storage, knowledge availability depends on access to powerful enough

computers and computer memory. As with interdisciplinarity, the
one limit is then economic. Powerful super-computers or portable
power-books are expensive, and rely on connections to information
super-highways to be of most benefit.[101] In comparison to the eulo-
gistic arguments proffered by early hypertext advocates and exponents, James Annesley has rightly pointed out more nefarious, even
dystopian, aspects caused by the internet and IT. His concern is the
creation of new social divisions 'between the technology haves and
the have nots. The feared result is an "outernet", a "cyberghetto"
inhabited by the "datapoor" [and] a new era of intensified surveillance [a] networked panopticon [. . .] able to monitor and punish
deviance with an unseen rigour and efficiency.'[102]

Like postmodern intertextuality, electronic hypertext and the
internet operate to counter notions of origination and nefarious
authority. Like intertextuality, the term 'hypertext' was also coined
in the late 1960s (1967/8), by T. H. Nelson, and enjoyed an equally
rapturous initial reception as liberating and inclusive. Nelson's term
should immediately be distinguished from Gérard Genette's imitative revamp in 1982 of Kristeva's, to which we will return in chapter
3.[103] Genette's is firmly print-text based and of specialist usage,
whereas Nelson's is electronic, subsumes print text, and is largely
common currency. (Nelson's) hypertext merely develops the status
of 'text' that is intertextuality's motor through digitalization. The
vocabulary central to hypertext endorses this delightfully: electronic
documents (including facsimile manuscript) of all kinds are *scrolled*
within frames and manipulated by the functions that were central to
scribal reproduction and production of new works, copying, cutting
and pasting other's texts. We shall be examining in the third and
fourth chapters how paradoxically close are hypertext procedure and
older forms of imitation and their copy-transmission processes.
At the same time, however, hypertext and the web reveal the
shadowlands or traces of intertextuality's conceptual base as in fact
lodged in the ideology of writing and the printed book. Whatever
effort Derrida and others have made to make possible a non-
representational account of signs, hypertext trumps these by being
the simulacrum of postmodern theory itself.[104] As the experimental
texts of the surrealists and *nouveaux romans* as boxes of unpaginated
sheets tried unsuccessfully to do, hypertext does so by simply erasing
the page.[105] By removing print text's fundamental boundary and
format, hypertext challenges two key ordering principles in the logic
of print and its theories: firstly, the (hierarchical) status of main text
to note, foreword, title or index is removed; secondly, the (authoritative) order of reading the page and manipulating what comes where
in textual reception is subverted. Hypertext can then also handle the

most complex of hyper*media* interactivity in ways that the Romantic *Gesamtkunstwerk* only dreamed of. Moreover, through hard-drive *memory* (a further scribal prerequisite) hypertext economically solves the biggest problem of all, the enormity and cost of procuring, buying and storing millions of pages, tapes, films, scores, CD-roms, etc., or retrieving one from such a collection. In its resources and resourcefulness, hypertext takes the triad 'multiplicity', 'heterogeneity' and 'exteriority', variously developed by Angenot and Kristeva, and transforms it as 'virtual texts', 'intercultural discourses' and 'users'.

This hypertext triad, then, returns reception and communication-orientated frameworks such as interdiscursivity and interdisciplinarity visibly to the equation. The hypertext triad, however, makes clear distinction between 'user' and 'reader' (in the sense both of person reading and anthology). In so doing, it again challenges ideologies of writing and text, not least Barthes's or Riffaterre's versions of intertextuality dependent on reader response, whether deriving pleasure from or bringing acumen to the text. Hypertext has no ideal, intellectual, highly self-conscious or pleasure-seeking user in view. Surfers may be in any of these categories or merely dabblers. Hypertext thus conjures the ordinary or general user from the shadowlands of print-generated culture, whether high or popular, since the qualifications of expert or competent literacy need not pertain. Clicking is even less taxing than two-finger typing or holding the pen.

However positive are the landmark contributions of the web, video or hypertext to the late twentieth-century global media revolution, no revolution, however virtual, is bloodless.[106] What does the double shift to virtual reality and its representations cover? The first answer to this ambiguously framed question is not negative and does not run contrary to the initial, utopian, educational vision of Nelson or Berners-Lee. The entry of reader or user to the screen of non-hierarchized material in the hypertext mosaic or web is by default the very energy of possibility which prevents any form of closure occurring, regardless of competence or interactivity. For the more academic or knowledge-agile user, response will be more positive to this plethora of choice where any word or image will have links to a more complex network of contexts which shape and inform it: historical, sociological, political, linguistic, national, generic, each of which open out centripetally and can themselves be chosen as the main, rather than subsidiary, path forwards. For less gymnastic users, sheer information overload, and the maze of pathways available, may present not a theme park experience, but a nightmare vortex. Given the exponential nature of hypertext linkage, the provision of orientation, assistance and exit links are recognized as essential features of good web design, and as ways of facilitating user competency.[107]

The cover is now blown, however, on the previously hidden controls and manipulations behind any web or hypertext design and its usage. Links or linking do not happen spontaneously, and are therefore not as fortuitous, innocuous or free as a user might first believe.[108] As the spider lures the fly, the power of the visual capitalized by advertising is magnified by electronic visual media, and rapidly becomes harnessed for economic gain, either by general 'consumer engineering', as Black terms it,[109] or for more nefarious trading, of pornography, arms or official secrets. Moreover, access to sites is not unlimited. Given the ease of copying, cutting and pasting inherent in electronic text manipulation, copyright law, originally devised for print text, has had to evolve to cover legitimate design, and to counter negative user activity such as illegal copying, counterfeit sampling or versioning. And the new acts of bloodless electronic terrorism are computer hacking or sabotage of a site, where the changing of crucial details may be more detrimental than the putting up of bigoted materials. As at once unifying means for all, digitalized text in all its forms is none the less divided as to its ends, reduced to the old cliché 'pure', or 'applied', but in a double helix. If essentially set up as media applied for profit, hypertext and the web will inevitably be developed along certain, not all, pathways and the richness of expanding inter-hypertextual diversity will be threatened. As purest, and most ecological, form of technology to date, IT as artificial intelligence and the creation of super-computers stand to eliminate the messy applications of the human altogether, whether as mind or matter. Such Manichean dreams surpass even the anti-metaphysical limits of late postmodernism.

Ends, aims or intentionality were the *bête noire* of Barthesian and postmodern intertextuality, to be removed for good by the death of the author and the assurance that there was nothing outside the text. Yet intention is the one question that splits artificial intelligence research and philosophy of mind.[110] By getting behind the hype of the 'hyper-' in hypertext, intention also provides an evaluative way of questioning the aims and objectives of the electronic media revolution as also deceptive, or exaggerated. In an unprecedented way, this evaluative role falls to the 'user' as strategic, both within the system and as the producer or employer of it. More than was required of the responsible (or irresponsible Barthesian) reader in the intertextual labyrinth of print texts, the hypertext or internet user is required to be a guarantor and arbiter of 'good' usage. Behind seeming serendipity or play lie choice, preference and decision. These imply a combination of utilitarian and non-utilitarian value systems, not least ethical and aesthetic. If the proper etymology of 'hyper-' meaning 'in excess' is recalled, the initial euphoria surrounding hypertext and postmodern intertextuality can be 'de-hyped' to weigh the relative achievements of electronic and print texts. The issue is then not the battle of the Moderns and the Ancients in new guise, computer versus print-text advocates, but the pinpointing of a scale of quality applicable to both. To choose canonicity or heritage already militates against newer media: criteria of relevance or accessibility stack the odds against older works. Equally, aesthetic or ethical value may depend more on temporal or national parameters and contexts. A more universal value system is to rate quality as the job hypertextuality and intertextuality perform at their best – extension of knowledge. How do hypertext and the web fare in distinguishing search and research as tasks and users as searchers or researchers?

In non-fictional texts, the table of contents and index are the equivalent of the electronic 'search' facility, where as yet, although Boolean searching can be sophisticated, there is no 'research' button. As with print texts, electronic searching works effectively only within a well-constructed, multi-use system, and only as well as the pertinence of the search question asked. Searchers of print and electronic resources ask questions that pertain primarily to information gathering or verification. If few direct answers or 'hits' are generated, searchers become researchers, asking lateral or other 'how?' and 'why' questions of the text or site, not least *via* other bibliographical and proper name links. To ask such questions, however, the *re*searcher will need prior general and specialist knowledge to gauge whether particular responses are irrelevant, incomplete or ambiguous, or if the initial search question asked was too complex or requires modification. Due to multiple links to other sites, electronic searching has one perceived advantage over certain print texts – range. This may, however, have the counter-productive result of throwing up a longer list of irrelevant 'hits'. To determine relevant from irrelevant, reader/user sophistication and familiarity with multiple contexts are essential to whatever medium.[111] In neither print nor electronic media, therefore, can simple word strings be the basis of more complex research. A test case is how ideological import, irony or parody can be ascertained in a given word string. As with translation, much more context will be required than finding all instances in a document of one word or word group. Theories of text, including intertextuality, deal with all these without difficulty since it is the paragraph or page which is automatically and unconsciously called upon. Indeed, postmodernist texts have taken irony to highly sophisticated levels, as magic realism has offered a powerful critique of oppressive regimes.

Another unquestioned assumption about electronic media is that, because they are immediate (up-to-date), information available on screen is somehow more accurate or unbiased than in (fixed) textual forms. What is forgotten, probably because sites are often anonymous, is that behind any material put up on the web, or included by links, lies the constructor, who fulfils exactly the same functions as the author or writer of a print text. S/he is responsible for selecting materials and presenting them in particular ways. It is the reader's memory, knowledge or interest which collates and sorts contents and form. Hypertext usage and its user are not essentially different. What is perhaps more invidious for searchers in internet sites as opposed to print-text-based ones is that poor quality, fallacious or out-of-date information will be less apparently indistinguishable from pertinent, correct, well-researched material. Print texts all have copyright dates: electronic sites do not always inform the user when they were last updated. It then falls to more sophisticated user-researchers to validate or correct false information because of access to other specialist resources not only *for themselves*, but also for subsequent general users of that site.

Ultimately, then, the 'user' of any medium is not merely an epistemological adjunct, enabling the extension of information (searcher) or knowledge (researcher), but is its quality controller. Accuracy (truth), fair or prejudicial presentation (ethical standards) and major flaws (aesthetic and moral values) such as missing texts or approaches (links) must all be evaluated. Print-text-based researchers have long undertaken such roles and published their re-evaluations. Hypertext research, due to its speed and immediacy, operates in a much shorter time frame. While this is advantageous for rapid updating, it is even more detrimental to material deemed 'irrelevant', and hence not included in the site.[112] As Gaggi remarks, 'For a *text* to be excluded from hypertext is likely to be even more crippling than its being excluded from the "canon" as presently constituted. The ease and speed of navigating between texts embedded in hypertextual networks has its flip side, a tendency to ignore texts that are not included, as if they did not exist at all.'[113] Only a specialist hypertext researcher can make good this gap, and, preferably, also check necessary links from any insertion to its site, and related ones. In strangely existentialist vein, then, the choice whether to change or ignore erroneous or biased electronic information is weightier than for print-text researchers, since obligation to users is more pressing in numerical and qualitative terms. The knowledge and information economies of electronic media therefore show no inherent advantage over print media, either to users or in their usefulness. For all its alleged democracy and openness, virtual reality and information technology paradoxically throw up the need for even greater 'censorship', but of the unreliable and the irrelevant. A website's authority in contents and presentation stops with the person of the expert as constructor and user. More than was betrayed by intertextuality, justice and truth in hypertext cannot be disconnected from utility or pastime. The now uncovered hidden agendas thus return some very old, humanist questions. Should poets and philosophers be part of good knowledge government? What is hypertext ultimately for, and for whom?

While cyberfiction already explores electronic hypermedia as dystopia and utopia,[114] their presence is set to expand, not contract. If this is not to be an increasingly barren, uniform or utilitarian knowledge environment, strategic lessons from print culture need to be incorporated into web and hypertext design. Models do not, however, have to begin with the ideal of all-inclusiveness, like some super-scanner system indiscriminately hoovering up and storing all texts.[115] More discerning models already exist and therefore offer good precedents to hypertext. As the fourth chapter will more fully explore, the literary translator is one such model of the kinds of encyclopaedic and specialist knowledge required by a hypertext designer.[116] Electronic hypertext has indeed proved particularly successful in mounting texts, variants and 'parallel' translations. The past, especially pre-Enlightenment texts and ways of thinking, can also furnish alternative models. Some of the most innovative hypertext sites – on the Bible, the classics, Shakespeare, medieval studies – build precisely on long-established, textual and interdisciplinary research traditions, including translations.[117]

It may, in fact, be pre-printing press cultures, which were as multicultural and diverse as postmodern ones, and their *summa* library fictions recorded on scrolls, that have most to teach and challenge electronic hypertext, especially at the interface between oral and scribal heritage. While hypertext will be significant in restoring preprint materials to hard-drive memory, oral-scribal heritage questions how human memory works, not least its principles of storage, recognition and retrieval. As Douglas Hofstadter says, 'It is the organization of memory that defines what concepts are.'[118] Machine memory may in fact not be an analogue of human memory, or its organization, as is evident in machine-memory users of hypertext. They frequently become disorientated, fail to rediscover digressions made previously, or cannot ascertain how to plot their position back to wider maps, not least because print and electronic information recovery has made active memory lazy. Oral heritage memory is altogether active, although it still needs signposts and recognized markers to guide listeners towards further complexity of plot or ideas. Epics, virtuoso mnemonics, mythical poem cycles, aboriginal song lines, dramatic repertoires in a number of cultural heritages all suggest the richness of memory and its value. In its recovery of pre-print vocabulary such as 'scrolling', electronic hypertext also needs to 're-member' the context of the original adepts of scroll and codex cultures, and how they solved the problems of being 'walking libraries'.[119] Exceptional memory was actually only one of several important skills that constituted true critical acumen and good 'librarianship'. Adepts (like hypertext expert arbiters) had to discern cultural value, discriminate real from fake texts, and provide a back-up system should retrieval fail (by fire, or pure geography), as well as locate items of knowledge in contexts seemingly unrelated to the problem in hand. As they were often specialist collectors across vast areas of knowledge that included bizarre rarities and arcania, theirs was not a role of knowledge censorship. Unlike the isolated academic scholar-bibliophile or scientific genius of post-Enlightenment models, these scholars worked in community, as part of schools. It was group debate that was the 'search engine' to channel thematic, generic, lexicographical, linguistic, analogical, rhetorical and other questions, to enable and reactivate the mind of each contributor. By 'scrolling' his [sic] personal memory and collection of papyri, and collective readings, an agreed wisdom on the matter in hand was arrived at and then recorded on a new papyrus, which might indeed begin with sophisticated *lemmata* and *capita rerum*, prefiguring Renaissance commonplace books.[120] The process of corporate assembly was thus self-correcting of human error and half-memories or intuitions, as well as receptive to more diverse approaches and multiple perspectives. Athenaeus was an exemplar and embodiment of the walking library re-created as a new text, the *Deipnosophistae*.[121] Yet this is no encyclopaedia or encomium of scholarly pursuits or of knowledge in the library of Greek culture and its scrolls (as proto-hypertext). It is primarily a creative composition about a banquet, with all the (pre-Barthesian) pleasure and seduction, humour and playfulness, that lie outside the treatise (*magnum opus*) or reconstruction of cultural fragments (postmodern hypermedia). Athenaeus' fiction combines virtuoso cultural and mental performance, entertainment and paedictics, organization by complex thought and playful combination of ideas, while losing nothing of the specifically Alexandrian and Greek cultural context and its expectations. This is therefore no digest or consumer text or modern 'reader'. It distinguishes itself by being truly a *hyper-text* in its Greek order of excess, in the superfluity, abundance and profligacy of banqueting as metaphor for a joyful sharing of knowledge. In the era of late-capitalist consumer culture, there are telling lessons here, then, concerning the 'aims and objectives' of hypertext and the role and acumen of its compositor. There are also morals of the story. Possessive or passive consumption of information may lead only to knowledge obesity or regurgitation. It is the combined pleasure and exercise of a mind fed on a very mixed diet of things, not least of familiar and unfamiliar 'foods' for further thought. As Proust so readily reminds his readers, memory is active and human, at the place between fiction and desire, experience and imagination, poetry and history, science and the world, *techne* and creativity.[122]

The researcher-constructor of hypertext is then not without models in the new Alexandria, which may be less the successor of the old than a belated recuperation of the latter's adept handling of knowledge. Unless such acquisition of learning, the celebration of extensive and eclectic scholarship, from 'old' schools of memory, is combined with information technology, the transformational, communicational aspects of active knowledge transfer will be lost. Hypertext is therefore not some huge electronic memory storage bin, or a non-canonical form to replace elitist print forms of thinking culture and its works.[123] Neither should it be envisaged as serving some memorial function, to preserve or store 'dead' text, but leave it relatively inaccessible on the outer reaches or links.[124] Rather its ideal task is to extend and deepen the impetus of pre- as well as post-Enlightenment knowledge accumulation, so as to uncover the elitisms and hegemonic exclusions exonerated by the 'scientific', technological and postmodern theory age. In these functions, then, hypertext and the web are media, not methodological, variations of Kristeva's intertextuality. Textual strategies have not been superseded, only reprocessed. Kristeva's emphasis on the work of intertextuality also applies to hypertext, to ensure the necessary permutation, heterogeneity and outsider–insider awareness of cultural productions for their future.

★   ★   ★

In the particular debates and history of intertextuality as upheld by critical readers and guides, the case of 'Kristeva' (in English and in French) spearheads some salient and wider questions for this chapter and this book. From close readings of Kristeva's text on intertextuality in the original French, it is now clear that her double erasure through translation and French philosophical tradition puts in wider context some of the ways in which sexed, gendered and ethnically different bodies are disinherited by becoming de-unified subjects, not least through critical reception.[125] It is also clear in the light of Barthes's or Riffaterre's versions that Kristeva's is the more malleable, and suitable for remanipulation in electronic hypertext or other media from its premise of translinguistic transfer. Indeed, the ways in which 'intertext' or 'the intertextual' are used in common parlance are precisely those glossed by Kristeva herself at the end of *Semeiotikè*:

> Intertextuality: supplants intersubjectivity; intersection of utterances taken from other texts; transposition in speech communicative of previous or synchronic utterances; polyphonic text; multiplicity of codes levelling out one another; removal revives and destroys discursive structures outside the text.[126]

There is much, however, for hypertext designers to learn from the strategically different spin put on Kristeva's term by Barthes and Riffaterre, not least how the user may respond (or not). In the era of the sound byte, a bored, disaffected, narrowly focused user or the super-nerd need both to be considered, if not encouraged to play or learn more extensively within the site. At the same time, the challenge to intertextuality brought by interdiscursivity and inter-disciplinarity by Angenot, Bruce and others reveals the blind spots in all postmodern theories based on relative meanings or kinds of meaninglessness. The return of the chronotope and the politics of meaning-making we uncovered in the often conservative institutions upholding interdisciplinarity also apply to deconstruction, and where it has been permitted to sit *within* the academy. As subsequent chapters will explore, reaction and counter-reaction (or Kristevan 'levelling out') prove to be the perennial motor of intertextuality, whether dressed as recycling, influence, imitation or reinvention, or the emperor's new clothes. Reiteration and repetition in 'other' words seem quintessentially part of the reformulation process that any cultural generation engages in. Kristevan intertextuality, if perhaps among its most complex theorizations, when distilled to its permutational motor, says no more than the old adage 'there is nothing new under the sun'.[127]

The voguish and modish, as Barthes highlights, are backwash and swash of a necessary cultural consumerism, and are not without a certain, and subversive, fascination.[128] They are also essential to the critical machine: 'the new and voguish "intertextuality" has served as a generational marker for younger critics who end up doing very much what their elders do with "influence" and its partners like "context", "allusion" and "tradition".'[129] The urgent question that hypertext raises is what happens when technological speeding up of such recycling ('inter-hypertextuality') increases? Can virtual media really generate completely new cultural forms? The New Alexandria has a lot to lose if it fails to address textuality's heritage in its fullest translingual, and transcultural, imagination.[130] It will create its own future only by faithful and hence unfaithful 'translation' of what has gone before.

This brings us full circle to Kristeva's introduction of *her* version of Bakhtin to Paris. Her transposition of his key ideas demonstrates the complexities of following and deviating from any text or precursor, and how any successor's contribution is never a new idea but a reinterpretation. Critical guides and 'readers' are also not exempt, although they purport to maintain fair representation, as Lear towards his daughters. Because blinded by deconstructive and postmodern premises, not least the metaphor of language as text, Kristeva and other theorists have been sidestepped, thereby leaving the all-inclusive middle of inter*text*uality as much these theories' aporia as their meta-critical structure. In the case of Kristeva, however, we have shown the more positive principle of the shadow-land in action. Exclusion by default (lack of translations) or uncritical, even misguided, appraisal of the received 'canon' keeps the outsider firmly on the outside. This is, however, exactly where intertextuality may begin, like Cordelia, to speak again, in spite of her rival sisters, the 'inter-' terms interdisciplinarity and interdiscursivity.

Intertextuality, then, shows a tenacity for the critical present, but also hints of a strong survival rate, proved through textual time, but in different guises. Because it has already been fractured and pulled in different and conflicting directions since it was 'coined', it may prove to be of most use as a primary identifier, of text-to-text or reading-to-reading relationships and the complex transmissions at work in text and reading in the first place. From identification must come clarification, as Lear also reminds us, for its secondary and fuller implications to emerge. The remainder of this book will examine these as existing but shadowland vocabularies, conceptual and critical terminologies that will ground aspects of intertextuality as their loftier sweep. Occlusion of the past is the necessary enlightenment of the present. It is to influence that we now turn as concept that intertextuality most had to inter to answer Susan Friedman's pertinent questions: 'Does the "birth" of intertextuality as a critical term insist upon the "death" of influence as its conceptual precursor? Is the "death of the author" as writer the precondition for the "birth" of the critic as reader?'[131]

2
Influence

As the last chapter demonstrated, intertextuality's protean and uni-versalizing thrust as facilitated by its 'inter-' prefix makes it a highly successful term as mediator and colonizer of spaces. However, the purloining of Kristeva's term by rival theorists, and the presence of parallel terms exploiting the same prefix, also make clear that a single definition or delimited application of intertextuality are impossible. For interest groups wanting to use such a capacious umbrella concept for strategic purposes, intertextuality offers rather small ideological leverage and surprisingly limited sites of operation before the need for distinctive terms re-emerges. Intertextuality's potentially inter-relational aspects cloak a relativism which may in fact be more in-vidious than the master narratives masquerading as universal standards it sought to displace.[1] Neither are all inter-relations benign, as the word 'internecine' demonstrates. It is to this family romance of the strangely similar but often lethally other, influence, that this second chapter turns, to uncover the asides and shadowlands which intertextuality backs onto and suppresses.

While intertextuality (like Barthes's 'dérive' as counter-current) claims to erase influence, not least by bypassing and surpassing its reliance on agents and intention as 'irrelevant', such a critical stance may prove less neutral than postmodernism would have it. The reception of intertextuality *vis-à-vis* influence offers an extremely interesting test case. Paradigmatic is Udo Hebel's comprehensive bibliography of criticism on and about intertextuality (1989), which omits influence and its cognate terms altogether. A second strategy is reduction by derision. Influence study is at best 'old-fashioned' and at worst retrograde, returning criticism to hierarchical lineages at odds with multiform and multicultural postmodernity. This adamant rejection of influence is, however, exactly the stance of Harold Bloom, conventionally intertextuality's favourite stalking-horse: 'Source study is wholly irrelevant here; we are dealing with primal words but antithetical meanings, and an ephebe's best misinterpretations may well be of poems he has never read.'[2] Is overstatement by both Bloom's 'anxiety of influence' and intertextuality some unacknowledged non-identical twinning between them? Paradoxically, of course, it is precisely influence study in its remit to investigate contexts that can address such a question. Rather than define the 'inter-' between Bloom and postmodern versions of intertextuality as previous guides and readers have done, this chapter will first uncover the contexts that make of influence the maligned shadowland of both. Throughout, this chapter will then up the anti (as in 'anti-thetical') of influence study. It will uncover something of the power structures at work in postmodernism and demonstrate that antagonism is not the only model for influence.

Bloom's 'anxiety of influence' in context

Among few critical works on intertextuality to have taken influence seriously as a competitor term of reference, Jay Clayton and Eric Rothstein's *Influence and Intertextuality in Literary History* (1991) is not, however, a plea to reinstate the first term or find equilibrium between them, as use of the copula might suggest:

> [T]he concepts of influence and intertextuality have been sites of generational conflict: to many people, influence has smacked of elitism, the old boy networks of Major Authors and their sleek entourages; [. . .] especially Americans have used the term 'intertextuality' in a context of enlargement [. . .] Concern with influence arose in conjunction with the mid-eighteenth-century interest in originality and genius, and the concept still bears the marks of that origin.[3]

Even if the editors overplay the subordination of influence to reinstate it in later discussion, the sub-texts of this passage speak volumes about another agenda, the importance of place in literary history. Influence here is less cultural and political privilege and elitism in general than dominating European imperialism in particular, even in its Enlightenment (post-French Revolution) and secular phase. Democratically defined, culture is more properly American libertarianism, reflected in postmodern genres and critical theory as well as in popular forms, upheld for their egalitarianism, inclusiveness and novelty value. For the new writer (as for the new country or new theory) an enlarged and contemporary heritage valuing merit and eschewing rank or privilege is essential.[4] Thus, influence, so strongly associated with authority figures, is automatically oppressive to newcomers struggling against an impossible weight of heritage that they can neither join nor follow, whether as writers or critics. In its re-evaluation of culture as communications network, postmodern intertextuality likewise sets itself against origins, lineages, inheritance or a heavy cultural baggage where knowledge of its multiple reference points is essential. For Clayton and Rothstein, influence studies are therefore all of unreconstructed traditional (European and modernist) academic literary criticism and its elitist tasks. Among these are the exalting and transmitting of lines and hierar-chies of writers in the Great Tradition, the upholding of canon, high culture and its genres, and the safeguarding of aesthetic values against mixed or popular cultural forms. The scornful, ironic and non-deferential critic, whether of deferral (Derrida) or neo-Romantic rebellion (Bloom), is everywhere preferable to those in a 'sleek entourage'.[5]

The dangers of any such blanket, monolithic or simplistically dichotomized overviews are glaringly apparent here, and serve as a good reminder that distinctions and nuances are ever needful in criti-cal inquiry. Moreover, critics versed in and from a European back-ground would map and date the rise of influence very differently and much more precisely than Clayton and Rothstein's rather vague 'mid-eighteenth-century'. They would point to the influence of the Greek classics on those of Rome and the role of both in shaping ver-nacular forms, especially during the European Renaissance. In this perspective, the avant-garde movements of post-Romanticism such as futurism, surrealism and, arguably, postmodernism are further replications and variations of a pattern for cultural regeneration already well established. In spite of similar experience with France of revolution and republicanism, the American view stems from a more recent history and reaction to European (high) culture, espe-cially modernism.[6] Whereas its European version was essentially political, in the USA it was largely aesthetic. Clearly, then, different cultural contexts shape perspectives on heritage and tradition, and inform aesthetic values, quite distinctly. As we saw with the very dif-ferent transplantations of intertextuality on both sides of the Atlantic, influence, too, has more than one seedbed.

Harold Bloom's 'anxiety of influence' is in many ways therefore a very American answer to the long tradition of influence in European high-cultural forms, as the ensuing part of the chapter will demonstrate.[7] The forging of difference from an alike is pivotal to its new-comer 'strength'. Hence, like any conversion, it is often more purist, dogmatic and complex in its reinvestments of the very precursor terms it vehemently rejects. Within the belated postmodern era, then, the similarities of response to influence are striking, both from Kristeva's European revisionism of Bakhtin's dialogism and hetero-glossia in *Semeiotikè*, and from Bloom's reinvestments of much older critical terminologies from the classics in his six revisionary ratios in *The Anxiety of Influence: a Theory of Poetry* (1973).[8] Both reinvest in Greek as the language of their overarching concepts. Both take up Freudian psychoanalysis as grounding for the psychic dimensions of their text-to-text or poet-to-poet dynamics respectively.[9] Both have much to say about the sublime, albeit from their distinctive per-spectives. 'The poetry of the sublime, Bloom argues, represents a manic triumph over loss: "a terror uneasily allied with pleasurable sensations of augmented power, and even of narcissistic freedom [. . .]". Kristeva, on the other hand, examines the depressive side of the sublime, the abject experience of loss.'[10]

Yet similarities and comparisons can be deceptive, especially if superficial likeness is not matched by deeper affinities. Kristeva's intertextuality is a recognized and redirected continuity with Bakhtin, whereas Bloom breaks with precursors by taking an overtly opposi-tional stance and by outdoing them. It is precisely Bloom's aggres-sive defence against tradition that makes comparison with Derrida's very similar 'misprision' (deconstruction) of Western metaphysics by far the more apposite.[11] As champion of misreading, Bloom is, in Lentricchia's words, Derrida's 'sibling rival'.[12] Where previous guides and readers, not least on intertextuality, would put them on opposite sides, several symposia on deconstruction include them in the same team.[13] It is the convergence between their theories and their similar entry into intellectual history prior to postmodernism that needs to be underscored, particularly if Bloom's contribu-tions to literary theory and intertextuality as conflict are to be re-evaluated.

Bloom and Derrida arrived on the critical scene in the late 1950s and early 1960s and were thus fully part of the intellectual and criti-cal *establishment* by the late 1960s, not foreign newcomers to it like Kristeva. It was in a context of post-Second World War indirection – political, postcolonial and intellectual – that they both experienced the sense of staleness and oppressiveness of a powerful and estab-lished 'arrière-garde'. Their oldest publications reflect the period of their critical and intellectual training and richly inform the keystone texts they had produced before May 1968 (as well as after it). Into the critical vacuum that modernism and its critics had left, while

different on each side of the Atlantic, any new and apparently original voice was going to be heard.[14] Derrida enters the fray in the wake
of the rather disillusioned existentialism and committed literature of
1950s Europe, not least in the light of the Algerian crisis.[15] By
rerouting aspects of these philosophies of writing by means of the
translation and critical edition of unpopular German philosophers of
language such as Husserl, Derrida is firmly *in situ* prior to *Tel Quel*
and at the ready to name *différance* and then deconstruction as the
philosophy and methodology underpinning Saussurian linguistics
and post-structuralism. At the same moment, Bloom is straining
against the lumbering, but particularly American, intellectual
framework of New Criticism, which, as its name implies, obviously
precluded successors.[16] Its elimination of the old brand of influence study – attention to sources, biography, anecdotal details about
authors' lives and literary circles – to instigate close reading of the
classics (European modernist high-cultural works) was the important
ground-clearing work that Bloom then turned on, from within. While
such revision from the inside appears 'conservative', the real radi-
calism of this move comprises several strategies – revisionism, 'misreading' and 'misprision'. Bloom thus purges an already American
critical movement of its focus on imported, non-American, works by
concentrating on the great belated *American poets*, who extend and
better the best of what European Romantics produced. By narrow-
ing, refining and redefining New Criticism, he sucks out its marrow
and leaves the picked bone behind. In a nutshell, this is Bloom's
'anxiety of influence' as practice and method to recultivate the
American critical wilderness, and just before the arrival of the next
wave of immigrants, French post-structuralism.

If their intellectual backgrounds find strong parallels, the constants
across both *oeuvres* are equally remarkable. While Derrida and Bloom
are perennially obsessed with tradition and its canonical works, more
important is how they reread such texts and as always in *advance* of
how other emerging critics might do likewise. To borrow Bloom's
terminology, both are strong misreaders, vying to be the strongest
of all. To achieve remapping of what are whole critical landscapes, not
merely duels with individuals, texts or movements, Bloom and Derrida
employ a two-pronged method of 'writing against'. Usable critical
concepts are first selected from their chosen establishment methodology, but given a strategically different 'spin'. To this is integrated terminology from an adjacent discipline, but one antagonistic to the
methodology of the official criticism. Take Derrida's 'trace' or Bloom's
'anxiety' of influence as examples, where psychoanalytical and arrière-
garde literary critical terms are grafted in wholly anti-Freudian and
anti-establishment ways, but so that an at least double rejection of

'authorities' occurs. Unless the reader or belated critic is as well read as they are – an often arrogant and arrant disregard for notes and bibliographies is a further concealment strategy – such reworked points of reference seem dazzlingly new, unassailable, and hence unsurpassable. Thus, Derrida's well-documented quest to demolish Western metaphysics matches Bloom's equally anti-humanist, but decidedly pro-American, endeavour to overthrow Hellenism and its European cultural progeny. The question to which the chapter will return is whether such writing against tradition (also called postmodernism) is new, or rather part of a longer anti-tradition?

Returning to Clayton and Rothstein's formulation above, a pressing question is how their criteria now apply to postmodernists such as Derrida and Bloom, since it is they who now sit in 'sleek entourages', the critical elites of Ivy League universities. Although prodigiously prolific, both continue to concentrate on (difficult, white) male writer-philosophers and critic-poets and largely discount alternative, feminist, gay or postcolonial critical work. Deconstruction and intertextuality clearly do not give America a pristine, democratic postmodernism free from European influence (whether cultural or critical) either, and Bloom's misreadings of belated American poets are hardly part of US popular cultural or mainstream theoretical fare. What indeed of the 'context of enlargement' and open critical debate that perhaps American postmodernism over others is deemed to uphold? If there are no origins or influences, only 'traces' and 'misprisions', where does the continuing authority of Derrida's or Bloom's *critical* voice stem or find ongoing impetus? In Derrida's case, if voice or critical writing are in deferral or without signature, how can work identifiably his be thus branded, let alone sustained? Similarly, how can Bloom's theory of belated strong poet-critics misreading other poets allow for assertive strong critics who are not also poets? Bloom is no Dryden (who is strikingly absent from Bloom's poet-to-poet lineages), yet he names and criticizes from some unnamable but no less vaunting super-critical position that is also Derrida's. Is this some belated but lingering trace of neo-Romantic will-to-power (Derrida) and quest for critical genius (Bloom), however cleverly forestalled and pre-empted by ironic interrogations and rhetorical questioning that identify such impasses before others do? Is Derrida's and Bloom's consistency and propensity to rework and develop their own theories by ironic self-reference a ploy to circumvent the dilemmas of postmodernity itself, *critical* belatedness without a subject (persons or topics)?[17] And does their aggressive defence of being 'first' preclude disciples who might outdo them, and allow only acolytes to extend the importance and impetus of their work?[18] Surely such positionings belie power, the very concept that is central to influence itself? As we shall see below, Bloom arguably includes power by adapting 'influence' for his own purposes and brings insight into the blindness of intertextuality and deconstruction, not least its amnesia regarding its own critical influences.[19]

This comparative contextualization and primary concern with where, as critics, Bloom and Derrida might be speaking from cannot occur without reference to an outside of the text or antagonistic poet-to-poet relationship. This is precisely where 'traditional' influence can step in, especially in its capacity to ascertain (re)sources – both works and people – and how these operate variously on one another. As Eric Rothstein states, 'no text is influenced, only authors. The inverse is that authors qua authors influence others only through texts; texts influence people.'[20] The problem, though, is more than clarifying definitions between people and things, or demarcating influence as having to do with agency and intention, since intertextuality is about random juxtaposition and collage of text. Bloom's theory of influence between often unrelated poets, as if to bypass their works, complicates the kind of simple, deterministic, one-to-one relationships 'influence' in postmodern theories has pejoratively been said to uphold. An electronic word search for 'influence', for example, especially in the scientific, geographical, historical, medical or sociological fields, will score thousands of hits and demonstrates both how wide is the range of its dictionary meanings and how widespread is its use in multidisciplinary contexts. Influence covers gods to persons, magic to mechanics to new media, and spheres as multifarious as astrology and astrophysics. Everywhere it connotes power(s) and empowerment, or their denial. As intertextuality, it engages with relations, but as forces and force fields, and how and why they are channelled in certain ways. In cultural ambits, both popular and high canonical, it is therefore strategic in how utterance, text and meanings are designed to affect, effect and persuade. While postmodernism's quasi-technical terminology, neologisms and jargon may claim that language is of itself neutral, a game or system, this nevertheless cloaks the same crucial matters of judgement, and which will count, that belong to older practices. As such, postmodern criticism may be more akin than it would pretend to the skills of casuistry, propaganda, advocacy, diplomacy, consciousness-raising and rhetoric. What has changed is awareness that use of 'ordinary' language to promote and demote certain perspectives and ideas may still arbitrate between life and death as outcomes. Heresy and inquisition, torture and salvation, blasphemy and blame, continue to rely on words for their defence.[21]

In this chapter, influence will therefore be investigated as an instrument to peel the masks from words. By turning next to a rereading of Bloom's alternative theory of influence, but unobscured by deconstruction spectacles, some of the power at work also in postmodern criticism will be revealed. The 'anxiety of influence' may then uncover the real stakes of criticism including its own, and return the repressed as neo-Romantic protest movements. How revolutionary Bloom's or Derrida's seemingly polarized versions then are can be ascertained only by reintroducing 'traditional' influence studies in the final part of the chapter. These not only provide a firmer grasp on what is meant by 'tradition', or its alleged anti-traditions. They also make manifest the multifarious influences – patronage, translations, Diaspora, travel, salons, war, printing or new media – that shape any cultural history. While worthy of a book-length study, and the next chapter will review the role of imitation in the transmission of cultural forms, at issue here is the particular importance for intertextuality and postmodernity of the writer-critic as interpreter, challenger or guardian of cultural and critical values. By reconsidering the even more maligned comparative criticism within influence studies, a critical method by synthesis rather than antithesis can be reinvigorated, not least for its relevance to multicultural contexts. Auerbach and Curtius and more recently Cave will be examined for their interpretations of complex European cultural exchanges, criss-crossing genres, history and geographical borders and languages to return influence's political, visionary and inspirational undercurrents to the debate. Understanding these as rich legacies, rather than disinheritance by profligate or vaunting forebears, then makes of influence less the obstructive father than the fairy godmother granting self-determination to disenfranchised newcomers to cultural expression. Influence as recognition then restores a place for belated subjects to speak again, like Cordelia, and sets the scene for a second glance at Bakhtin's work for its social, not intertextual, dialogism with a context of censure. By recognizing Bakhtin first as an intercultural critic, his method of engaging with political, religious, moral and cultural censorship may be a timely critical legacy.

Influence thus provides a way of discussing the overtly singular within the plural or universal, and distinguishes instead of relativizes the orders of things. Its continued deletion from postmodern critical theory begs many questions about the latter's politics of critical correctness. If influence is constructive rather than obstructive, does it have an advisory, even supervisory, role to play as we engage with a multimedia hypertextual explosion? Can influence have a redemptive function in its gifting or safeguarding 'minority' cultural values in the face of global capitalism's drive for financial profit? Can influence be an agent for socio-cultural change?

Harold Bloom

If there is a perceived joker in the pack of literary critics, it is without doubt Harold Bloom, whose 'wonderfully Byzantine theory' provoked immediate and strong response.[22] Serious critical theory in the USA, France and Italy greeted *The Anxiety of Influence* (1973) with antipathy and derision.[23] Based on the metaphor of father–son inheritance and Oedipal struggle for poetic supremacy, Bloom's work automatically excludes those not central to the family romance or the Great Tradition, such as women or the politically marginalized. Feminists (as later postcolonial critics) were quick to point this out, but found in Bloom a major impetus to establishing their own canons.[24] More interesting, though, is why white male theorists of the mainstream overtly sidestepped or refused to confront Bloom's work and in the terms in which he openly framed it, especially Freud.[25] Indeed, the excuse that Bloom's esoteric vocabulary and evaluation of poetic antagonism and conflict are alienating to newcomers seems hypocritical, given that initiation into the terminology and ideas of deconstruction is no less so. Yet it and related postmodern theories are actively promoted and taught. At the very least, Bloom the joker challenges the suit of deconstruction's upholders, and the canonization processes which make these the acceptable 'avant-garde' and 'difficult' theories as against other blatantly anti-establishment, but unacceptable, candidates. By prejudicing reading of 'influence studies' in general, postmodern critical theories including deconstruction can lump Bloom's version in the same lot and conceal their most antagonistic detractor. For Bloom, this occlusion has paradoxically allowed his own work to escape the net of deconstruction, especially what he calls the 'anguish of contamination' caused by any strong rival.[26] Since Wisdom as Folly returns at critical moments in cultural history as a regenerative figure to be reckoned with, a rereading of Bloom as 'trickster theory' with close attention to the contexts of his arguments may offer new light on his ideas and provide a viable alternative by which to assess those of his closest arch-rivals.[27]

Bloom's most (in)famous *The Anxiety of Influence* (1973), published the same year as Barthes's *Le Plaisir du texte*, seems to present a case for reading Romantic poets, not their poetry, by applying Freudian psychoanalytic theory of Oedipal conflict to their antagonistic struggle of 'an ego seeking to recover a primary narcissism from which it is withheld by its immediate precursor'.[28] The creative misreading that emerges as the new poetic writing is like a quest narrative, but has a clearly demarcated six-part process, the 'ratios' named 'clinamen', 'tessera', 'kenosis', 'daemonization', 'askesis' and 'apophrades' respectively.[29] Apart from 'clinamen', these are all Greek theosophical terms repackaged to form what Bloom calls 'revisionism', a tradition of belatedness, in which all poets and critics are engaged. Parallel Freudian terminology is included by Bloom at each stage, with a tripartite, kabbalistic condensation of them incorporated in his diptych text *A Map of Misreading* (1975).[30] Whatever the framework vocabulary, these six Bloomian poetic labours may be more understandable (or laughable) when translated into dance rather than conceptual moves, especially since Bloom overtly eschews common physical experience.[31] The first is a sidestep away from the precursor's footwork. The second is a leap invented by the precursor but used as a different dance step by the newcomer. The third is a flat-footed jump to claim independence as dancer from the precursor's dance tradition. The fourth describes a dance movement so quintessentially anchored in dance that the precursor's use of it seems amateur. The fifth is a dance movement of withdrawal of movement as dance, leaving the sixth a dance movement that so retranslates the precursor's most original dance step that this appears derivative.

Demystification is of course contrary to Bloom's intentions, which aim less at difficulty than at complexity and dexterity. If Bloom serves up a rhetorical, theosophical, psychoanalytical, New Historical mytho-poetics with sideswipes at both New Criticism and deconstruction, it is then to make such contributions so elaborately 'simple' that they can be reduced to 'master tropes'. He thereby also gauges the strength of his own critical acumen over theirs.[32] While outdoing precursors may thus seem Bloom's primary motive, there is more to his 'anxiety of influence' than beating off and overcoming rivals. The real bid is for superlative status, to become the greatest of all so as to defy future replacement, and hence break for ever the cycle of ultimate failure caused by succession. The very reason that Bloom therefore situates himself overtly outside deconstruction is that its claims to relativism and democratic inclusiveness cannot fit easily with a theory of the superlative, or elites. The quest model behind Bloom's six 'ratios' and their Freudian or kabbalistic revisions make this abundantly clear: 'All quest-romances of the post-Enlightenment, meaning all Romanticisms whatsoever, are quests to re-beget one's own self, to become one's own Great Original. We journey to abstract ourselves by fabrication. But where the fabric already has been woven, we journey to unravel.'[33]

Yet the elitism of this doing, undoing and outdoing is more elite than the highest of high-canonical literary traditions or a heritage of influence studies, as de Man noticed in an early response to Bloom.[34] It is a threefold cord of which the first strand is Bloom's choice of the post-Enlightenment poetic tradition, especially Romanticism, to read the 'strongest' poets in a heritage before and after it.[35] For Bloom, the Romantic poet's personal quest for poetic supremacy – desire to elevate self, language and interpretative power – is his self-creating misinterpretative strength. This is measured by an assault on strong forebears' poetic being, their very language, which transcends history.[36] Thus, the world, common humanity and tradition, the prosaic and its penchant for irony (that is the deflation of elevated forms but in historically limited contexts) are the inverse of sublime poetry, which always reaches beyond.[37] As the art of only a rarefied elect, poetic sensitivity, sensibilities and intellect are then open to inspiration, from the mightier few who came before and from invisible sources outside the human realm altogether.[38] While Bloom draws initially on the Muses, angels and other spiritual forces, it is oracular and visionary gifting that qualifies the strongest poets.[39] Thus the poet's power (*agon*) is assessed on a scale of 'strength' on several fronts, creative, critical and prophetic. In such a neo-Romantic super-league, however, it is in the most belated and American modernists such as Whitman and Emerson that Bloom most sees such attributes made manifest, since their 'psycho-poetic' struggle is necessarily the most intense.[40] While Bloom's view here chimes with Clayton and Rothstein's very American position on influence and tradition above, Bloom's understanding of the psychodynamics of American poetic vision points to the second formative strand in the elitism of the strong critic misreader, Freud.

For many critical movements in the post-Second World War period, Freud is singularly the force to be reckoned with. As early as 1975, Bloom expressed views that are only now more fully circulating, that Freud is less significant as the founder of the 'science' of psychoanalysis than as strong literary critic. Bloom's use of Freudian terminology to match the processes of Romantic imagination (the six ratios), however, has been confused, even by Bloom's advocates, with what the 'anxiety of influence' demonstrates.[41] This is Bloom's own wilfully revisionist reading of Freud's highly original reading of Oedipus to interpret patterns of cultural overthrow.[42] To lever himself over Freud, Bloom openly 'out-Freuds' him in at least two domains. The first is recognition of Oedipus as location of the dynamics and antagonistic drives that keep culture going. Whereas Freud sites this famous complex in the unconscious, and builds his psychoanalytic edifice on the 'id', and on sexuality as the terrain of its sublimations, Bloom situates antagonistic rivalries in the realm of the 'superego' and its psychic defences.[43] It is the blind Oedipus confounded on his path to visionary and 'oracular godhood' that is the most telling part of the story for Bloom.[44] While Bloom thus applauds Freud for expanding consciousness, and for doing so without returning it to some primordial plenitude (unlike Jung), sublimation and the unconscious are taken to task because they move in the wrong direction, downwards instead of upwards.[45] It is on the (poet's) super-sensible that Bloom insists, his quest for the sublime.

To nail this strong 'misreading' of Freud's Oedipus, Bloom corrects his precursor in a second major way, the field chosen to insert such theoretical insights. It was Freud's (and Nietzsche's) underestimation of poetry that provides Bloom with the golden opportunity to make this his domain. Where Freud had taken on the mighty Greek dramatists and the tragedy of Oedipus to found psychoanalysis, Bloom takes on epic poets, but in their belated post-humanist guise, to determine the 'anxiety of influence', especially celebration of sublimely singular exploits. In this move, Bloom's wrestling match with Freud is to determine who is not only the greater reinterpreter of myth as 'master-trope', and hence the strongest revisionist, but also the better guardian of such insights. For Bloom, the inventor of the Oedipus complex designed the 'talking cure' as therapy to help the many find in their own prose the resolution to their conflicted worlds with the analyst as arbiter of the right interpretations. Bloom would qualify his audience as an elite poets' society so as to reserve his insights for the (critical) salvation of the very few. This scene of instruction only enhances the strength of acts of strong misreading, but so that the *genius* of the supreme masters, himself included, is unequivocal. To return to a quotation that allegedly links Bloom's work to Kristeva's intertextuality, the real differences are clear. 'Influence as I conceive it, means that there are *no* texts, but only relationships between texts. These relationships depend upon a critical act, a misreading or misprision.'[46]

It is this 'critical act' that is paramount, for not only does it return the subject to the place of 'the death of the author', and intersubjectivity to intertextuality, it also highlights the Bloomian critic as supreme interpreter, vastly superior to the inventor-analyst of the prosaic talking cure. If critics of Bloom have been generally hostile to his ideas, they agree on one thing: Bloom is supremely the critics' critic.[47] Unlike that of the humble editor-mediator in traditional influence studies, Bloom's critical position serves neither texts nor writers, but seeks to assert itself by correcting their imperfections with greater perfection.[48] Bloom as interpreter-critic of Romantic poets as belated 'brother-poet,[49] of Freud as belated misreader of Oedipus, and of Derrida and de Man as belated Nietzscheans fully authorizes his own critical terrain. In so doing, he neatly pulls the rug from beneath intertextuality and deconstruction as 'merely' deferred or overwritten text with no human, let alone critical, interventions. The 'anxiety of influence' does then return the repressed of postmodern critical theory precisely at the point of its authority to theorize or criticize, since 'texts' in themselves can do neither, or any such work of hypothesis. Derrida's directive and consistent overwriting of Western metaphysics therefore stands to be questioned and corrected by Bloom's 'anxiety of influence'. Likewise, Bloom's work discloses in Derrida's critical appraisals and other postmodern overwriting – allegedly operating only by terminological frameworks, 'grammars' and grilles, not by humans – more than a 'trace' of Nietzsche's 'Übermensch'. Where indeed is the critic of deconstruction and intertextuality, let alone the chief technician, in the text as laboratory of artificial text reproduction? Does Bloom's 'anxiety of influence' actually provide the insight that dispels the myth of human overseeing in postmodern critical theory? Like the story of 'The emperor's new clothes', postmodern critical theory looks uncannily like a remake of 'The sorcerer's apprentice' if the director of the laboratory is *in aporia*! Thus, with regard again to the prefix, overwriting as process is the 'sibling rival' of 'overriding', which the Collins dictionary glosses as 'to . . . disregard with superior authority or power', 'to supersede or annul', 'to dominate or vanquish by, or as if by trampling down'. The neo-Romantic and antagonistic roots of intertextuality and postmodernity lurking below the surfaces they claim are all there is are now revealed.

It is pertinent, however, to up the anti again here, and recall the antithesis of the 'overwriter'. An underwriter is one who guarantees, endorses, sanctions, countersigns, backs, finances or provides security for something and is a useful metaphor for the role of the 'traditional' critic eschewed by both Derrida and Bloom. Bloom clearly is as much an overwriter as Derrida, since his assertions and fault-finding perfectionist criticism stem from the same will-to-power, unassailable critical expertise. Yet Bloom as ever would want to distinguish his strong(er) belated critical misreading from those of his nearest rivals, to oppose and surpass deconstructive criticism's technical virtuosity. Returning to some concept of critical genius is too overtly 'Romantic', yet Derrida's equally unholy critical spirit already deconstructs wind blowing from some pseudo-Greek *Sophia* as a heady mix of sophistry and sophistication. What is that third strand which makes Bloom's elitism more than that of the strongest proponents of the anti-metaphysical?

The answer is at once devastatingly simple, yet superlatively Promethean, the neat replacement of 'super-' as prefix for 'over-'. By going back before the Western metaphysicians proper (Plato and Aristotle and their overwriters) to the Sophists, Bloom can sidestep

Derrida and draw on a poetry that came by prophetic inspiration, the supernatural influence from the stars and gods, which are among the first definitions for 'influence' in the *OED*.[50] What is paramount here is that such oracular poets are obviously part of a priestly elect.[51] Bloom's 'superman to supermen' response to the Sophists discerns kindred spirits where Bourdieu's *episteme*, for example, can only describe the nebulous spirit of an age. Against Greek philosophical tradition in its doubled-pronged heritage, 'official' Western orthodoxy, including epistemology and its inversion, deconstruction, Bloom therefore opts for a differently Greek *gnosis*, personal and 'super-personal', as opposed to impersonal, modes of knowing. This sets him free of the mire of traditional influence studies and intertextuality's depersonalization, such as Kristeva's 'materialist gnoseology' in chapter 1. Bloom's elitist stance, however, equally avoids the idiosyncratic or eclectic for itself, which would doom him to inward narcissism (Freudian or mythological), or the outward Romantic and nihilist act of self-destruction. Gnosticism as alternative tradition to Greek Platonism permits Bloom to join the chosen few of the critical elite. These figures (theosophists, poets, interpreters) are the foil against which supreme individuality shines more brightly by redefining the very lights of the elite themselves. The tradition of Romantic and strong poets, including Freud as creative misinterpreter of Oedipus, is dismantled by Bloom in order to read their 'individualism' as part of literary and cultural tradition's longer shadowland, and his own, heresy.[52]

Bloom's core works, *The Anxiety of Influence* (1973), the diptych *A Map of Midreading* and *Kabbalah and Criticism* (both 1975), *Agon: Towards a Theory of Revisionism* (1982), and *The Breaking of the Vessels* (1982), openly declare the centrality of Gnosticism and particularly Kabbalah as critical paradigm for reading poetry. 'The word "Kabbalah" means "tradition" in the particular sense of "reception" and at first referred to the whole of the Oral Law.'[53] Critics' strong prejudices against Bloom have deflected their own unwillingness to countenance the theological, esoteric, mystical, or anything counter to rationalism and secular enlightenment. This is exactly the critical pressure point that Bloom's work targets. Critical understanding or appreciation of Bloom's alternative view of literary tradition and its modes of transmission and regeneration has consequently been superficial. By mapping Gnosticism briefly, and by drawing on Gershom Scholem's magisterial history of Kabbalism, Bloom's kabbalistic criticism can be given a fuller critical hearing than cursory judgements have hitherto allowed. It will either prove a more preposterous merry critical dance, or provide a password beyond the closed doors of postmodernism.

Gnosticism is no one heresy or even purely mystical sect. It is a term gathering together various religious-philosophical protest movements that were most active at the time when the rival religions, Christianity, Islam and Judaism, were setting out their doctrinal and orthodox positions about the one true God. The melting pot was Alexandria in the third century AD. While the Gnostic sects continued their existence throughout the medieval and Renaissance periods (the Cathars are a prime example), it was not until comparative religion became fashionable for academic study in the nineteenth century (influenced by Romanticism) that Gnosticism was unfettered from various prejudices – that it was pagan, akin to magic or without a Jewish version. Its central tenets as negative theology, and protest movement eschewing accepted statements of faith, are particular redolent of Bloom. As Kurt Rudolph succinctly elucidates:

> The Gnostics understood themselves as a 'chosen people', as an élite that, in opposition to the 'worldly-minded' has perceived the strong connection between the world, humanity and salvation. With the help of 'insight', the objective of Gnostic teaching is to free the elect from the fetters of this world. [. . .] It involved an 'exegetical protest' against the older traditions, that is, the interpretation of older traditions in a manner contrary to their original sense. The area of activity involved two things. First, their customary world-denying ascetical ethos. Second, an ideologically inevitable curtailing of sacramental rites in favour of a salvation achieved only through 'insight' (*gnosis*).[54]

While Bloom's elective critical stance of exegetical superiority, insight, protest is now accounted for, one final ingredient of his elitist stance is missing, precisely that element which defines Kabbalah from (any) other Gnostic heresies. It seems no accident that Bloom frames himself firmly in the inner circle of these heresies, specifically of the already elite and chosen people, the Jews. The anti-religious Jew in Bloom, his heretical Judaism in the rich tradition of Jewish Kabbalah, may further explain why he wilfully locks antlers both with the heretical *midrashic* interpretative tradition of Freud that produced psychoanalysis, and with the primacy of the scene of writing that is Derrida's anti-metaphysical fetishization of the text.[55] The distinctiveness of Kabbalah as Jewish Gnosticism therefore provides for Bloom an elective elite of elites which surpasses Greek heritage – Plato, Western metaphysics, Pauline theology – and its 'heretical' counter-movements stemming from Heidegger, nihilism and deconstruction.[56]

Gershom Scholem's scholarship, as Bloom consistently endorses, provides a full background and history of Kabbalism. His *Major Trends in Jewish Mysticism* (1946) is no manual of esoteric lore or mystical initiation. It presents and distinguishes this late twelfth-century arrival on the Gnostic map from other Christian and Islamic forms. As first an orally transmitted interpretation of the universe, its textual formalization occurred in Spain round the *Zohar* (The Book of Splendour). Its golden age was the Renaissance through the teachings of Cordovero and the Safed Kabbalist, Isaac Luria. It is Scholem's seventh lecture on Luria and his slant on theogony and cosmology that is most significant. It is from this that Bloom extracts the tripartite terms that will replace the six ratios. Luria's *Tsimtsum* (concentration, contraction, withdrawal or retreat, which Bloom transliterates as *Zimzum*), followed by *Shevirath hakelim* ('the-breaking-of-the-vessels', which Bloom borrows for a title), is completed by *Tikkun* (restitution or reintegration). Bloom's *A Map of Misreading* not only gives a pithy resume of Luria as Scholem presents him. It also openly acknowledges these Hebrew terms so as to show off the strength of his own superior reformulation of them in his manifesto for literary criticism as revisionism:

> [T]he revisionist strives to *see* again, so as to *esteem* and estimate differently, so as then to *aim* "correctively." In the dialectical terms that I employ for interpreting poems in this book, re-seeing is a *limitation*, re-estimating is a *substitution*, and re-aiming is a *representation*. I displace these terms from the context of later or Lurianic Kabbalism, which I take as the ultimate model for Western revisionism from the Renaissance to the present.[57]

It is Bloom's understanding of strongest poets down the ages as part of a particular 'kabbalistic' lineage from the *Zohar* to Milton, from the Romantics to Stevens and Whitman in America, that constitutes his 'insight' into the blindnesses of postmodern criticism, not least its lack of a meta-critical term for tradition itself.[58] He, on the other hand, can judge such lack by appealing to Kabbalah, as surpassing both the tradition that undergirds Western and European canon and its anti-canons. By inserting kabbalistic criticism into these conceptual spaces, Bloom would then claim critical supremacy, his own insertion by election into Kabbalah's highest elite as exemplified by Luria, since 'every master of Kabbalah has stressed his own continuity rather than his discontinuity with previous spectators.'[59]

As he did with Freud, however, Bloom must also 'out-Luria' Luria, not only by making himself the improved reincarnation of this kabbalist grand master's theosophical speculations, but also his aegis. As Scholem elucidates, 'Mystical knowledge is not [Luria's] private affair which has been revealed to him [. . .] On the contrary, the purer or more nearly perfect it is, the nearer to the original stock of knowledge common to mankind it is.'[60] Within Luria's esoteric restoration of divine sparks to their fullness by elect Jews, there was none the less in Kabbalah a wider redeeming or 'soteric' function.[61] In and for his age, Luria pondered the horrors of exile, the Shoah, and the Jew's place in the redemption of nations. Bloom, on the other hand, rejects common humanity, to play only for elitist and elective poetic influence, for the tradition of the individualistic talent, to bowdlerize T. S. Eliot, as highly intellectual interpretative and unorthodox heritage.[62] Bloom understood in the light of the tradition of Kabbalah, therefore, makes critical responses to his work on poet-to-poet combat for visionary 'strength' as essentially irrelevant or mainly Freudian pale. At the very least, the 'anxiety of influence' dislodges the oppositional frameworks from within postmodern criticism itself.

Yet there are two, and seemingly contradictory, turns of the screw in the 'super-kabbalistic' critical position that Bloom would adopt. Both pertain to the specifically Jewish counter-tradition that he wishes to uphold. The first is Bloom's awareness that, while he has gone beyond Luria as regards the poet as 'redeemer' of the demiurgic mission, the very belatedness of Kabbalism and Luria's place in it puts their reputation at stake, and consequently his own. To resolve this dilemma, Bloom makes the same counter-move that allowed him to sidestep Derrida's potentially rival misreading of Western metaphysics. As with his return to the poetry of the Sophists, Bloom needs some pre-kabbalistic heresy by which Kabbalah can then be regrounded as belated improvement of it. It is on the heresiarch of heresiarchs, Valentinus, chief among Gnostics, that Bloom calls as proleptically *Jewish* Gnostic in the making. In 1982, Bloom indeed ascribes his own personal standpoint as Jewish *Gnostic*.[63] If critics of Bloom have noted his 'Valentinism' in passing, none has explored this properly.[64] Clarification of the salient features of this particular heresy can be summed up in the following quotation:

> The principal ingredient which Gnosticism derived from Christianity was the central idea of redemption. [. . .] Even in those sects which stood closest to Orthodox Christianity, such as [. . .] the Platonist Valentinus of Rome, the Gnostic attitude to matter as alien to the supreme God required the rejection of any genuine incarnation [. . .] The influence of fatalistic ideas drawn from popular astrology and magic became fused with notions derived from Pauline language about predestination to produce a rigidly deterministic scheme. Redemption was from destiny, not from the consequences of responsible action, and was granted to a pre-determined elect in whom alone was the divine spark. [. . .] The Gnostic initiates were people of the spirit, the elect whose salvation was certain and indefectible. Ordinary church members, with faith but not 'knowledge', were only of *psyche*, while the heathen were merely earthly clods without even the dimmest ray of light.[65]

Christ as redeemer is either elided as pure spirit providing the knowledge (*gnosis*) necessary to escape the demiurge or evil creator God,[66]
or erased altogether by the 'predestined' redemptive elect possessing
the 'divine spark'. Valentinus also adopted the Christian idea of the
Pleroma (the outpouring of the Holy Spirit after Christ's resurrection), but did not name its part in the Trinity to give expression to
the ineffable (without name). For the elect, it was the (Adamic) force
to rename. Bloom's own self-validation, his 'Lurianic Valentinism' or
Gnostic yet Jewish investment in redemption by the spirit-spark, can
now be clearly compared:

> A Gnostic 'place', like the classical topos or 'commonplace,' is always
> a name, but [. . .] a Gnostic or Romantic name comes by negation; an
> un-naming yields a name. A written space has been voided of its
> writing, so that the Gnostic place displaces a prior place. This is why
> the best model for Post-Romantic poetic place or image of voice is the
> Valentinian Pleroma or its curiously similar analogue in the Lurianic
> *tehiru*. The Pleroma or *tehiru*, like the Romantic and Modern poetic
> place, is both a fullness and an absence. [Therefore it] implicitly
> commits Gnosticism to an aesthetic that is neither mimetic, like Greek
> aesthetic from Plato to Plotinus, nor anti-mimetic, like Hebraism from
> the Bible to Jacques Derrida. Gnostic writing, when strong, is strong
> because it is super-mimetic, because it confronts and seeks to over-
> throw the very strongest of all texts, the Jewish Bible.[67]

We will be returning to many of the problems of mimesis in the next
chapter, but this passage is remarkable for its combinations of
Valentinus, 'the greatest of the Gnostic speculators', [68] and Luria,
'most inventive of Kabbalists',[69] as theory of the 'super-mimetic'.
This is not on one count but on two. Bloom inserts himself in the
line from Luria's disciples working to restore some of the Jewish
sparks to the 'crisis of postmodernism'. At the same time, he can
promote the (Greek) Pleroma-*Sophia* aspects of Valentinus's heretical reformulation of *Gnosticism* beyond its status as Christian heresy.
For Bloom, Valentinus is no Platonist, but, and here we have it, a
belated Sophist, centred in negative theology and antithetical criticism that constructs, not deconstructs:

> Protagoras and Gorgias are the authentic origins of an antithetic
> criticism [. . .] Let us, as critics, abandon Aristotle to the Formalists,
> and Plato to the Platonists (which these days may mean the Decon-
> struction Road Company) [. . .] [Protagoras] teaches, as Gorgias will,
> the relativity of meaning, but meanings for him *are* presences, not
> absences, though these are flickering presences, perpetually in flux.
> The crucial term in Protagoras is *metron*, 'mastery over something',
> which for the purposes of literary criticism I would translate as 'poetic
> misprision'.[70]

In short, such super-mimesis is Bloom's attempt not only for revisionary mastery beyond Luria *and* Valentinus, but also to bring forth
from behind them a kind of extra pure *gnosis* that none the less has
an elitist, 'Jewish', stamp upon it. Safely removed therefore from any
Urzeit of the Sophists, it is paradoxically to be found in its preposterous and belated, yet pristine, time and space.[71] This transpires to
be exactly where Bloom is, the America specifically in the light
(sparks) of Emerson.[72]

   This is the second 'super-kabbalistic' critical position that Bloom
would adopt, an American poetic and intellectual elite separate from
any Western European traditions. His own role in this is truly of the
super-elite, pseudo-Messianic, yet deeply kabbalistic, for he will be
the teacher and enlightener of the elite of intellectual Jews, the
redeemer of wandering poetic meaning (as opposed to 'deferred'
meaning) for a select and reconstituted group of Diaspora Jewries.[73]
If Valentinus is heresiarch of heresiarchs, then Bloom takes up for
himself the double sense of this word: the founder of a heresy and
the founder of a school. Bloom's kabbalistic criticism is designed precisely for the adoptive, and non-Greek, homeland of America. The
interpreter turns his other face, teacher, but in the hieratic and vatic
modes. Teaching is the passing on of strong tradition – Hebrew
mishnah and Kabbalah – not the conservationist 'blend of antiquarianism and culture-mongering' or instruction as 'antithetical
teaching'.[74] In one move again, Bloom adopts the role of kabbalistic
rabbi in his 'scene of instruction', which neatly overwrites both
Freud's 'primal scene' (all-important for psychic formation) and
Derrida's 'scene of writing'. To counter general deconstruction and
late capitalist relativism in which all, including Jews, are assimilated,
Bloom's scene of instruction attempts to clarify a specifically 'Amer-
ican-Jewish' project, since America is a country built on election. This
is the revalorization of an elitist American tradition 'affirming the self
over language', and a language that is the strongest of all, American-
English poetry.[75]

   Bloom forgets one thing. This elect cannot be the elite of elites
and fully part of democracy, which is also open to all-comers. The
hierarchy of elites in Bloom we have now traced in Kabbalah and
Gnosticism has a fatal flaw, a dark shadowland in all its embodiments, including Bloom's postmodernist 'American' form. It is
exclusively (but not inclusively) male. Scholem, as authority of all
aspects of Bloom's Kabbalism, is unequivocal:

   One final observation should be made on the general character of
   Kabbalism as distinct from other, non-Jewish, forms of mysticism.
   Both historically and metaphysically it is a masculine doctrine, made

for men and by men. The long history of Jewish mysticism shows no trace of feminine influence. There have been no women Kabbalists; Rabia of early Islamic mysticism, Mechthild of Magdeburg, Juliana of Norwich, Theresa de Jesus, and the many other feminine representatives of Christian mysticism have no counterparts in the history of Kabbalism. The latter, therefore, lacks the element of the feminine emotion which has played so large a part in the development of non-Jewish mysticism, but it also remained comparatively free from the dangers entailed by the tendency towards hysterical extravagance which followed in the wake of this influence. [. . .] This exclusive masculinity for which Kabbalism has paid a high price, appears rather to be connected with an inherent tendency to lay stress on the demonic nature of women and the feminine element of the cosmos. It is of the essence of Kabbalistic symbolism that woman represents not, as one might be tempted to expect, the quality of tenderness but that of stern judgment.[76]

The next chapter on imitation will return to this 'demonic nature of women' in a different guise. The Kabbalists evaded 'feminine', autobiographical and subjective writing about mysticism, for reasons of 'muscular', masculine illuminations and only for an inner circle. These visionary revelations were delivered by oral instruction and transmitted only to male disciples. Such channels remove any need of 'female' or 'feminized' intermediaries such as the Muses or Sophia in certain theosophical traditions. Thus, Bloom's 'anxiety of influence' as essentially Gnostic and kabbalistic can accommodate special male belatedness, but cannot countenance great poetesses or strong feminist critics, since a female canon is a contradiction in terms. For Bloom, woman is not part of election, or his 'America', which rests on Emerson as exemplar of male individualism, intellectualism and poetic acumen. As the description of Valentinism above suggested, Woman for Bloom is but a 'clod', with infinitesimal light:

There are very good women poets writing in America even with Miss Bishop dead and gone [. . .] I find it fascinating to speak of a poet whose work I do not admire, the prophetess, the great shaman or shamanessa, Miss Adrienne Rich. [. . .] in what is supposed to be a recent body of work which tries to establish itself in the true body of the high feminist canon that there is scarcely a passage in which the actual poetic language consistently being struggled with is not that of another poet, on the whole one whom I do not greatly admire [. . .] Robert Lowell.[77]

Of course, the feminist critical camp reacted quickly to reject such blatant arrogance and misogyny, but failed to investigate where its authority came from. The dismissal of him by their male counterparts for his 'brooding, neo-Gothic self-seductions of style' or self-justificatory vocabularies[78] is potentially much more dangerous. It should now be clear what authority Bloom's 'anxiety of influence' does possess.[79] As manifesto of an exclusive male elite it deposes most male traditions and canons by 'feminizing' them in the Gnostic sense above. One quotation will suffice to demonstrate Bloom's outrageous unpolitically correct criticism on all these counts: 'Most feminist poetry, of course, is like most black poetry. It isn't poetry. It isn't even verse. It isn't prose [. . .] I have no name for it [. . .] they are all ideologues.'[80] Such extreme superciliousness should sound strong warning bells. Bloom's open advocacy of a superior and exclusive caste, set on perfecting an already elective elitism which is not determined by birth, class, national identity or respect for the past *per se*, makes plain a super-egotistical bid to circumvent (male) creativity and (female) procreativity completely. While such a move is consistent with many Gnostic heresies, Bloom's aspirations to a kind of *non*-genetic engineering of supermen precursors to attain a perfectability of self smacks everywhere of a psychic eugenics. Such authoritarian experimentation reminiscent of Nazism shares a similar and fanatical disregard for any higher intellectual and spiritual authorities with power to redirect or correct error. It is this, after all, which is the lot and also safeguard of the whole human race.

As with any ethnic cleansing, Bloom's ruthless mastery over, or purging of, other traditions actually pronounces profound disregard for 'minor poets' or even the great texts of his chosen heritage. Bloom has very little to say about any of the strong poems he reads, except to extract their vital marrow to demonstrate his own 'strength'. Beyond any Barthesian bruising as mark of pleasure, texts in the Bloomian mindscape can therefore be raped, assaulted, disemboweled, violated or cannibalized to any degree. Is the cover on the real perversity, even pornography, of Bloom's 'anxiety of influence' now blown? Is this the return of a repressed Sadean homoerotics of the mind, a belated 'disrememberment' of Orpheus, to grasp his vital 'spark' as strongest poet of them all? Octavio Paz reminds us that:

> [t]he Orphic cult arose after the destruction of Achean civilisation, which caused a general dispersion of the Greek world and a vast reaccommodation of its peoples and cultures. The necessity of reforging the ancient links, both social and sacred, created a number of secret cults in which the only participants were 'uprooted, transplanted beings [. . .] who dreamed of fashioning an organization from which they could not be separated. Their only collective name was that of "orphans."' (I should mention that *orphanos* means both 'orphan' and 'empty.' Solitude and orphanhood are similar forms of emptiness.[81]

If Bloom's assault on high culture's epic of strong poetry is a will to unrivalled power, its extremist Promethean and Sadean narratives fall flat in two major respects. The first is that his plundering of Luria's Kabbalism may appear new to literary criticism, but its motor of anti-traditional exile flows from the same artesian spring as Orphic and other ancient 'poetic' mystery cults, and hence is not new at all. As critic or iconoclast, Bloom is neither a Milton, nor an orphan of mad genius as a Nerval, nor even an extremist fanatic such as Bobby Jones. While Bloom's theory of influence does clarify and exalt the role of the critic, the banal reality is that criticism of whatever stable is secondary to literary creativity. Consequently, while the critical acts that Bloom perpetrates on literature are at times insightful, they never rise above the prosaic. The translation of Bloom's ratios into dance steps at the outset of this analysis reduced their exoticisms to banality and potential ridicule. Eccentric and private language can never safeguard its creator from 'bloomers' of this sort.

Extreme positions in times of cultural exhaustion or indirection, as indeed when Bloom and Derrida entered the critical fray, are indispensable critical thermometers. Bloom's work differs only in degree from other strong critical approaches which ever take what they want from cultural heritage. Deconstruction equally abstracts its supplements from predisposed lodes of philosophical and literary tradition. As important anti-model, even strong antidote to the blandness of relativism, or ironic and cynical undecidablility, singularity of view or vision, can be applauded, since values such as genius, inspiration, mad reason and prophetic crying in the wilderness can be reappraised. As the Romantics before him, Bloom and his bold 'scripture',[82] his strong culturally critical response, challenges the values undergirding materialism, empiricist or pseudo-scientific models for excellence, an economics of the global marketplace, or virtuoso technologies as models of cultural reproduction. He also entertains longer traditions and anti-traditions than strictly Enlightenment and secular ones to return myth, the esoteric and religious significance to art and literature.

Canonical poetry, culture or criticism is not born of a piece from Zeus's head, but made. Bloom's refashioning of the 'Great Tradition' of his New Critic father, Frye, demonstrates unequivocally that critical consensus conspires to oust certain writers or genres and promote others. Bloom undoubtedly understands roots of traditions (influences) much more than most postmodern or feminist criticism is prepared to countenance. Dismissing iconoclasts such as Bloom out of hand is not a good object lesson. Not only did Gnosticism exclude women, it was also largely such heresies that shaped orthodoxy itself and its canon of texts:

[I]n practical and sociological spheres, Gnostic foundations were of
direct and tangible importance for the development of the Church,
e.g. polity and church order (the episcopal system), the exclusion
of women from community leadership (advocated particularly by
Tertullian), and forcing the laity into the legal and hierarchical
institution of a state Church.[83]

In its theosophy, Bloom's work is therefore intensely theological.[84] By
exploring a psychic history of schism and its dynamics, Bloom takes
the 'anxiety of influence' beyond Freud, Kabbalah and literary
criticism, including postmodernism, to a richer understanding of
Western traditions. We will answer Bloom with Girard's alternative
reading of such processes in the next chapter. Bloom's so-called
arcane vocabularies now appear less so once their heretical
antecedents are understood. By at least aspiring to critical distinctiveness, and to a hyperbolic degree, Bloom's terminologies also
disrobe the equally sublime, potentially ridiculous or blasphemous
coinages in postmodern critical theories. Masterminding such jargon
is what will distinguish the super-critic (whether a Bloom or a
Derrida) from the acolyte attempting to master it. However ingen-
ious, postmodern critical theory and its rival 'anxiety of influence'
will remain equally idiosyncratic and rapidly outdated critical babble,
unless their public comprehension and comprehensiveness are taken
into account. Only accessible and open celebration of the teeming
richness of ubiquity will assure durability. In the light of Bloom,
Derrida now emerges as 'strong' theorist of the negative anti-
tradition, whereas Bloom himself is exemplar of its double negative.
His blatant, extreme and elitist masculinism at least leaves no doubt
as to where he speaks from and makes him a match for the anti-
humanistic artificer of deconstruction. As non-identical twins,
Bloom and Derrida thus sit as latter-day interpreters in denial of any
Holy Spirit yet firm believers in the critical spirit.

Bloom's 'anxiety of influence' thus throws down the gauntlet to
other critics to be more correct if not political. Gender and postcolonial studies clearly have a call to take up tradition as seriously as
Bloom, particularly his dedication to lifting the interpretative burden
of oppressive orders, and his operation from within the several
legacies of 'tradition' to forge one for himself. Is then the strongest
response to tradition and its Gnostic anti-traditions either a theory
of inclusiveness of all 'men' (humanity) or the harnessing of the 'stern
judgement' of women so feared within it in Scholem's account above?
The feisty judgements of a Deborah or a Jael certainly provide
models of an extremely strong 'Jewess' tradition, to which many
'belated' women poets and critics, such as Adrienne Rich, certainly

belong. Such alternative critical responses to the very elitisms central to Bloom's work are not, however, hypothetical, but 'always already' exist. They are the shadowlands of both postmodernist and Bloomian attack, 'traditional' influence studies. It is to this doubly maligned other that the chapter will now turn.

'Traditional' influence

Even before post-structuralism or Bloom took it to task, influence study had been variously charged with irrelevance. The New Critics had already disposed of its manifestations as outmoded biographical criticism or source-hunting. Equally, Hassan's theory of artistic expressionism in the mid-1950s was deemed too vague or impressionistic to be useful: an artist's work could be explained by a reflection of his/her unconscious, or by the susceptibilities and affinities to the similar values, impressions or worldviews found in other writers.[85] On the other hand, comparative criticism was accused of promoting a specifically nationalistic cultural imperialism, in spite of its alleged cosmopolitanism and comparative approach.[86] It was agency that was problematic for the recipient's perceived powerlessness, 'under the influence of' the forebear or canonical heritage. Postmodernism and intertextuality neatly solved the problem by denying agents and intention altogether. As the quotation from Clayton and Rothstein (1991) at the outset of this chapter established, the term 'influence studies' means a hierarchical order of 'influence over'.

A trawl of dictionary definitions for 'influence' rapidly demonstrates that this is only one side of the story. The other, and positive, 'influence for' reverses hierarchies or understands influence as complex and plural. Contrary to Bakhtin's concept of monologism and intertextual glosses on it, a so-called authority may also be multiple, dialogic or reciprocal, just as a number of strands plaited together make a more diverse but stronger rope. Or, more radically, a truly influential work may be one that knows its own increase by being central to others subsequently. Power is in having given to, not usurping from.[87] It is in pre-Enlightenment and European traditions, which were openly receptive of new texts, ideas and movements, that this view is exemplified. Thus, because influence has been seen only monodirectionally as 'x's' influence on 'y', where 'y' comes temporally always after 'x', the wider possibilities of 'y' as positively influenced have been occluded. As Baxandall so cogently puts it,

> [i]f we think of Y rather than X as the agent, the vocabulary is much richer and more attractively diversified: draw on, resort to, avail oneself of, appropriate from, have recourse to, adapt, misunderstand, refer to,

pick up, take on, engage with, react to, quote, differentiate oneself
from, assimilate oneself to, assimilate, align oneself with, copy, address,
paraphrase, absorb, make a variation on, revive, continue, remodel,
ape, emulate, travesty, parody, extract from, distort, attend to, resist,
simplify, reconstitute, elaborate on, develop, face up to, master,
subvert, perpetuate, reduce, promote, respond to, transform, tackle
. . . – everyone will be able to think of others. Most of these relations
just cannot be stated the other way round – in terms of x acting on y
rather than y acting on x. To think in terms of influence blunts thought
by impoverishing the means of differentiation.[88]

While many of these ideas are the subject of the next chapter, on imitation, including negative manifestations of the copy as intention to
deceive or plagiarism, the notion of negative influence as debt and
debit is everywhere exchanged here for credit, to 'y'. The thesaurus
of similar terms emphasizes the enlargement and enabling of successors, whether these are traditions, authors, texts, critics or readers.
By viewing influence from 'y', influence in its widest and most multiform senses is revivified. The changes to 'x' that 'y' as predominant
entail, such as redefinition, recognition or adaptation, makes 'x'
essentially contributory, that is primary by being secondary. As
opposed to the hierarchical, astral, Bloomian paradigm, the pertinent
model for influence here is 'that which flows into', a tributary that
forms a mightier river by its confluences, or the main stream that
comprises many contributors. Influence as baton to be passed on
thus understands the 'situatedness' of texts not as a synchronic
system or electronic network, but as a complex process of human
(inter)cultural activity in spaces and times including those of subsequent readers. Texts are the productions of multiple agencies and a
plethora of intentions, from pleasure to instruction, exemplification
to enlightenment. The contexts of influence and the influences of
context are therefore the 'how' and 'why' questions any text will
variously address, even if it is concerned primarily with form or a
language game.[89] Stylistic manipulation is never neutral, but the
particular weave of the writer, however hidden, so that the fabrication is understood in certain ways. Thus, the reader is the trans-
mitter and interpreter of a work as cultural artefact that has relevance
to real worlds but is not a mere video recording of them.

Influence study in this positive sense, however, goes further than
investigating the multiple contexts and purposes of a work. Like
interdisciplinarity in chapter 1, influence is also at home with generic
or other groupings as combinations and syntheses. The difference is
that it concentrates more on meta-level inputs than outcomes. As
proposition or hypothesis generated by lateral thinking, influence,
like an incoming tributary, generates something which was not there

previously, whether qualitatively or quantitatively. While such nebulousness has been the bane of source studies – did author x actually read text y? – influence here is not subjective or impressionistic. Rather, it is a facilitation of informed imagination, and hence is closer to scientific speculation which can then be confirmed by detailed analysis.[90] Clearly, influence of this order can begin to postulate and address such questions as 'What is literature for?' In response, postmodern intertextuality can only reply, 'for itself' as ultimate language game, whether ornamental, ludic or acrostic. Bloom's 'anxiety of influence' is no less solipsistic and self-serving: it is to demonstrate the genius of the later critic or poet.

Positive influence, on the contrary, aims at a variety of responses, not more of the same. It is therefore intrinsic to understanding change, revolt, regress and progress, depending on factors such as, for example, censorship or ideological control. These may have both negative and positive effects on artistic production whereas, in periods of stability, consensus and democracy, cultural production may become an expendable part of consumerism and toy mainly with its own putative triviality, proliferation, even obsolescence.[91] Beyond tradition, positive influence thus tackles mimetic and anti-mimetic ends and means and can enlist a variety of stimuli. For newly emerging branches of cultural production – Afro-American women's writing is paradigmatic – such influence is vital in the establishment of appropriate forms within the wider cultural frame of reception.[92] Because influence permits a reference to persons in different histories and other geographies, it has been a strategic weapon for women to recover their forgotten foremothers and set up alternative stories, as well as ways of telling them, about official canon and tradition and their exclusions.[93] Influence then is a 'y' that changes 'x' indelibly, but by resorting to more than causality and chronology. Jazz is an obvious example, and also of what Awkward calls 'denigration', 'this infusion of Black cultural "spirit" into Western "matter" [. . .] alters that matter in essential ways.'[94] 'Y', the would-be 'victim', is now seen to embody a uniqueness of constitution and relationships (beyond text-to-text or poet-to-poet), a nexus that is a *community* of consciousness outside categories of sex, class, creed, race, or time and place. Girard's exploration of the power for change of the scapegoat will return to these ideas in the following chapter.

Positive influence as multiple and braided expression is also not limited by specific spatio-temporal parameters or direct interpersonal relations. Cultural production includes a further and more holistic transformational impact, a response to material and human circumstance. This is not a universalism or definition of the world by fixed archetypes and essences. Rather it is the site of facing extremes of circumstance, to find a self transcended, a circumstance overcome, and an ability to reach out once more.[95] Doubt, pain, catastrophe, terror, despair, melancholy, pessimism, or the heights of passion, love, celebration, jubilation – the gamut of human emotions find a language of personal and cultural response that then infiltrates the cerebral.[96] Art in this sense richly provides precursors who faced similar exaltation or vicissitudes to find enlarged, creative responses to reality, empowerment through cultural memory, or other imaginative frames of human reference. In the teeth of extreme adversity, the positive influence of art may also revive a will to survive, to hope, to endure. Deeply experiential, intuitive or inspirational works thus defy or bypass didactic, directive or partisan levels of representation or recipes of form.[97] Something of a greater wisdom and understanding flowing erratically down the generations, yet channelled by sure knowledge of the right way to retell the old story, provides deeper recognitions than are possible within traditional source studies, which concentrate on a single lineage, or intertextuality as orderly web of previous texts.

Such open intention, rather than postmodern refusal of intentions or Bloom's highly strategic ones, is the ultimate challenge that positive influence levels at critical theory and shows is the contradiction within it. If postmodern and Bloomian criticism refuse past sources, they cannot then envisage a site for their own future as entities or springboards for renewal, but only as stardust or fallen stars. Positive influence, on the other hand, permits proleptic recognitions, since it acknowledges those of the past. It 'backs into the future', as Knox reminds us is quintessential to early Greek imagination.[98] Such open agendas also assume change as central and multiple, but because of a constant human import. By contrast, postmodern theory, including Bloom, relies on invariable models for texts or poets as network or antagonistic overthrow. These models of course preclude complete change, since there is no alternative outside position that might ultimately oust them, only variations of the master plan. This dogmatism – all views are equal but one is more equal than others – reveals the real intentionality and disqualifiers behind both deconstruction and Bloom from opposite ends of the same spectrum, whether cloaked as ultimate arbitrariness or concerted rebellion. The critical grilles or master tropes a Derrida or a Bloom then impose on text or poetic lineage respectively, together with their supporting underling terminologies, constitute the motors by which criticism itself – whether Marxist, feminist, postcolonialist, genetic, psychoanalytic, New Historicist, postmodernist – supplants texts and 'poets'. It is the confrontation with works and artists who seek to influence positively and generously that reveals such arbitrations and prescriptive beating of texts into an 'appropriate' shape for certain purposes.[99] Influence that openly recognizes different others again confounds any programmatic or even systematic mode of textual criticism, however socio-critical, interdisciplinary or formalist, and offers a site for cultural renewal.[100] As a way of opening up and disrupting closed orders, of calling for the past to be added to the future, positive influence reneges on limiting options. If this is not to result in bland optimism, are there critical approaches that take positive influence forward to map *qualitative* understanding of complexity and confluence of traditions?

Positive influence studies already in fact include two confluences for addressing renewal, yet both have been demoted by criticism and critical theory through the rejection of influence as negative. The first concentrates on internals within one cultural context. At the micro-level, reconsideration may come from genetic critical approaches that focus on manuscripts and versions of one author's work before it is fixed in print. This recent area of specialist endeavour on the insta-bilities of 'text' has revivified source-hunting and the academic production of critical editions, especially of canonical writers. It is indicative of the way in which influence and authorial intention have become partner terms for describing the dynamics of literary creation in a work that includes its author's own revisions, the impor-tance of various contexts, as well as serendipity. Genetic criticism thus challenges the Romantic notion of creativity as 'of a piece', inspiration from on high, or accountable by the 'genius' of the writer or artist.

Critical understanding of the past of one cultural heritage, better known as cultural or literary history, also has a wider brief than patri-otic endorsement of traditional historiography and source-hunting in its wider socio-political and national contexts. Cultural criticism demands highly flexible, yet pertinent, interdisciplinary interpretative frameworks to recuperate and describe elements that are deeply ingrained in a given cultural fabric, such as genres, narrative modes or plots. These necessarily evolve and develop over time because local context will influence how any paradigm, to remain relevant, responds to changes at the legal, social or other level. Within one tra-dition, anti-models are not necessarily breaks, but links within more complex meshing of influences to form 'traditions' within a tradition. These may actually strengthen rather than weaken the genre's or plot's ability to survive. We will return to canon and generic revital-ization as constructive imitation in the next chapter. To illustrate this socio-political point, of note is the Chinese *xia*, or knight-errant tra-dition. This spawned the *nüxia*, or female knight-errant tradition, and has since become an ideal vehicle in which to insert the modern New

Woman, for it was already a tale of intrigue, integrity and transgressive, yet appropriate, conduct.[101] Reshaping the Grand Narrative in this way is in fact hugely economical for the later writer. So much can quickly be evoked by shorthand cultural reference or dependence on the reader's familiarity with a tradition, its particular authors, canonical texts, styles or generic conventions. Influence from the past of a national heritage is thus positively embraced as mode of enhancement, even if the new narrative refutes the absolute authority of previous canonical works in the same vein. Miner and Brady also point to the Indian preoccupation of ceaseless retelling of a few immense works, or the fact that, 'in east Asia, literary language is, by definition, precedented language and if there is anxiety, it may be more properly be termed the anxiety of not being influenced.'[102] To unlock such interpretational frameworks requires a critical method immersed and versed in a long-sighted reading of national heritage and its developments, not some 'tunnel vision', however deconstructive, from the present.[103] Necessarily the remit of such long-sighted cultural criticism will include more than one century, one generic specialism, a single thematic line of investigation, one level of cultural production, and will be informed by a deeply rooted knowledge of context, language, history, geography and ethos of the culture concerned, as well as its organs of censorship. Referring to Frederic Jameson's dialectical criticism and Hans Robert Jauss's *Rezeptionsästhetik* at the time, even in 1981 Jonathan Culler suggested that 'one source of energy for criticism in the coming years may be the reinvention of literary history. The historical perspective enables one to recognize the transience of any interpretation [. . .] and to take as object of reflection the series of interpretive acts by which traditions are constituted and meaning produced.'[104] Note the word 'source' even in the thick of post-structuralist work here. Perhaps more interesting in retrospect is how feminist and gay studies have already got inside the 'ungendered' agenda that Culler tacitly suggests here. Recuperation of authors in mainstream culture sidelined for their sexual difference, politics or social representations has been a central part of gay and lesbian studies, while gender studies and feminist criticism more broadly have, for a long time, been challenging tradition as monolithic. These fields are already restoring the shadowlands of traditional literary history and recent theories of textuality to cultural histories dedicated to national frameworks.

The second contributory channel of positive influence study draws on externals, on renewals of one heritage that come through dialogue with neighbouring, or more 'foreign', traditions.[105] A tired or stagnant form, plot or narrative convention at the end of its national life cycle can be transformed through transplantation from another. As with vital organs, however, the import none the less has to share fundamental similarities with the host if it is not to be rejected. Comparative criticism already has such tasks within its centrifugal remit (for literature, art, film and other cultural forms). Yet, due to the pejorative downgrading of 'influence studies' of all kinds, this approach has been stigmatized as outmoded, or as a larger version of source or allusion-hunting as 'comparisonitis'.[106] As Hermerén, however, specifies, a properly searching comparative critical method will distinguish between surface similarities and 'the extensiveness, precision, and exclusiveness of the similarity'.[107] Comparative criticism's close considerations of multiple contexts, influences and linguistic considerations in fact represents the 'always already' that is the *Urform* of postcolonial criticism. In this light, not only is the old charge of paternalism associated with comparative study ill-founded; comparative criticism's potential as cosmopolitan criticism is therefore more wide-reaching than certain brands of postcolonial studies which sever the colonial past or invert the old colonial hierarchies by overemphasising the new. By being able to reconnect pre- and postcolonial and examine the continuities and transplantations of linguistic heritage, for example, comparative criticism has the further advantage that it can evaluate heritages within postcolonial criticism itself.[108] Where the past is too openly painful for articulation, as in Holocaust studies, postcolonial criticism is better served, not by deconstructive 'trace', but by recognitions within the wider gamut of comparative criticism.[109]

Partnership criticism, whether of plural traditions or from perspectives of the newcomer on the forebear, are also matched, however, by other kinds of so-called old-style overviews of national and European heritages. Here, critical undertakings focus on movements or periods, such as medieval or Renaissance studies, which already tackle 'mixed' questions about parts and wholes that pertain to multiracial, multilingual and cultural exchange. 'Melting-pot' cultures are not in fact new, as 'Mediterranean' studies amply demonstrate. Critics in these domains demonstrate the multidisciplinary toolkits and range of critical expertise required to tackle questions which everywhere risk anachronism or culture blindness. This kind of comparative criticism is poles apart from canonical criticism of Grand Narratives. Two cases in point are made by Ernst Robert Curtius and Erich Auerbach. In *European Literature and the Latin Middle Ages* (1948) and *Mimesis: the Representation of Reality in Western Literature* (1946) respectively, they demonstrated that insider–outsider *exclusions*, not inclusions, can perhaps be more influential in shaping culture-generous and insightfully non-racist questionings of values beyond the political. As German-Jewish intellectuals writing during and just after the Second World War, their critical identity was altogether scholarly and cosmopolitan, rather than national or ethnic. Their resplendent identification with 'classical' scholarship goes far beyond its representations in Western European texts, or their learnedness and knowledge. It is the openness to learning itself as informed by personal circumstance and a set of values beyond race, creed or class that counts. Auerbach's enforced period of exile as Jew brought *Mimesis* to birth.[110] Significantly, Auerbach and Curtius shared a *Swiss* publisher and the fortune of having the same translator. Combinatory and positive influences were crucial to the impetus, and reception, of their work.

That Auerbach, Curtius and Bakhtin all trained principally as medievalists begs questions of current critical theory's value(s) as critical training programme in cultural studies for its future. Terence Cave as belated scholar in the Auerbach–Curtius tradition, but in Renaissance studies, demonstrates the necessity of both extensive and intensive study but, more importantly, the value of inspirational models for criticism itself, without which reseeding of ideas cannot take place. Cave's *Recognitions: A Study in Poetics* (1988) is a book about the 'scandal' of recognition as trope, interpretative device and mode of describing revelation, but it also amply demonstrates how any criticism based only on knowledge as information of facts, or on grids of interpretation, can limit or be a trap. The importance of scandalous critical thinking will be taken up again in the next chapter. Everywhere Cave brings into central critical debate those elements that critical theory cannot countenance since all texts are of allegedly equal status: trivia, intuitive leap, accident, tangent and seeming irrelevance. These of course constitute the 'telling' clues in detective and crime fiction.[111]

Comparative criticism as critical genre, therefore, goes far beyond reiterating the battle between the Ancients and Moderns on the side of the Ancients. Its insistence on tradition as combinatory, and on influence as open critical method, provides ways of recognizing what was programmatic in grille-based theorization of culture in its various twentieth-century 'economies'. Beyond excellent critical purviews of one national heritage, comparative criticism's most valuable recognition is that bi- or trilingual understanding produces rather different angles of vision to monolingual approaches. George Steiner, for example, manifests how intensely constructive and anti-deconstructive are modes of occidental critical endeavour which are multilingual.[112] Thus, without wider linguistic frames of knowledge, even gender or postcolonial criticism can readily become parochial or localized. In contrast to imitation, influence then also signals the *multiple* and often 'foreign' differences that make up what appears a single channel of expression. Influence studies, therefore, are not confined to identifiable details, images, borrowings or even sources – though they may include them – but enlist the pervasive, the organic and vital beyond one tradition or genre to aspire to the very meta-levels of intercultural reference itself.[113] As George Steiner writes:

> 'Interanimation' signifies a process of totally attentive interpenetration. It tells of a dialectic fusion in which identity survives altered but also strengthened and redefined by virtue of reciprocity. There is annihilation of self in the other consciousness and recognition of self in a mirroring motion. Principally, there results a multiplication of resource, of affirmed being. 'Interanimated', two presences, two formal structures, two bodies of utterance assume a dimension, an energy of meaning far beyond that which either could generate in isolation or in mere sequence. The operation is, literally, one of raising to a higher power.[114]

Comparative criticism thus offers more than comparison or comparison and contrast: it is concerned with reciprocities, recognitions, differences understood through definition of dissimilarity from similarity. More than the virtuoso intellectual metalepsis that Bloom discovers through his Lurianic map because it frees only one intellectual strand, comparative critical plaiting and braiding cannot be monodirectional, monologic, monochrome or monolingual. Relying on translation of critics or second-hand criticism in any domain is not enough.[115] Rereading the *French* Kristeva in chapter 1 and the misrepresented Bloom of critical-theory readers above amply makes the point. The underlying issues here will be taken up in the next two chapters, on imitation as transmutation (not second-hand copy) and translation as quotation in other words (not unquestioned same). As we will see, they build directly on the paradox that repetition with variation is potentially more different than radical difference or *différance*.

The coda of this chapter belongs to the critics who read influence as multifaceted, just as they expect their audience to be. Criticism about older traditions, or critics in their greater maturity, some also in danger for their lives, *serve* as models instead of asserting them. T. S. Eliot is paradigmatic of the critic who understands the developmental and generational patterns of criticism as well as creativity. Youthful, energetic and polarizing criticism of affinities and dislikes (postmodernist critical endeavour) melds into a maturer, more complex understanding (pre-postmodern European critical heritages) issuing from greater experience of other cultures, languages and traditions, and from life itself.[116] From his critical and creative modernist position, Eliot comprehends the reciprocal, but not identical, exchanges between criticism and creativity and that there are equally valuable kinds of critic (even in one and the same person) as there are kinds of text.[117] His one blind spot, like Bloom's, is that the critic is unequivocally male.

The critic therefore stands in the place of influence as mediation or intermediary, not to predict the future or guard the past, but to alert the current generation of other versions of reality.[118] Such alerting, not asserting, includes reminder, speculation or the ability to present alternative views. While part of everyday critical activity, these are most crucial in moments of great national, political and cultural upheaval when 'authorities' vie for supremacy, and are most ready to eradicate any who refute their angle of vision. Here, Bloom's wilfully heretical kabbalistic criticism pales before Bakhtin's politically soteriological, but no less radical, conservatism, his anti-revolutionary call to unofficial disruption of oppressive and authoritarian order from the inside.[119] As no less of a modernist than Eliot, his view of the carnivalesque is deeply informed by the intensities of political censorship, social realism as propagandist form, and the dangers of any political or representational monologism. Censorship can then work paradoxically as positive influence on the renewing of cultural versions of double-coding (irony), open secrets (dramatic irony or recognitions), or the long tradition of inversions of authority by fools and on feast days. Bakhtin's carnivalesque further warns the most seemingly democratic of multicultural nations that built within relativism is an equally ugly self-regulatory censorship that is monologic, not dialogic. Aporia spectacles permit only aporia vision.[120] Unless a culture can laugh at itself publicly, it is unable to harness the energies of its multiformity and will proceed to adopt the conformity of its most powerful. Literary or cultural criticism is therefore not expendable, anodyne or even heretical, but essentially about being critical as influence for change.[121] Europe, especially Russia, still has something to say to America – and vice versa. Both have as yet to engage with 'their' traditions in alternative Chinese forms, including Japanese.[122]

This chapter has focused on what influence as critical term offers that intertextuality, for all its potential diversity, cannot, but had thus to banish as negative. Indeed, influence studies reveal intertextuality's terrible potential sameness and how it did the banishing. The *OED*'s seventh definition of influence is 'conduction of externally-driven forces'. Positive influence, on the other hand, provides meta-critical terms of reference outside texts and textuality, and can encompass many influences from both within and outside one cultural ambit. Influence is not a term affirming a simplistic or utopian desire to recover lost (pre-postmodern) origins or holistic world-views, but a toolbox of many instruments to get work started. It can say nothing about the direct outcomes, but in this lies its liberating potential. Not least it also allows the complexities of postmodernity (Bloom *and* deconstruction *and* Kristevan intertextuality *and* post-colonialism) to be named for their various roles in bringing cultural productions to where they are. More importantly, influence also redirects postmodernism forwards from many pasts and their traditions. Influence thus never endorses directly oppositional thinking – the 'anti-' of hierarchies and binary oppositions – or its inversion, accumulative but changeless all-inclusivity. Influence is very concerned with the so-called belated, for it sees any 'after' as a new 'before'. It is thus an active, synergetic way of re-examining received ideas from the past, including critical 'givens'. By remembering that influence is quintessentially a metaphor of motions and fluids, applied to waters that swell a greater river or freeze as blocks in seas, its many self-contained general and specific uses need to be reinstated not least for its power to map flow, force, currents, divergence and convergence. Beyond man-made canal (Bloom) or complex irrigation system (intertextuality), we have in influence a force to describe cultural change, erosion, watering, silting up, destruction, increased or decreased pressures due to the 'geology' and geographies of its channels. Whether cultural forces are then explained with reference to the gods, magic, self-delusion, mechanics, the role of other human agent, texts or other cultures, influence recuperates for criticism its intentions and agency for tomorrow. To postmodern critics, the tasks ahead for positive influence, renewed as braided 'source studies' to include cultural histories, comparative criticism and gender studies, are perhaps too vague. Yet to disregard tradition as plural will close down change and ultimately bring satisfaction with cultural stagnation and its simulacra. Copy of copy thus returns us to the big questions about mimetic theories of referentiality, authenticity or derivitiveness that are the subject of the next chapter, on imitation. This also challenges T. S. Eliot's critical claims for influence, that:

> [a] poet of the supreme greatness of Shakespeare can hardly influence, he can only be imitated: and the difference between influence and imitation is that influence can fecundate, whereas imitation – especially unconscious imitation – can only sterilize. [. . .] Besides, imitation of a writer in a foreign language can often be profitable – because we cannot succeed.[123]

3

Imitation

In their different yet co-extensive ways, intertextuality and influence have both revealed their double anxiety about singularity and convergence, identity and difference. Postmodern versions of intertextuality capitalize on textual and technical virtuosity to outdo the past just as Bloom's bid was equally to ward off past and anticipated rivals. Quantitative (the world is a plethora of texts) and qualitative (power is having overcome the strongest competitors) overdetermination amount to the same thing, anxiety about having precedents. The shadowland that both therefore occlude is a longer history of imitation and prior models whereby the new suddenly appears not an innovation at all, but a variation of similar cultural patterns. For both postmodern intertextuality and Bloom, it is rather 're-novation', as d'Haen terms it, 'a self-conscious exercise in the hierarchical realignment of convention' that counts.[1] More precisely, it is the realignment of the givens of text-to-text or antagonistic relations that is at stake, to avoid inherent imitation at all or on any level, and hence the possibility of being derivative. Barthes's *dérive* thus clearly sums up postmodernism's attempted contraventions of, as well as countercurrents to, the past, whether its models or conventions. As shadow behind a foil, however, imitation in this chapter will not merely prove the doubly denied of both intertextuality and influence together. It also challenges cultural valorization or daemonization of appearance, semblance and resemblance, and reopens the knotty questions of the distinction between figurative and non-figurative language, between symbols and signs. Unlike the additional and accumulative 'inter-' of intertextuality, or the confrontational and divisive 'anti-' of influence, imitation will demonstrate the more radical paradoxes of its 'para-' status. As approximation, protection and anti-parallel, imitation deals with particularization within iterability and the strongly repetitive within any subdivision. In other words, alikeness is not necessarily sameness, just as dissimilarity is not necessarily difference. Imitation, then, is key to cultural representation in whatever form, and plays deliberately with simple equations and category mistakes.

Imitation in context: mimesis or anti-mimesis?

In the glossary to his book on intertextuality, Graham Allen defines mimesis as '[t]he idea that art directly represents reality. Mimetic views of art are severely challenged by theories of intertextuality, which argue that art works, or "texts", refer not directly to external reality but to other works.'[2] Imitation, however, would synthesize this seeming polarization between pre- and postmodern overviews, and counterbalance Allen's positive valorization only of the latter. This is apparent if imitation's place in influence studies is compared with its allegedly different role for postmodernism. For influence, whether positive or Bloomian, imitation is like familiarity: it breeds contempt. Imitation is therefore highly pejorative, for it designates redundancy, stagnation, stasis and inertia, everything that is the opposite of dynamic rejuvenation, energy and power. As Cordelia rightly intuited, imitation is indeed 'the sincerest form of *flattery*', the emptiness of mouthing formulae, yet their necessity for social interaction. Caught on the horns of the dilemma that is imitation itself, Cordelia understood that it is at once an authentic and inauthentic answer, depending on the interlocutors' ears and expectations. Imitation thus represents for influence the blocking of creative response since, in being too faithful to have life of itself and too derivative to circulate further, it will fail both its new and original contexts. In the light of the final quotation of the previous chapter, a hypothetical imitator of Shakespeare can be inserted into Eliot's formulation. She or he will never rise to the model's greatness even by the most clever pastiche and attention to authentic language, as both belie the original and originator. Any successful redramatization of Shakespeare, as Stoppard for example has demonstrated, needs to rework and mine the original for its relevance in a different context. A second solution, as film versions of Shakespeare's plays have shown, is to adapt his stagecraft for a different medium and audience. If models remain, they are springboards, not mirrors. 'Proper' creativity will better the model.

For postmodernism, imitation should fare rather better, since cultural recycling is among postmodernism's key dynamics. Imitation is

like imitation fur. It may be a good copy, affordable, morally preferable as regards the preservation of endangered species or prevention
of cruelty to animals, yet irreparably, wonderfully and flagrantly
fake. In the electronic age of virtual copy, perfect imitation names
the only taboo: complete imposture passes off copy that is counterfeit.[3] Pirated copies can then be caught out and distinguished from
licensed versions only by retrospective detection of the chronology
of their appearance, like plagiarism in print forms. In contrast,
legitimate postmodern copy, such as sampling, is authorized-user
reproduction and manipulation of material, but not verbatim.[4] By
thus circumventing *in toto* 'imitation', postmodern intertextual recycling highlights the process, not the product, and so defines both its
status and regenerative stature.[5] Only repeatable and reusable items
retain replication value, making copy tantamount to copiousness,
meaning the possibility of retransmission by displacement and
re-placement elsewhere in the network. Copyability as constant redeployment is thus the only convention, leaving uncopied remainders
in limbo in the darkest corners of the network memory, or ultimately
deleted. Worse even than non-replication for postmodern intertextuality is imitation as total replication, for it is this empty mimicry that
reveals the unforgivable sin, presumed identity.[6]

Thus, what mimetic and anti-mimetic theories of representation
equally abhor is the deception and deviousness of perfect mimicry.
This is the category mistake in Allen's definition, which falsely
polarizes art's so-called pre- and postmodern reference points, to
nature or other works of art respectively. Elided here are in fact
Platonic and Aristotelian theories of representation, which, although
different, are none the less on the same side of culture against nature
as prototype. Mimesis in either its Platonic or Aristotelian form thus
situates art respectively as either an illusion or an imitation of nature.
In both, it is the degree of duplicity or illusion that distinguishes
faithful from unfaithful replication, 'good' from 'bad' mimesis (or
anti-mimesis). Like imitation fur, however, mimetic value is both true
and false.[7] This is because mimesis depends not on innate aesthetic
or ethical criteria, but on supplemental systems of qualifying values
related to a given cultural moment, such as the swing of fashion,
taste, or the vogue of novelty, complexity, difficulty, simplicity,
naïvety. All cultural forms are therefore in the thrall of imitation's
double act, its *dichotomously* similar heritage harking back to Plato
and Aristotle. As Worton and Still (1990) note:

> Neither Platonic nor Aristotelian imitation is to be understood as
> imitation of nature. In the case of Platonic imitation, the 'poet' always
> copies an earlier act of creation, which is itself already a copy. Plato

terms 'poetry' a realism that is partial and deceptive [. . .] For Aristotle dramatic creation is the reduction, and hence intensification, of a mass of texts known to the poet, and probably to the audience as well. [. . .] Aristotle holds that we learn [. . .] through imitating others and that our instinct to enjoy works of imitation is an inborn instinct; both Cicero and Quintilian emphasise that imitation is not only a means of forging one's own discourse but is a consciously intertextual practice [. . .] Imitation is thus not repetition, but the completion of an act of interpretation which is, as Gadamer says, a highlighting in which the reading and writing translator declares her/himself, while also engaging in the practice of self-alienation. [. . .] For Cicero and Quintilian, the stylistic exercise of imitation is not an end in itself: it serves as an apprenticeship in improvisation, facilitating a liberation from over-investment in admiration for past masters and revealing and actualising the 'inner principle of proliferation' which is the essential feature of language.[8]

This lengthy quotation reiterates variously a very simple point. Neither those forms that follow a strictly Aristotelian lineage (genre classifications, Formalist theories of literary properties, rhetoric) nor those that follow a strictly Platonist line (the *mise en abyme* of representation itself, including intertextuality and deconstruction as its postmodernist variants) can deny the ultimate importance of *imitation per se* or mimesis as central device in Western metaphysics and its cultural representations.[9] The double bind of Platonic and Aristotelian mimesis therefore finds only interim and provisional resolutions, since the tow of the one will be counterbalanced in due course by the pull of the other on either side of the *same* balance. The recurrent pattern will rapidly dispel any moment of 'victory' on one side of the arc. Consequently, relative not oppositional values hold sway, such as proportion, perspective, recalibration, symmetry or asymmetry.

Imitation, then, is not about breaks in a continuum (time or national heritage), but about cyclical checks and balances. Consequently, pre-modern (classical) versions are sure to return when the predominant mode, in this case Romanticism (influence studies) and postmodern anti-mimesis, has reached the top of its wheel of fortune. Indeed, as this chapter will demonstrate, the counter-movement often starts from within, not outside it.

Our concept of shadowlands is highly redolent of imitation's returns here. Both genre study and rhetoric, for example, have been subsumed within postmodernist intertextuality, although this chapter will reveal their presence, and in imitative guise.[10] As Marjorie Perloff has pointed out, however, 'the more radical the dissolution of traditional genre boundaries, the more important the concept of genericity becomes.'[11] Indeed, she argues that 'the most fundamental questions about postmodern culture – epistemological, ontological, political, and aesthetic – are derived from considerations of classification and genre. The underlying rationale for genre [. . .] falls within the larger category of post-Enlightenment culture [. . .] There is no unity of genre, but only the historical determinations of "genres".'[12] Postmodern 'genre' is then not a new entity but a conglomerate of popular and high-cultural genres. While old pre-postmodern genre hierarchies and their classifications may then be collapsed or abolished, the law of global business conglomerates applies. Postmodern cultural productions have no option but to increase by further merger. This both removes competing, differentiated, models and produces monstrous amalgamations.[13] Like any simulacrum (clone) or complex hybrid, these in the longer term may generate only unsustainable, infirm or infertile forms.[14]

Is imitation then a universal pattern, or a law like gravity? If it is a suppositional model of change, the swing of the pendulum, is imitation a key to the most complex modelling and copying systems, the two hemispheres of the human brain rather than super-computers? Moreover, if imitation is a theorem of the re-emergence of mimetic theories, could it then be used as a predictor for what comes after postmodern intertextuality? Or have we got our ideas about art as model and copy, production and reproduction, reformulation and form, even model and emulation, wrong in the first place?

Cultural impersonation and imposture may be 'empty' mimicry, but this has its own peculiar agency in nature. Mimicry and dissimulation here are key survival tactics, and in many species of flora and fauna. As disguise, such as camouflage to blend with surroundings, it is a mechanism to hoodwink predators. As conjuring trick, as the cuckoo exemplifies, deception enables reproduction. Imitation *in* nature (not *of* it) is therefore highly specialized and, as Richard Dawkins makes clear, never mixed-mode.[15] On the evolutionary scale, it represents a variation or sub-species, not an innovation or new biological species. Mimicry is thus positively valorized, as adaptation to context, both as environment and species' ecosystems. It is similarity, not complete difference, that is the motor that allows predator and prey, strongest and weakest in the food chain, to have equal chances of the trick succeeding, life or death.

Outside cultural representation, human use of mimicry for survival is little different. Under adverse conditions such as persecution or authoritarian regimes, political or ethnic dissembling may be the only chance for survival and even subversive change or counter-protest.[16] Double imposture plays an equally central role in successful espionage and counter-espionage for protection of national interest. Consequently, fool figures and human tricksters play an important part in the long literary tradition of inversion of codes, social norms and conventions. Crime writing, spy thrillers and detective fiction similarly represent and demonstrate dissimulation tactics, not least attempted hoodwinking of the reader. These genres (also beloved of postmodern meta-fiction) do more than present the problem of perception, or play with representation and its mirrors, however distorting.[17] Imaginary imitations of life and death dissembling put pressure on theories of 'pure' mimesis (Platonic and Aristotelian) at its most vulnerable spot: art does not (should not?) represent 'life'. As paradox of this chapter, imitation itself will show when an imitation is not imitation, but the real.

This chapter will therefore turn first to imitation in life, to nature not culture, to search out alternative imitative models to those by which contemporary critical theories and their Platonic–Aristotelian mimetic informants live.[18] By returning science and particularly genetics to the foreground, the seemingly different mimetic models of postmodern hybridity will be shown in their true colours. Not least, the metaphor of (nineteenth-century) science and progress that has dominated artistic and cultural development, including structural linguistics, can also be questioned. By looking at these from a science-eye view, Richard Dawkins's replications of Darwin through his popularization of evolutionary theory as 'the selfish gene' and 'meme' theory, some of the category mistakes in thinking the mimetic can be flushed out.

This path cleared, the chapter then turns back to imitation for the arts, the rich and double heritage of the 'figure'. This will consider a pattern that includes bodies and design, rhetoric and poetics on the one hand and form (genres, architecture) on the other. While the Renaissance in its upper- and lower-case meaning provides important models and explorations of both, it is the lifelong work of Gérard Genette which holds both 'figure' and 'architexte' in balance. His *Palimpsestes* (1982) is of course crucial to any discussion of intertextuality and imitation. However, the chapter will focus in particular on his earlier, less well-known, *Mimologiques* (1976), which is contemporary with Dawkins's 'selfish gene', and the various theories considered in earlier chapters of this book. Its investigation of forms of representation such as parody, pastiche, satire, caricature, travesty, that mimic by reversal but which are also distinguishable from plagiarism, sets the scene for several lines of discussion. Among these is the pivotal place of *Mimologiques* among Genette's most design-orientated works after 1976, including *Palimpsestes*. How far this is indeed a plagiarism or imitation of Kristeva's theory of intertextuality is a moot question. By showing how Genette has recast her template term as hypertextuality, the chapter forcefully returns to the reproductive-imitative dilemma inherent in Western metaphysics and its representations. Where can one turn if models of imitation operating on laws of symmetry or simile always bring back representation, whether language or other signs such as art and sculpture, as refiguration?

It is to models operating outside and inside simile, metonymy and metaphor that constitute the final part of the chapter, symbolic orders of imitation, such as ritual and inscription on bodies, not materials. René Girard's examination of imitation as the scapegoat complex offers a window on the pre- and post-print imagination and its legacy of surrogate imitations. Girard's work then disclosed a further two, seemingly paradoxical, models, whose position is in counter-point on the pendulum swing that is imitation, but at its furthest span. At the one extreme is the material, symbolically represented by the gold standard. It is this that allows the minting of coins or paper money, but these laws of economics are what also enable their twins, counterfeit and forgery, to exist. At the opposite and counterbalancing extreme, the immaterial, similar dilemmas of doubling and distinction occur. Divine authority or supreme truth (the Law of God) is mimicked by supreme falsity, the Devil's laws of deception and imposture. This opposition of God and Mammon, both with their counterfeits and doubles, is what paradoxically returns imitation to its singular, the real and the anathema of copy as idolatry (the mimological mistake of the representation being the represented). The Hebrew interdiction on representation of God in graven images thus offers an alternative model of art and representation to the Greek versions of Plato or Aristotle, and, in an uncanny turn, flips *Urzeit* back to virtual reality. Without anticipating in 'whodunnit' fashion, this track it takes runs strangely parallel to Darwin's interpretations of human origination read through the geomorphic. Thus, on both the high road and low road of culture, imitation will prove far from static, even if it leaves no more than the afterglow of form or echo of voice to charge us to seek out authentic twenty-first-century models to live by. 'Breaking through the anaesthesia of familiarity is what poets do best. It is their business. But poets, too many of them and for too long, have overlooked the goldmine of inspiration offered by science.'[19] Dawkins's own attempts at 'poetic science', the crossover potential of examining form and imitation from both scientific and literary perspectives, seem the obvious starting point.

Richard Dawkins: genetics and 'memetics'

The most fundamental questions about any discipline, not just postmodern culture as Perloff above contended, are derived from considerations of classification and generic distinctions. In the sciences, taxonomies determine how larger or smaller groupings can be named, investigated and compared. The mistake is to assume that similar terms in different disciplines apply, or apply to the same level of classification. As the main principles for understanding evolutionary modelling and *genera* developments in Richard Dawkins's *The Selfish Gene* (1976) are like and unlike literary genres and sub-genres, his first need to be distinguished before they are compared. The following extracts combined together sum up the key parameters of his work for the purposes of this chapter:

> Chosen examples are never serious evidence for any worthwhile generalization [. . .] Species are grouped together into genera, genera into orders, and orders into classes. Lions and antelopes are both members of the class Mammalia, as are we; [and] the properties a successful unit of natural selection must have [. . .] are longevity, fecundity, and copying-fidelity.[20]

> Development is change in the form of a single object, as clay deforms under the potter's hands. Evolution as seen in fossils taken from successive strata, is more like a sequence of frames in a cinema film. One frame doesn't literally change into the next, but we experience an illusion of change if we project the frames in succession; [and] successful buffaloes don't duplicate themselves around the world in the form of multiple copies, they duplicate their genes. [. . .] Successful buffaloes don't become more frequent. Each buffalo is unique. It has a frequency of one. You can define a buffalo as successful if its genes increase in frequency in future populations.[21]

To test these principles for the arts, let us replace the named mammal species above with well-known fictional works: *Don Quixote* and *Tristram Shandy* are both members of the class 'cultural representation',[22] as are *Madame Bovary* and *Middlemarch*. Following the buffalo example, the genetic success story is prose of a particular kind (and hence 'not-prose' as variant form), while the genus is novel and the class is literature. Imitation is therefore not novel-to-novel, but prose-to-prose. Mechanical replication of multiple copies of *Madame Bovary* could happen in the animal world only by cloning. By deliberately choosing four canonical novels, some of the false assumptions that are everywhere apparent in taxonomies of literary genres and in postmodern theories emerge clearly. Any list of individual examples can be pressed into a category, but cannot constitute 'serious evidence for any worthwhile generalization'. This is because the examples hide a number of category distinctions and mistakes, particularly if a postmodern intertextual or deconstructive approach is taken.

Take the leap from the species, Spanish *Don Quixote*, to class, *international* cultural production, which elides sub-orders, genres, orders and classes. Where does classification of the picaresque novel, the realist novel, the English novel, or meta-fiction operate? Are these species? But what then of the translation of *Don Quixote*, which was vital to the development of other picaresque traditions? Is the French version part of the same 'species' as *Madame Bovary* as 'French' novel to begin with? This distinct uncertainty regarding species definitions, as Duff notes, 'is that in "genology" or genre theory, unlike in botany or zoology, there is no "species" term to accompany the "genus" term *genre*. [. . .] We talk today of "subgenres" and even "microgenres", but this assumes a measure of agreement about relative size or stability of the type of entity called "genre" [. . .] that in reality does not exist.'[23] Postmodernity's conflation of prose and prosody, for example, or media, only further complicates the issue and endorses Perloff's insistence on the centrality of 'genericity'. From Dawkins's perspective, the shapeless plethora that is postmodern 'cultural representation' would probably be identified as the 'primordial soup' or the 'gene pool', which starts the genetic process, rather than naming its most evolved states. Comparison of taxonomies in the sciences and arts clearly demonstrates here that abolition of all categories and rules is extremely problematic, and that some intermediate, and relatively stable, levels of classification are essential if major changes and anomalies, or equally important minor variations, are to be plotted.

In terms of qualifying evolutionary success, how does prose fare, since we know that successful genes require longevity, fecundity and copying-fidelity? The last term is a potentially ambiguous, but most important, prerequisite, to be distinguished from clone-copy. Note that Dawkins does not use 'copy-fidelity', but the more dynamic 'copying', which emphasizes process and operates like imitation as action. In *The Selfish Gene*, Dawkins interestingly names the prototype to the complex DNA molecule the *replicator* gene, not *replica*. This incorporates all of the key features of success above, but its especial quality is copying-fidelity, the highly patterned, but not exact and foolproof, replication of genes. It is this margin for slight error that constitutes potential for evolutionary improvement in the gene pool.[24] Moreover, without inexact copying-fidelity as counterbalance, longevity and/or fecundity alone would overbalance reproduction to turn it eventually into counter-reactive destruction. To put this back into literary critical terms, too much traditional replication of the same order (longevity) would be as non-productive long term as too much novelty and innovation for its own sake (fertility). Neither strict adherence to tradition or canons nor postmodern playfulness is the

formula to keep cultural representation evolving. Equally interesting is that Dawkins's replicator is the successful messenger, not a
medium. In cultural terms therefore, circulation by a limited number
of copied manuscripts or by mass-production of cultural representations by print or electronic copy methods are but two expressions
of the gene pool, not of imitation itself as process. It is the all-
important prose 'gene' that has survived, multiplied and evolved in
both. The particular factor that explains this survival for Dawkins is
the altogether 'Darwinian' contribution to what would have otherwise remained either a 'steady state' or a completely destabilizing
environment, the element of *competition* contributed by the error
factor in otherwise completely successful replicators.[25] Copying-
fidelity begins to find other rival copying-fidelities at work, and it is
these that enhance the survival and evolution of all the truly successful copying-fidelity sorts. It is here that Dawkins's idea of the
'selfishness' of replication comes in. No successful replicator gene
can afford to be altruistic in the survival game, but ruthlessly opposed
to loosing out in gene pool evolutionary survival. To return to postmodernism, this appears the most selfish form of all as it removes
rivals by hoovering them up. However, because it has overplayed on
initial multiplicity and conglomeration at the expense of specialist
strike or protective defences, its exponential activity will not enjoy
longevity or fertility, since its 'success' is in fact an internal decay
mechanism. Indeed, postmodern representations are also open to
attack from other rivals, such as electronic hypertext and hypermedia at genus level, and non-mimetic arts as alternative class. Imitation theory as elucidated by Dawkins's replicators therefore only
endorses the discoveries of chapter 1. Without longevity and fertility, intertextuality is very much at risk from electronic media forms
of cultural production and interdisciplinarity. Textual imitation, then,
as a kind of *replicator* molecule, affirms continuity and complexity as
recipe for long-term success and evolution, but with similarity *and*
some difference as the all-important leven. It is pattern and variation
that counts. The prose 'gene' can then look forward to discovering
in its DNA-like double helix of dramatic, poetic and prosaic build-
ing blocks its own 'genome'. As against the rivalries understood
between genres in genre theory since at least the Renaissance, this
may be just the variant that makes the difference.

But what of Dawkins's own rather different version of genetic evolution and cultural evolution which he coined 'meme' theory? Is the
above discussion merely a copy of this, or rather an intertext, a
recopy*ing*, a critical imitation? These alternative definitions for the
same processes will be particularly important when we turn next to
Genette. For the moment, memes must speak in order for serious

similarities and differences between zoology and cultural criticism to
be appraised.

> Cultural transmission is analogous to genetic transmission in that,
> although basically conservative, it can give rise to a form of evolution.
> [. . .] Language seems to 'evolve' by non-genetic means, and at a rate
> which is orders of magnitude faster than genetic evolution. [. . .] The
> new soup is the soup of human culture. We need a name for the new
> replicator, a noun that conveys the idea of a unit of cultural transmis-
> sion, or a unit of *imitation*. 'Mimeme' comes from a suitable Greek
> root, but I want a monosyllable that sounds a bit like 'gene'. I hope
> my classicist friends will forgive me if I abbreviate mimeme to *meme*.
> If it is any consolation, it could alternatively be thought of as being
> related to 'memory', or to the French word *même*. [. . .] Examples of
> memes are tunes, ideas, catch-phrases, clothes fashions, ways of
> making pots or building arches. [. . .] If the idea catches on, it can be
> said to propagate itself, spreading from brain to brain. As in the case
> of genes, fecundity is much more important than longevity of par-
> ticular copies. [. . .] Some memes, like some genes, achieve brilliant
> short-term success in spreading rapidly, but do not last long in the
> meme pool. Popular songs and stiletto heels are examples. Others,
> such as the Jewish religious laws, may continue to propagate them-
> selves for thousands of years, usually because of the great potential
> permanence of written records [. . .]. Here I admit I am on shaky
> ground.[26]

At precisely the point where Dawkins realizes his limitations (as
zoologist), he *replicates* an old chestnut, the ingrained dichotomy of
'popular' and 'traditional' cultural forms, or between the Ancients
and the Moderns.[27] His problem may be due to the lack of specific
classificatory handles at his disposal in this different field. A second
stab at 'meme' theory in *Unweaving the Rainbow* (1998), to explain
how and why memes 'cluster', similarly fails to convince. 'Just as a
species gene pool becomes a cooperative cartel of genes, so a group
of minds – a "culture", a "tradition" – becomes a cooperative cartel
of memes, a memeplex.'[28] The previous chapter, on influence, especially Bloom's version or feminist approaches, altogether demolishes
the utopian scenario painted here. Where Dawkins lambasted poets
for not taking a leaf out of the vast book of science, the same criticism can be levelled at 'meme' theory, but with the show [*sic*] now
on the other foot. Because he has not taken a leaf out of the vast
science of the book, his 'meme' theory is equally shaky. It is also
derivative, because 'meme' theory already exists and in several sur-
viving and thriving forms, including the idea of replica.[29] It is present
in any linguistic performance, whether in dead or 'modern' living lan-

guages, as discussion of the prose 'gene' above endorses. It is also present as the very mimetic energy of cultural production in its Aristotelian or Platonic variants, in etymologies, *scribal* miscopying or jokes (the 'show on the other foot' is intentional to illustrate both points in one example). 'Meme' is to mime, therefore, as 'intertext' is to reference. The first in each pair is a coinage: the second is its flexible, fecund and living form because it exists as both noun and verb.

While the question of imitation as mime will be considered below, Dawkins's theory of 'memesis',[30] however, is wonderfully disruptive of mimesis, perhaps indeed its very nemesis! The analogy from nature of the *replicator* gene and the process of imitation (as noun with verbal force like copying) has uncovered a number of ways of catching the slipperiness of mimesis and imitation for cultural criticism, including postmodern intertextuality and deconstruction, and revealed from a science-eye view several category mistakes within it. Not least, the notion of imitation as exact copy, empty mime or replica (plagiarism) can now be rejected, since all successful replicators include noticeable variation, and hence potential for future evolution. Their complex double-helix structure and principles of order, not anarchic randomness, in the gene pool also challenges the notions of non-representational signs and sign systems within Saussurian linguistics and semiotics. Replicators may even be another way to rethink 'transcendental signifieds' for theories of language.

> There is no way to delineate the limits of the semiotic system or to determine a centre round which such a system might be structured. If one denies the existence of 'transcendental signifieds', then every signified is also a signifier, and the sign can have only a provisional coherence. Further, if the sign functions through its differential relations within an unlimited and shifting network of signs, then it is neither identical with itself nor present to itself, but always marked by the changing trace of what it is not, where it is not. What Derrida's critique of the sign leads to is a general semiotics of Platonic bad mimesis, a conception of signs as simulations of themselves that mime their identity while remaining other.[31]

The analysis of the prose 'gene' above is therefore not a mime of Dawkins's meme, but a critical imitation in the spirit of Dawkins's own work, especially *The Selfish Gene*.[32] As model, this richly encourages *rigorous* critical cross-pollination across the arts and sciences when it comes to consideration of the categories and classifications that are intrinsic to disciplines and hence interdisciplinarity. Boundaries and limitations, whether by species and genera or genre classifications or by specialist knowledge, also prove essential for longer-term critical regeneration and evolution than complete freedom to interconnect (Kristeva) or disrupt (Bloom, Derrida). In this light, the work of Gérard Genette is paradigmatic of specialist concern with genres, classifications and taxonomies. It has also wrestled with the problem of mimesis and imitation, and ingested intertextuality to give it more rigorous taxonomies. While other critics and critical readers have always treated *Palimpsestes* (1982) alongside, and as the better redefinition and transformation of, Kristeva's term,[33] the ensuing discussion questions the relationship between intertextuality relabelled by Genette as 'hypertextuality' and imitation, not, as undertaken in chapter 1, further forms of 'intertextuality'. Comparing like with alike is not the same as comparing like with like. How far does Genette's recopying of Kristeva amount to creative imitation that in fact reinvests older rhetorical terms and models with more contemporary clothing?

Gérard Genette: rhetoric and the mimologic

If Riffaterre responded directly to Kristeva's too catch-all term 'intertextuality' by making good its 'omission', the role of the reader, on which he grounded his own theory, Genette's project was the more ambitious rewriting of her theory in *Palimpsestes* (1982). The evaluative time lag (as for Angenot) of second-wave response, however, allowed Genette a precision in two directions. The first is his systematic redefinition of Kristeva's term as the five-pronged hypertextuality, intertextuality, metatextuality, paratextuality and transtextuality. It is his extensive 'hypertextuality' that replaces Kristevan 'intertextuality', while her coinage is redefined to mean only micro-levels of 'allusion' or 'quotation' within a new work. By attending least to this category, Genette performs a double negation: he dismisses the 'authority' of Kristeva's invention of the term, and 'authority' modes marked by speech marks, whether explicit (quotation) or implicit (allusion).[34] By so doing, Genette also avoids hermeneutics and authorial intentions,[35] yet, second, can redirect Kristeva's term more strategically, its 'strict' relevance to poetics (poetry and narratology).

Critics have in the main applauded Genette's *Palimpsestes* for its 'open structuralism'[36] or 'pragmatic' reworking of Kristeva.[37] Equally, critical readers offer mainly paraphrase of the salient points, with little analytic, let alone comparative, evaluation in the light of Genette's lifelong critical interests.[38] Only those sceptical of Genette's heuristic approach have questioned how 'systematic' the redefinitions are, discounting them as 'arbiträr',[39] or finding in the palimpsest 'like *bricolage* and the invisible *matrix* of text [. . .] another heuristic metaphor that reveals the paradox of structuralism and semiotics.'[40] Its sequel *Seuils* (1987), known in English as *Paratexts*, seemly endorses such capitalization on designations for textual play. Exhaustively mapping the margins and borders that frame poetic works – titles, blurbs, epigraphs, forewords, conventions for chapter layout or tables of contents – *Seuils* puns on the paratextual name of its publisher. Clever use of the epilogue (also a paratext) charts what, in spite of its vast repertoire, it does *not* cover – translation, serial publication, illustration – and potentially allows Genette to fill the critical gap in true serial or soap opera fashion. Through post-modern spectacles, then, it is tempting to see in such a move, à la Derrida and à la lettre, a rival deconstruction. Genette as the master critic of the exhaustive encyclopaedic limit not only traces but also designates the *critical* limit. Like Bloom, Genette the master critic is in a limited company with the master of *Limited Inc.* (1988) or *Marges – de la philosophie* (1972).

Like and alike, however, are not the same. Genette's lifelong enter-prise is no Promethean deconstruction using ambivalent or double terms for their troubling edge or irony. His constructivism, while reflecting rather well the virtuosity of the critic as architect, is instead a Herculean venture.[41] As his more recent *Figures IV* (1999) demon-strates, Genette's concern has always been to rethink the figurative through imitation taken to other degrees. In the Renaissance tradi-tion of imitation as rhetoric or poetics, effective redefinition and recategorization of terms and precursors were imperative for the work of later innovators. In a nutshell, such imitation is Genette's model, field of poetic endeavour and method. His appropriation of Kristeva's intertextuality in *Palimpsestes* is then not plagiarism or parody, but licensed imitation. This is also not an isolated incident in Genette's critical evolution, for Louis Marin's 'architexte' had already been bor-rowed openly in the preceding volume.[42] Genette's imitative critical indebtedness in fact derives from many critic-compatriots and col-laborators since the 1960s, most notably Tzvetan Todorov.[43] It is Todorov's rich Russian Formalist background and erudition from *Théorie de la littérature* (1965) onwards that Genette exploits, and in whose work he finds a common ancestor, Aristotle.[44] It is thus their related and different Janus response to 'imitate' anew 'the Art of Poetry' that sets the critical agenda for the grand projects of both Todorov and then Genette, to refigure the circumference, and the inner circle, of poetic language. What is urgently needed is compara-tive critical study of Genette and Todorov by Russianists versed in French to demonstrate how each complements, adapts and counter-balances the work of Russian Formalists and their successors, includ-ing Yury Tynyanov, Viktor Shklovsky, Boris Eikhenbaum, Roman

Jakobson, Yury Lotman, Vladimir Propp, Mikhail Bakhtin and Pavel Nikolaevich Medvedev.[45] European genre theory will be the richer for such variety of insights, but perhaps especially Todorov's contribution, which, like Kristeva's, spans a Central European and French heritage.

Genette's work and method are thus renewed as increasingly complex constructions of the figurative nature of literary language by use of figures in all senses, including persons. The *OED* defines 'figure' (eytmologically of the same root as *fingere*, fashion) as '1. form, shape (of geometry or persons); 2. represented form (image or likeness); 3. devised form (diagram, illustration, dance movement); 4. a written character (or number); 5. *Rhet*. Any form of expression that deviates from the normal (also in grammar or logic).' Genette is nowhere interested in resuscitating rhetoric *per se* or its codes,[46] but rather is concerned with renaming its taxonomies and terminologies for a theory of literature that has its roots firmly in the tradition of critical commentary or *explication de texte*, which we noted that Riffaterre also shares.[47] Its critical method of precision, particularization, explanation, expansion, extension matches imitation's principles for creation. Stress is not only on inventiveness or innovation, but also on imitation in the pre-modern sense of invention, *inventio*: the discovery of appropriate material to imitate. Worthy material is then arranged anew, yet in accordance with pre-disposed parameters (*dispositio*).[48] Freedom of personal expression is not the rejection of models, but the espousing and reshaping of them in one's own words (*elocutio*). In Genette's own personal critical odyssey, his dialogue with Proust about French literature, these three terms of the five making up the classical 'Art of Rhetoric' have more recently been complemented by the remaining two, memory and communication, in *Figures IV* (1999) and *Fiction et diction* (1991).

Introduction à l'architexte (1979), *Palimpsestes* (1982) and *Seuils* (1987) undoubtedly represent encyclopaedic redefinitions of literary tropes and figures, classes and genres, and constitute a modern kind of Renaissance pattern book. This trilogy, however, is arguably more important for its efforts to distinguish forms of writing (genres) that are often mistaken for modes. The most obvious is parody (which Dawkins might reclassify as an order or a class), considered as 'supra-generic', especially in postmodern popularization and disintegration of high-cultural forms.[49] Parody is of interest to Genette, not as one of several counter-genres, such as satire or travesty, or 'hybrid' genres, of which the novel itself is a chief example, but for transformations of texts. As *Palimpsestes* makes abundantly clear, individual works can be parodied through particularization, but genres, because generalizations, can only be imitated.[50] This then resolves a key

problem for postmodern criticism, that, if parody is always intertextual, intertextuality is not always parody.[51] However, by staking
the case very clearly for genres (as Dawkins would endorse) as the
main vehicles for change, Genette's theory of imitation subsumes
equally necessary distinctions. For example, a genre cannot readily
be subdivided to encompass parodies of the parodic novel genre, or,
because it eschews rhetoric, discuss irony.[52] Genette's work is therefore equally problematic when it comes to classifying pure language
games, or games of imitation such as pastiche.[53] Thus, while it is an
essential contribution to the refiguration of poetic language, Genette's
trilogy none the less collides with the old impasses of classical
rhetoric between grammar and stylistics, with generative and structural linguistics replicating the issues of the former, and formalism,
structuralism or semiotics the latter.[54] What is gained on the swings
is lost on the roundabouts. Genette's architext, hypertextuality and
paratext in all their manifestations and vagaries may offer the fullest
modern testimony to print corpus figures and figurations, but equally
determine their undoing by being hoisted by their own petard.
Electronic media have already rendered Genette's 'hypertext' obsolete and challenged the boundaries of the *printed* page, whether in
high- or low-cultural form.

As Genette's work before and after this trilogy shows, however,
imitation is all about renewable energy sources (Dawkins's
'longevity') generated by its internal dynamic, the pendulum swing.
The impasse or border ('seuil') is an opportunity, not a block.
Genette's greater contribution to imitation is his critical rereading of
core Western texts on mimesis itself. The generalization and particularization at work in *Introduction à l'architexte* (1979) on Aristotle's
Poetics allow the key errors made subsequently in critical reiterations
to be uncovered, notably the accepted tripartite division of genres
into epic, lyric and drama.

> Gérard Genette has conclusively demonstrated [. . .] that the attribu-
> tion, though ubiquitous, is erroneous, and that the 'seductive triad' is
> really a conflation of two separate genre theories: that of Plato (which
> distinguishes between three different modes of literary representation:
> narrative, dramatic and mixed) and that of Aristotle (which differen-
> tiates literary types according to mode *and object* of representation, but
> reduces to two the number of modal categories). Neither system, it
> should be noted, assigns a proper place to lyric, which is only incor-
> porated into the supposedly Aristotelian triad by much later acts of
> substitution and amendment.[55]

If Duff squares the circle of how such a mistake should have
remained undetected for so long by seeing mistaken attributions

as inherent in any systematic construction of taxonomies of genre, Genette's reading prompts more serious questions for critical readers and theorists of the word-processor era. How far do critics and critical readers simply scan and repaste others' commentaries without checking the arguments or sources? How much has rejection of 'source' study precluded scholarly imitation à la Genette? We will return to imitation as counterfeit at the end of the chapter.

If it is Genette's direct imitation (copying-fidelity) of Aristotle that unmasks replication (unquestioned critical gloss) and provides renewal for his own 'architexte' and the ensuing trilogy, it also represents an important departure (*seuil*) for Genette's *oeuvre*. This was the impasse created by the limit of his previous work on imitation, the massive *Mimologiques* (1976). In spite of belated translation, *Mimologiques* is still little discussed, but provides essential reading for post-postmodern critical ventures out of the minefield of the anti-mimetic and deconstruction (quintessentially the idea that the signifier does not equal the signified). Given the context of its date of appearance, *Mimologiques* is Genette's provocatively erudite reconsideration of cratylism (the idea that the signifier equals the signified). In Plato's *Cratylus*, Cratylus believes in the natural appropriateness of names as correct designations of their innate being. His antagonist Hermogenes is the believer in the arbitrary nature of words. Their connection to things is only by agreed convention. Socrates mediates between them and extremes of subjective or objective naming, of false etymology or exorbitant analogy, and of any suspect valorization of one language as natural, the root of all tongues. *Mimologiques* thus holds up a mirror to the imitations of these models and debates in contemporary linguistics and poetics, and does so with *poetic* licence on several counts. As noted in Genette's other works, the title and main idea owe much to precursors, in this case the nineteenth-century Frenchman Charles Nodier. By acknowledging and recuperating him in a history of cratylism and natural language since Plato, Genette stands on Nodier's shoulders as a way to delimit the ideas underpinning his own reformulations. While Genette thus retains a critical position and idiom throughout *Mimologiques*, this remains constructive, and includes 'poetic' play with the subject matter and form.[56] Excessive punning, caricature, cynical rejection and deconstructive critical ambivalence are avoided as not conducive to the doubly mimetic and poetic import of *Mimologiques* itself. Genette thus neatly incorporates parallel theories of natural language (cratylism) and their alternative history within French rhetorical tradition into a critique, which is also a pseudo-travelogue.

As structuralist fellow traveller, Genette in *Mimologiques* revisits cratylism in its primary modes – eponymy, onomatopoeia, mimophony – and its reformulations in the heritage of secondary mimesis, synaesthesia, homologies, homophonies, mimographic equations of vowels and consonants with colours or meanings. The discovery everywhere is the powerful undertow and lure of the non-arbitrariness of language in its *compositional* forms, particularly in poetry. Like Plato's Socrates before him, Genette cannot therefore make any final arbitration, or defend 'hermogeneity' as clear winner against the seemingly preposterous, but ebulliently gargantuan, cratylism. *Plato's* text (and hence Genette's) is then more than what Thaïs Morgan suggests it is, 'a treatise on the problem of language as a kind of lying. Words suggest an infinite variety of imaginary connections to things, yet the more we enjoy the name game, the further we find ourselves from the ideal of truth.'[57] *Mimologiques* abundantly illustrates the deceptions and self-deceptions of any language position, however rigorously upheld, that excludes its opposite. Language as truth or falsehood lies in neither extreme nor even in some compromise between them, but in the premise upheld by both: strong *belief* in some form of connection or non-connection between words and things. Since one form will not fit all, the only stance is to operate some mixed balance, located in the place of mediation, Socrates.[58]

This 'solution' to the debate shared by Plato and Genette, however, raises more questions than it answers. If language itself has no ontological guarantee, and is not total randomness, its poetic and critical functions rest with a secondary mimesis (and mimologism) as a form of language convention that is at the same time separate from cratylian or 'hermogenizing' models. If the 'Socrates' position is the proper place of arbitration for both poetic and critical language, how can it then be ascertained? The impossible mimetic circularity and vortex cannot be underestimated. The corrector, 'Socrates', is already a hypothetical (fictional) representation of a person as a state of language (secondary mimesis), as well as the figure and arbiter of such usage. Genette's work on Platonic secondary mimesis and his later work on Aristotelian replications of genre and poetics amount to the same thing: the double bind or two-way mirror of mimesis in Western heritage is Platonic *and* Aristotelian. Genette's impasses and *seuils* are the same moebius strip of imitation as secondary mimesis both creative and critical. Successful replicators are everywhere a double helix! For Genette, the metaphor is, as everywhere in his understanding of mimesis, Proustian; the experience of the two ways may amount ultimately to the same, but this does not make the critic give up on an *A la recherche de la figure perdue*. The extremes of pure poetry (Cratylus) and urbane critical sophistication (Hermogenes) do then have some potentially recoverable site of unity. As the ending of *Mimologiques* and Proustian narrative suggest, and as child psychologists and psychoanalysists endorse,[59] this is the position of childlike naïvety, a place of complete arrogance, and the delusions of the 'let's pretend'. If *inventio* for Genette is childlike rediscovery as opposed to mimicry or repetition, this is hardly innovative. Any generic development or evolution at its most mature moment or apotheosis is a degeneration awaiting death and rebirth. As Tony Hunt has convincingly argued for Villon's *Testament* as mature creative writing that 'authorizes every conceivable operation which may be performed on a text by a reviser or commentator', thresholds and palimpsests ever go hand in hand as 'points culminants' and 'points de départ'.[60] As we will discover in the next chapter, commentators and their authorities are equally symbiotic.

Genette's contribution to intertextuality as imitation, however, is to critical precision, recollection and, paradoxically, the rhetorical functions of *correctio, distributio, expolitio, interpretatio* and *interrogatio* combined as a poetry of criticism.[61] His various volumes represent repositories and museum art collections of designs and figures, with *Introduction à l'architexte* as their neatly arranged and concise catalogue. Like a *kunstkamer* miniature,[62] this advertises the architecture of his double designs on both its sides and the cement that holds them conjointly. The enormity of Genette's *oeuvre* may then discourage plagiarism or copy, but its own taxonomies may prove ultimately unusable, because too complex, already dated or pedantic. For some, his cavils and quibbles may constitute a sophistry of the peripheral (*seuils*) which only detracts from properly pivotal issues.

If Genette's work has avoided the ultimate ends of hemlock, deadlock or gridlock, his replications of mimesis do not break its double chains, the true/false representationality of simile, metaphor and analogy. These tropes, like the titles that are the cornerstones of Genette's critical endeavour, concern poetic writing and resist nostalgia for speech as more authentic imitation or site of limpid communication, such as direct revelation. Genette thus remains firmly on the side of culture against nature, of civilization (especially French) against the horde, of poetry versus technology. He thus leaves the Grand Narrative of mimesis and anti-mimesis intact, and ways of rethinking its secondary behavioural, social, linguistic or cultural models. Is there no way out of the vicious circles of mimesis that are its altogether ancient and newly towering, architextual Babel?

René Girard: scandal and excommunication

Another French critic, René Girard, writing on French literature at the same time as the early Genette and of *Mimologiques*, was about to stumble upon that same block and cornerstone of mimesis, as (Aristotelian) forms or (Platonic) Form. He was, however, to surpass Genette's conclusions with a more startling one: realizing that, if both versions of mimesis are in fact the same, then neither a radical unhooking of antagonistic binaries nor their synthesis would solve the representational problem. To see opposites as a continuum rather than two poles, or to promote figures such as the paradox or synecdoche, were not sufficiently *radical*.[63] Even the most diverse forms such as medieval imaging of *pars pro toto*, the microcosm or miniature as analogous version of the macrocosm which might include an idea of God, or the undecidability or ambivalence that anti-religious deconstruction everywhere proffers, only return or reinforce a deeper mimesis.[64] Indeed, Girard realized that analogies had often been more of a hindrance than a help, because they deferred facing a 'real', a more basic premise openly concealed since time immemorial.[65]

> The standard view, derived form Plato's *mimesis* via Aristotle's *Poetics*, has always excluded one essential human behavior from the types subject to imitation – namely, desire and, more fundamentally still, appropriation. If one individual imitates another when the latter appropriates some object, the result cannot fail to be rivalry or conflict. Such conflict is observable in animals; beyond a certain intensity of rivalry the antagonists tend to lose sight of their common object and focus on each other, engaging in so-called prestige rivalry. In human beings, the process rapidly tends toward interminable revenge, which should be defined in mimetic or imitative terms.[66]

From here, Girard elaborates the scapegoat mechanism, society's ultimate mimetic safety valve of self-preservation, whereby victimization processes hold together the sacred and the violent to expel the latter.[67] Although it is already extensively described in his earlier publications, it is in his work from 1978 onwards that Girard extends his view of imitation to bind together the literary and anthropological questions we have examined above in Dawkins and Genette. Instead of making science the ultimate touchstone or antagonist to the arts, Girard turns upside down the order of reason and reason's orders of knowledge by asking some key questions:

> If mimesis, like all primitive gods, has two 'sides', one that disrupts the community and the another one that holds it together, how do these two sides relate to each other? How can the conflictual and destructive mimesis turn into the nonconflictual mimesis of training and learning, indispensable to the elaboration and perpetuation of human societies? If mimetic desire and rivalries are more or less normal human phenomena, how can societal orders keep back this force or disorder, or, if they are overwhelmed by it, how can a new order be reborn of such disorder?[68]

The disclosure of a constant pattern in world mythologies, anthropological investigations of rituals, and a few truly exceptional texts from no single heritage[69] all suggest for Girard the source of the cultural patenting process, religion, not science and technology. It is here that the 'real' event, collective murder and its aftermath, and the rituals for its prevention, are ascertained. From this real(ization) radiate multiple human representations – myths, religions, art – but also the sciences of man, including astrophysics, genetics, behavioural sciences, cultural studies and critical theories. While these disciplines all consider causes and effects to varying degrees – we saw how far influence helps to explain these – a powerlessness to identify, let alone arbitrate between, 'end things' as positive and/or negative inhabits each.[70] If positivism is dead, the relativism that has replaced it can have no final answers.

In a move similar to the Greek *opiso*, 'the backing into the future', to recall Knox's words in the last chapter,[71] the future for Girard cannot be determined until and unless the past of religion has been properly scrutinized and discriminated.[72] Discrimination as (final) judgement between things, and mechanism of discernment to arrive at such a singling out or marking of difference, is paramount here. What Girard stumbles on is the realization that, if the scapegoat mechanism conceals and reveals the mimetic in many variations of human culture, then the mimetic is also the key to the underlying principle behind its many manifestations.[73] Its very mechanism, 'the *all against one* of collective violence'[74] derived from its many replications, uncovers an originating event and process of its repetitions (like Dawkins's copy*ing*-fidelity). Yet inherent in the mechanism itself is the solution to its cessation, a scapegoat to end all scapegoats. It is not sufficient, however, that this ultimate scapegoat victim embodies some hyperbolic doubled polarity (positive and negative in their purest form). Such self-cancellation merely repeats the same scapegoat mechanism all over again, as rituals amply endorse. What is needed is a breaking of the mimetic cycle itself, for the scapegoat principle and its mechanisms to be revealed for what they are, that is, transcended. Imitation as supreme representation cannot do the job unless it is at the same time supreme *embodiment* to commemorate the originative murder and its apotheosis. Transfiguration names this one final resolution to break the iteration of the scapegoat mechanism past and future. The real is then alpha and omega. For Girard, this is no utopian or logical conclusion to come. The one perfect victim and sacrifice, Jesus Christ, has fulfilled and transfigured the scapegoat of scapegoats, and made a show of the mechanism openly on the cross.[75] Crucifixion was not enough to end the mimetic cycle. Only resurrection could transcend and transfigure it and make possible the truth of the real. Consequently, the touchstone (discrimination, discernment) is discovered in imitation of the real that Christ transfigured reveals, not in imitations of imitation.

But as with Bloom's discovery of tradition as Kabbalah, and Genette's uncovering of the double face of the mimetic, why had no one before Girard envisaged the scapegoat as the way to break the cycle of imitation and the mimetic? In an interview response to just such a question, Girard first admits to insight as central to the process, and its 'privilege'.[76] However, because it stems from overwhelming evidence, and overwhelming conviction in truth itself as conceivable and *public*, Girard's position is not overweening (Bloom, Derrida) or brilliantly intellectualist (Genette), but a more humble *recognition* of a combination of circumstances – the preparatory 'codicil' in the work of Kenneth Burke, certain ideas as 'in the air'[77] – to enable his insight. This is not revelation alone but a way of seeing that embodies the other meanings of the Greek *theoria*, contemplation and speculation.[78] The final piece in the jigsaw was an open mind to discovery itself, and acceptance of every resource, including the Bible, but perhaps especially the Gospels.

The reverberating scandal of Girard's theory of imitation, then, is the *skandalon* itself, 'the obstacle against which one keeps stumbling'.[79] In *Things Hidden since the Foundation of the World*, Girard's challenge to criticism of all kinds is a simple choice to countenance religion or not. 'Here at last is a fine new scandal for the closing stages of the twentieth century, something that should cause real panic among moderns avid for new sensations.'[80] In other words, blindly continue 'old' mimesis in full realization, and self-deception, since its mechanism has been revealed, or work from the truth of mimesis: imitation of a transfigured Christ is the blueprint for how order can be restored. The *skandalon* as stumbling block will remain such for those who choose not to see it, but become the foundation stone for those who do. Although Girard does not elaborate here, the call is to move from metaphor to the ethical action and charge of parable. Jesus reveals the truth of the real, that the stumbling block is the chief cornerstone, in two ways. First, he quotes Psalm 118: 22–3 as prophetic word of which he is the fulfilment (metaphor/incarnation), but this revelation is framed in a parable, the story of the vineyard and its stewards, a 'story' quintessentially about how to discern 'end things'.[81]

Accepting or rejecting Girard's theory because it requires the 'leap of faith' is not the issue. Rather, the challenge is that any 'theory' or ideology requires an act of belief to adopt it, and discrimination in both senses to choose it and reject others.[82] Indeed, theories of relativism may be the most dogmatic,[83] since their reliance on pendulum swing and counterbalance (mimetic effects) must be propped up by some form of dualism, duplication and duplicity.

> One cannot imagine starting with a structuralist system containing two differential elements that have the same degree of value. There is a simpler model that is uniquely dynamic and genetic – but also completely ignored. This is the model of the exception that is still in the process of emerging, the single trait that stands out against a confused mass or still unsorted multiplicity. It is the model of drawing lots, of the short straw [. . .] only the shortest straw or the longest, is meaningful. The rest is indeterminate.[84]

The exception not only proves the rule. It cancels interim judgements with a final one.

In terms of models of language, then, is Cratylus' one-to-one correlation of signifier and signified paradoxically closer to the truth? Is Girard's Jesus the transcendental signified, not the transcendental signifier so ruled out of court by structuralist and postmodern models?

> The signifier is the victim. The signified constitutes all actual and potential meaning the community confers on to the victim and, through its intermediacy, on to all things. The sign is the reconciliatory victim. Since we understand that human beings wish to remain reconciled after the conclusion of the crisis, we can also understand their penchant for reproducing the sign, or in other words for reproducing the language of the sacred by substituting, in ritual, new victims for the original victim, in order to assure the maintenance of that miraculous peace. The imperative of ritual is therefore never separate from the manipulation of signs and their constant multiplication, a process that generates new possibilities of cultural differentiation and enrichment.[85]

From this, Girard's work would suggest that Jesus (incarnate and transfigured) is the supreme transcendental *sign* and arbitrator between uses of such signs. It is not then difficult to understand why belief is so close to excommunication, and blasphemy the inverted use of sacred names.[86] By a misplaced worship of arbitrariness itself, that words and things are merely 'signs' pointing nowhere, postmodern theories and cultural fetishism may then be the most recent re-enactment of the *ritual* implications of this transcendental sign. Girard's work, however, reveals the dangers of such positions against the backdrop of global capitalism and the re-emergence of fundamentalist groups of all persuasions as signs that do point clearly, to persecution and discrimination. Girard's work therefore provides a means to reveal the scapegoating mechanisms that all non- or anti-religious theories have colluded in *collectively*, an end-stopping of all that is not 'reason' by excommunicating myth, religion, the primitive, nature. By the same token, and more shockingly, religious dogmas and theologies are revealed as being equally complicit in scapegoat mechanisms, especially persecution, crusade or jihad. By relying on sacred texts as authorities for these, they uphold a no less sacrificial or exclusionist interpretation and scapegoating ethos.

Girard's theory of imitation thus throws the gauntlet back to the models of the previous two chapters. Postmodern intertextuality pertains to be all-inclusive of text, including the Bible. Yet its anti-religious spirit of interpretation, that all texts are text, in fact delivers tokenism and taboo packaged together. Influence studies, especially comparative, allow greater space for religious questions and religious traditions across historical periods. Cultural tunnel vision or political correctness often airbrush anti-humanitarian parts of culture out of the picture or clothe them more comfortably. Holocaust studies have much to recuperate from consideration of Girard. Heretical criticism, such as Derrida's deconstruction and Bloom's 'anxiety of election', which both employ antagonistic positioning and concerted overwriting of strong precursors, can also be reconsidered in a very different light through Girard's work. Bloom's is perhaps the most uncanny counterfeit of Girard's discovery. Overwriting Freud's interpretation of Oedipus as superego, Bloom remains blind to this figure as scapegoat victim, and to Gnosticism in whatever form as unhooked from the touchstone of soteriology.

Girard's theory encapsulates a vision that runs parallel with the central idea of this book, that shadowlands lie behind, and belie, the importance of what covers them. However, by theorizing the scandal of what has been most occluded as the place to uncover truths of a greater moment than more overtly trumpeted ideas, Girard also opens wide the future of reinterpretation across and within disciplines. Interdisciplinarity has much to reconsider if religion, not science, is its model and in the light of the kinds of research that Girard has undertaken with others in the fields of anthropology, ethnography, religious studies, literary, cultural and psychoanalytic criticism.[87] Quite how such transfigured interdisciplinarity becomes a workable blueprint to rethink the sciences, social sciences and arts in the twenty-first century is the moot point of Girard's work. If a clean sweep has been made on all mimetic critical models, little is in place to begin such work. Girard none the less does not mince his words concerning its urgency. The escalation of nuclear arms stockpiling, global terrorism, religious fundamentalisms, persecution and backlash are strong reminders of the actuality of scapegoat *effects*.[88]

Clearly if Girard is right that the source of the cultural patenting process is religion, and that Christ has revealed the scapegoat mechanism, then the greatest challenge of all is to a Christianity that takes on the real, rather than further refinements of theology as cloak of authority.[89] We will return to authority and its authorities in the next chapter.

Girard's method also challenges theory that operates grilles of interpretation, or endorses only certain texts or approaches, as quasi-theory, for it is more concerned with the intricacies and refinements of its application and hence justification.[90] It was not applied theory that led to his own discoveries, but direct dialogue with, and contemplation of, primary sources, including the Bible. Girard would then advocate secondary critical divestment, but without a return to a Romantic worship of canonical texts for themselves. His is radical rethinking that listens to opposite views and responds to lateral and imaginative approaches in order to be discriminating. Such 'theory' cannot be safe, confining or cosily replicating and has no taboos on what it considers. As intensely political in its concern for public matters, an approach à la Girard, or *via* Girard, has much to offer socio-criticism and postcolonial criticism.[91] As privileging no genre, Girard's work on the mimetic as scapegoat mechanism permits radical reappraisals of the novel, theatre and poetry, and hierarchies and cycles of return, catharsis, recognition, purgation or *analusis* as represented, for example, in Bakhtin's carnival, Greek tragedy and fairy tale.[92] For disciplines such as myth, cast out for its universalism or essentialism, Girard's work again provides a vehicle, which cannot but endorse the speaking of 'things hidden'.[93]

Revelation of 'things hidden' as release may still not encompass freedom for all, however, but rather imprison some even more. However convincing Girard's scapegoat theory may be, like other overarching theories by Marx, Nietzsche, Freud, Bloom, Derrida and others, it cannot shake off its status as yet another 'Grand Narrative', and a strikingly male one at that. Girard is adamant that his theory is positively discriminatory and 'pro-women', indeed richly addresses the scapegoating and victimhood of women. By arguing that they are not the primary agents of violence, Girard sees women's place of 'real moral superiority' as outside the scapegoat mechanism proper, the circle and power games of men.[94] Thus feminism for Girard is a further mimetic effect, detrimental to women, since, in seeking to join the very power games that have oppressed them, they also lose their real moral superiority.

Feminists would of course argue that male designations of women's 'moral superiority' have formed a powerful weapon to enforce their role as the gatekeepers of morality in the home, to marginalize them from the real power and authority of male public and political space. Such dichotomization of function has also provoked the double victim status of women in the male psyche (including its secondary mimetic structures such as art or psychoanalysis) as saints or witches, good mothers or whores. Feminist criticism of many hues has therefore been a vital instrument to challenge these accepted orders, and the institutions, canonical texts and laws used to authorize such positions. By pursuing theories of difference, alterity or otherness, but in very different guises from the traditional, hierarchical binary opposition, the spectrum of feminism has visibly challenged patriarchal models. By having the revision of the whole Western cultural project in their sights, feminists have thus made major and visible inroads into rewriting woman into history, from her point of view. If feminism (and, in its wake, gay and gender studies and masculinities theories) can be charged with replication of mimetic effects, as Girard would contend, it may be because of unwitting replication of first premises in post-Enlightenment rationalism and its rebuttal of all mythical, religious or theological inquiry, rather than the motives behind such a project.[95] Feminism therefore cannot but confront the processes of mimetic desire externally and internally to itself – feminism is already plural – but this does not change its desired remit, to uncover the gendering at work in any construct, perhaps especially ones like Girard's scapegoat which claim not to be gender-specific. For example, if feminism has been made the 'scapegoat' for masculinist backlash, which blames a largely monolithic and mythical 'Feminism', it is feminism which can add these speech marks, and suggest how such backlash also testifies to the real fear in men of discovering the very victim status they cast firmly on women. Feminism cannot offer a final solution to the problem, but, by gendering the problem, it at least opens a space for different answers. In the two fields (overlapping strongly with Girard's) that feminism has only belated begun to rework – an ethnography which is andropological, and feminist theology[96] – feminist theorists continually discover the minefield of the revictimization of women at secondary mimetic levels *because of* feminist work on representations of the female body and cultural embodiments for women. If feminism has only begun to realize the complexity and difficulty of its task, this is because, like Girard, awareness of how deep-rooted imitation is has only slowly emerged. Even if the mimetic is supposed to have been broken in the singular man of God, it has always already, and across all cultures, been regarded as *woman's* chief vice and virtue. Can there be a way out of the magic circle that labelled women as witches if woman's imitation is made a *skandalon*, or out of her representational disenfranchisement due to her status as muse or of 'naturally' secondary artistic merit? How can the (false) myths of culture be so deemed, or fictions and theories be discriminated or told apart from counterfeit versions of a 'real thing'?

Countering the canon: imitatio v. plagiarism, forgery, counterfeit

Although Girard's theory nowhere informs her work, Elin Diamond's contribution to feminism and theatre puts female role-play and the display of female bodily performance centre stage as a primary pressure point on cultural representation. In other words she reveals what is concealed as *skandalon*:

> Desire, politics and gender struggle are *persistent irritants* in Western theater and its literature. Historically women have been denied power in the theater apparatus yet signs of female sexuality have been crucial to that apparatus's functioning – a contradiction that can be read as the signifying processes of almost any play. Theater itself may be understood as the drama's *unruly body*, its material other, a site where the performer's and the spectator's *desire may resignify elements of a constrictive social script* [. . .] *occluding its own means of production.* [. . .] Conservative and patriarchal, the theater is also, in a complex sense, the place of play, and unlike other media, in the theater *the same play can be played not only again, but differently.*[97]

Diamond sees clearly the urgency for feminism, particularly feminist theatre, of tackling mimesis à la Plato and à la Aristotle. To formulate the subject as masculine, the 'universal standard for determining the true', men equate 'Woman' with mimetic non-identity, imitation or its counterfeits and also with the place to identify mimesis itself.[98] In Western culture, 'Woman' is therefore at the same time 'good' mimesis and 'bad', the very 'embodiment' of deception, duplicity, impersonation, illusion. Her play-acting nature epitomizes the worst of mimetic behaviour as feminizing, whatever is contrary to proper and appropriate male action. Hence, Plato sought to remove theatre from his Republic, not so much as false mirror or lie, but because it was improper and an imposture for male action. It is this impropriety of 'Woman', her deception and ability to deceive, that made it an easy step for theologians to formulate 'Woman's' nature itself as evil, of the very counterfeiter, the Devil incarnate.

For Diamond, it is therefore woman who can unmask this modelling system by female gender doubling and unmasking of 'Woman' from the inside and as secondary mimesis, 'pure' spectacle. It was when theatre was at its most flourishing that the scandal occurred, in the work within Restoration theatre of Aphra Behn. We have already mentioned the importance for Renaissance art of imitation as positive use of previous models for new ends. Here was a woman playwright not only doing this and well, but also challenging the very modelling systems themselves. It is Behn's staging of women who are playing women and 'Woman' in all her mythical identifications that makes the show of 'Woman' openly. Taking the prejudice and hypocrisy of the social codes of her period at face value, Behn's theatre everywhere names the stumbling blocks of mimesis and reveals their real counterfaces:

> No playwright, and certainly no woman playwright, could ignore the persistent denunciation of theater practice as moral and spiritual contamination. The Patristic revulsion against theater, typified in tracts from the third-century Tertullian to those of Renaissance Puritans like Philip Stubbes and William Prynne, builds on the Platonic condemnation of mimesis as the making of counterfeit copies of true originals. In a sense Prynne and his supporters were pragmatic semioticians; ignoring reationalizations from Horace to Sidney to Dryden that dramatic poetry was designed to 'delight and instruct,' they perceived that meaning was made by impersonation – the deliberate contamination of natural or God-given identity – and by enticing spectators to respond pleasurably to such deceptions. Moreover, the Fathers and their followers condemn actors in costume and cosmetics as hypocrites whose shape-changing derives from the devil. [. . .] Restoration actresses were so clearly identified with the pleasure of theater spectatorship that the Puritan dicta, through periods of all-male theater practice, seemed prophetic. To the Puritan mind the presence of women on stage was an affront to feminine modesty, but more damning was the fact that the means of illusionism – use of costume, paint, masking – involved specifically female vices. The nature of theatrical representation, like the 'nature' of woman, was to ensnare, deceive, and seduce. [. . .] Disguise allows women and men to pass not only as the other gender but as members of a different class. After the Restoration in 1660, the theatricality of everyday life was strongly in evidence, extending beyond lavish court masquerade into the private lives of men and women.[99]

For Diamond, Behn's work shows that art and life in theatre are not two separate spheres divided by a procenium or in the round. Through Behn's wider critique of 'Woman' as the site and seat of mimesis in (male) theatricality, by woman's mimicry that can *unmask*, Diamond's project opens up the space for feminist playwriting within and against mainstream theatre which itself can now be gendered. Luce Irigaray's theories of female mimicry in *Speculum de l'autre femme* (1974) and its anti-mimetic reconstruction of Plato's cave as a womb-theatre provide the all-important key.[100] This is not 'empty' but rather 'full' (excessive) mimicry, a conscious and self-conscious role-playing that conforms to the viewer's worldview (identification with the mimetic model), yet frees the performer as also other person (female identity outside the mimetic). Performance is therefore not just the seen of bodily enactment which conforms to spectator expectation. It is an unseen (or *gestus* à la Brecht and Benjamin), made visible by (personalizing) gesture, which maintains the fiction of the enactment but also allows the woman to embody herself at the same time.[101] The mimetic is thus revealed by double excess, the non-conformity or going beyond the model or stereotype, and the physical presence of the woman actress in excess of the role.

Behn's theatre as spectacle of embodied recognition for Diamond operates in similar ways to Girard's *skandalon*.[102] Girard, however, would foreclose mimesis in the singular and non-repeatable trans-figurative embodiment of Christ's work on the cross, whereas Diamond requires a space for women to begin to reconfigure their own symbolic, representational and real identities and identifications. Beyond this remit, Diamond's valiant critique, of much relevance also to gay studies, allows 'live' performance in theatre to be further distinguished from fixed, 'canned' versions of plays in film, television or video forms. The inherent problem within it, however, is that it cannot make a final spectacle of secondary mimesis as *theatre*, so as then to recuperate it as specifically female or feminist. The deeper contaminations of the mimetic still at work against embodied woman (full mimicry) are in fact revealed but concealed within Diamond's own formulation above. How is the woman actress in her costume and paint playing a prostitute, or indeed more scandalously women icons of virtue, to be unequivocally discriminated from woman the seducer/prostitute, enacting and mimicking the *desiring* woman and woman as desire? The mimetic tangle between prostitution, imper-sonation, hysteria, female bodily exemplification of woman as either supreme bride or supreme harlot (the 'originator' of sin and evil) has as yet to be resolved by feminist study, although Marina Warner, Elaine Showalter and Sandra Gilbert and Susan Gubar have all made vital contributions.[103] No feminist staging or counter-acting can as yet of itself break these mimetic traps, even through clever mimicry (as in Dawkins) for different ends. As with any myth or mime, true versions can easily be interpreted as false, just as many women continue to be imprisoned or tortured for speaking out against 'authority'.

Something about theatre as performance and embodied imitation in its most crystallized or stylized form does, however, persistently point to, but cannot explain, the *skandalon*. We can connect this piece to another in the jigsaw that Hawcroft has noted with regard to the rise of rhetoric and the demise of religion as sign of civilized society in the mid-sixteenth century, on the one hand, and the apotheosis of rhetoric (in its written forms) and drama, on the other.[104] Are public oratory, acting and performance eclipsed because of the circulation of print for the same ends of persuasion, conviction or testimony, but for private consumption? Does Renaissance imitation of the classics move imitation itself into a private (book) sphere so as evade public denouncement of its own appropriations? Did the Renaissance help turn imitation from an 'Imitation of Christ' to imitation in its secular renaissances? Can fair copy be distinguished from false, real from illusion, because imprimatur makes forgery and plagiarism important issues for the first time?

While there is no one agreed explanation for the concentration of imitative practices in Renaissance arts, it is undoubtedly the period of increased legal and social responsibility for the individual (male) subject.[105] Laws regarding primogeniture and property highlight the position of the individual in society. Judgement on the proper and improper, original and copy were no longer matters for the Church, but the self as notary. The true continues to be male and universal measure. While drama was flowering, not least by plundering plots from the classics, and 'feminizing' (in Plato's sense) court society, it seems no accident that this same pre-modern period also spawned 'heroic', 'muscular' genres where the written pre-empted the spoken. Of utmost, and inimitable, importance to self-reflection and criticism were Montaigne and Dryden. They did not concentrate on drama, but transcended it in other forms such as the epic, opera and the essay as critical and creative vehicles. It was the voicing of the self as ultimate arbiter and critical (authority) of taste, propriety and aesthetic standard that had particular pre-eminence.[106] Montaigne and Dryden were master performers, however, of flagrant plagiarism, but turned to *public* advantage – the reinvestment of the Greek and Roman classics as French *belles-lettres* or a properly English canon. As master collectors à la Genette, not art thieves or forgers, their appropriations and ensuing copyright masterpieces have made copy, imitation and, particularly, plagiarism vexed questions since. The 'copy' can better the 'original' in certain cases so that imitators are left no option but to be derivative, by following such models openly, or legally reprehensible plagiarists.[107]

For Romanticism and its successor postmodernism, the ever-constant anxiety is not of influence, but of imitation (positive or negative) *before* it in both senses, the lack of new ways to write what is already attributable. Romanticism chose to break with classical imitation often by impersonation, invention or fabrication of mythical heritages. *Ossian* is a key example. Postmodernism has further perfected the art of flagrant plagiarism: recycling is a euphemism for unlimited activity in the electronic 'pick-pocket-book'.[108] Everyone is therefore an electronic magpie, or virtual plunderer, and hence outside the law. Thus, whatever the epoch, plagiarism (like cloning and IVF) shows up the knotty complexities of imitation's appropriations as legitimate and/or illegitimate, forgery and/or cleverly creative. The importance of the slash is illustrated in the creative but fake 'discoveries' of the early works of known writers, 'translations' from other heritages, pseudonymous works, or ghost writing as modern economic replication of the work of scribes.[109] Blatant but overt copy of another's style is called pastiche, while anthologies and readers are copyright reproduction of major parts of others' work. If anxiety about plagiarism spearheaded copyright in 1767,[110] and copying and reproductions of copies thereafter as creative and illegal, it also legalized and legitimized processes and principles of production and reproduction. 'Good' imitation and creativity were firmly on the side of art, fabrication and complex mechanisms, but this measure was aesthetic and moral. The ultimate justifications for art and its ownership as the domain of the male subject were now in place. 'Woman' was not merely imitation of nature, but artful deceiver through her more dangerous forgeries: adulteries and (il)legitimate issue constitute 'Woman's' proper work, her indubitable maternity.

Artistic imitations then only endorse the similar polarizations in anthropology, ethnology and histories of religion that have been used to explain the overthrow of matriarchies and goddess religions by patriarchies and their gods. The pendulum swing seemingly furthest towards 'culture' inevitably reveals equal counterweight of 'nature'. Marion Hobson speaks to both when she reminds us that '*Mimesis* in art is the remnant of its magical and cultic origin' and that 'Art is not a scandalous illustration of the divorce between appearance and essence, but a fascinating play between them.'[111] Art probes the heart of discernment as meanings of illusion (error, mockery, 'the work of the Evil One') or appearance, 'different modes of being like (simulation and dissimulation) and of appearing (seeming and pointing beyond); they are structured by two different theories of truth. The first is correspondence theory, *adequatio rei et intellectus*; the second, revelation, uncovering or disclosing of the hidden, *a-letheia*.'[112] Hobson's important book maps the ramifications of seventeenth-century oppositions of illusion and appearance as *vraisemblance* through to the eighteenth century's premising of illusion on *vraisemblance* so that '[b]y the end of the eighteenth century, illusion has hardened; it has become either the designation of a private state of mind, which can be true or false, or the designation of the art object as copy, true or false to the model.'[113] One might speculate on the intervening worldview of Rousseau here for Hobson's appreciation that 'Any appearance may be epiphany or simulacrum, immediate manifestation of the divinity or derivative action of the *phantasmagoria*.'[114] In post-Renaissance secularization and separation from Church and faith, oppositions such as 'true or false', 'illusion or real', 'good or bad' expunge good/evil by human judgements and their critiques. To what extent have rationalism, the Inquisition and its critical theories made the real taboo the Devil and not Christianity in case criticism is itself a forgery? Does Hobson's choice of 'scandal' to describe art reveal a critical truth that we can accept or reject (a Hobson's choice) about the monstrous nothing behind the mask?

If theology little attends to a hermeneutics of evil, the representations and construct of the Devil or his laughter out of court are running threads in art. Indeed, they may be important indicators of moments when cultural self-reflection can be expressed only in tropes of falsification, imposture, mockery, dissimulation and (self)-deception.[115] A further manifestation is cynical irony. Postmodernism, therefore, amply qualifies on all these counts, but, with the exception of Harold Bloom's heretical and Gnostic criticism,[116] it is especially allergic, not to *phantasmagoria* but to *pandemonium*. Arbitrariness and free play, not human or demonic forces, 'operate' the game of language. Play, however, is imitation and mockery in another form,[117] and not necessarily benign amusement, for power operates at some level. What maintain the game are rules of possibility and probability of seemingly open and two-way design. This duplicity, by which punters enter and enable the game to continue, then plays on their folly within what is a double game. As with gambling or lottery operators, the real power to generate money (as new theory or more power) is always at the expense of the punter. The ultimate cover that cannot be blown is the operator who names these two-way rules, but in fact stacks power with the rule-maker. In chapter 1, we saw 'choices' and options of virtual reality or hypertext as also the disempowerment of disorientated or marooned mouse-clickers. Chapter 2 revealed Derrida's ultimate, critical, ironic control over the rearrangements of words to keep deferral endlessly deferring, yet back to himself.[118] If benign game leads to addictive imprisonment in cycles of repetition to increasing the stakes of victory as ultimate defeat, then malign game plays with total order of winners over losers. As Nazism and all totalitarian power demonstrates, warmongering to announce external power cloaks the internal power agenda, ethnic cleansing, or the daemonization of the enemy within.[119]

Power therefore lies behind all imitations, lotteries and theories of chance, which have their roots in Greek tragedy and epic in the form of the gods or *moira*. Epic is about the pitting of absolutes against the other, magic, fate, cosmic and personal power struggles between good and evil.[120] Key cultural moments of transition and chaos therefore return to reshaping epic. In literary history, Dryden transmuted it for personal quest (genius) and 'autobiography'. Global capitalism and stock markets marshal epic to speak of bears and bulls to pit the gold standard against money, paper stocks and shares. Power like *pandemonium* or Mammon is a signifier, which signifies everything and nothing, and is the lure behind which is imitation's single determinant, Desire (the lottery operator). All desires replicate the order of Desire and its power structures, but Desire's own desire (and power) remains concealed. Secondary mimesis of all kinds, especially art, mirrors and conceals this process but cannot speak its name. Oughoulian is right to pinpoint Desire not as instinct, need, drive or mimetic appropriation, but desire for (the other's) knowledge, which, because hidden (secret and ungraspable), is perceived as the essence of identity. Omniscience is therefore the desire behind Desire, summed up in Satan's words to Eve, 'You will be like God . . .'[121] The Devil is in the detail regardless of the theology. It is the 'like' which is not equal that is the lure selling equality, yet always delivering difference or otherness. In the Middle Ages Satan was even known as 'the other' and hence never pinned to the one, the here and now.[122] The 'like' is also seat of power to sow dissatisfaction, difference, discrimination and exemplified by Satan himself. As Lucifer, the (false) light-bringer or (fallen) angel of light, Difference is the supreme antagonist of God. The 'as if', therefore, is the key to all secondary mimetic desires, power and cultural representations. It also names the place *of* language and hence the indiscernible difference between words as figurative and non-figurative, truth and lies. Paradoxically, it is suspension of belief in fiction as fiction that allows negotiation of the place of the 'as if' to occur. The mask is now off. The equation of Eve with evil (the other), or 'Woman' with the site of mimetic desire, fantasy and its structures, is the lie of another order. Only acceptance of the reality of 'the Devil' as construct can provide a key to understanding this mimetic order or, as Girard would have it, the mimetic disorder of things.[123] Girard's essay on Satan as the ultimate *scandalon* Jesus denounced by making himself a *scandalon* to reveal its works, dares to speak of these things openly, and in ways which put theology,[124] and all theories with claims to open-mindedness, to shame.[125]

The history of science, art, cultures and criticism demonstrates how this Hobson's choice has been made, but differently to Girard. Thus, these forms of secondary mimesis continue the principles of appropriation, imitation and discovery of untruth where truth was

thought to lie. As in all epics, counter-theories can be released only
when authorities are proved false and their injustices overthrown.
Authorities will be the next and final shadowland of this book.
However, until some final judgement comes along, criticism of all
kinds has to do with interim truths and rediscoveries of the same
questions. It is this process which brings to light new discernment
which is more than Dawkins contends, '[a] minimal test [. . .] of
reliability',[126] or even common sense from the stock of cultural
memory.[127] Any nostalgic remembrance of the past and 'the act of
recognizing ourselves' must always be complemented.[128] Discernment always tests imitation against time to find singularity and identification amid its many others, and their models. Is it art that is the
Hobson's choice about such a place?

The models of cultural heritage tacitly assumed and openly negotiated in this chapter are *representational* and Greek in some form,
whether as mimesis, Pauline theology or modern science. The
Hebrew tradition, however, equates imitation with idolatry, and
hence has no indigenous theatre. This taboo stems from the interdiction on making images of God, since the 'I am that I am' surpasses any Form or forms. Because the Hebrew model does not
feature theatre, it immediately offers a way of untangling classifications, genres and conventions within Greek representations and their
hierarchies, but without conflating them as postmodernism does, or
like science, separating arts from non-arts. As Goethe would 'discover' as the hub of *Urdictung* – the ballad, fairy tale, lamentation,
hymn, prayer, incantation – from which emerged the three spokes of
drama, epic and lyric,[129] the nub for Hebrew tradition is the oral
genre. However, where mimetic problems endure between orality
and literacy in 'Greek' theories, Hebrew tradition confronts the same
problem, but solves it by a different route. It grounds both oral and
written forms in the same *single* authority, the commandment. First
given to Adam and Eve (Genesis), then to Moses (Exodus) and later
to the Israelites (Leviticus), the Pentateuch has a triune rather than
neatly tripartite iteration of 'myth', 'history' and 'Law' as three ways
of exhorting humanity to keep covenant with God and one's neigh-
bour, so as to avoid covetousness (mimetic desire and its orders of
mimesis). Keeping of the Law was therefore more than pharisaical
prohibition and obedience to its letter, but interpretation of its spirit
by active response and remembrance. 'Storytelling' and 'testimony',
as well as public reading and teaching of the (written) Law, amount
to the same thing: transmission of the covenant for the present and
next generation. Talmud (laws) and midrash (interpretations of the
Law often in story form) are not then hierarchically arranged grafts,
but balancing, narrative forms in unison.

In contrast to the visual and dualistic thinking inherent in Greek traditions, its principles of priority, binary opposition and mimesis, it is the aural/oral that unites Hebrew narrative forms. Hence, canon plays a strikingly different role in Hebrew tradition as something to be performed, and as closely as possible to the 'script'. It is the telling (or writing) of the 'old' story for a contemporary audience that makes it vibrantly present, not a repetition or plagiarism. Canon, then, is not some institutionalized monument to, and apogée of, male achievement, but an *aide-mémoire* in the most instructive, creative, formative and inspirational ways.[130] Aural/oral imitation is canon's renewal and creative energy. It is also transformation, of cultural self-awareness and expectation, in respect of, and thanks to, the worlds of the other. In the light of this definition of canon, plagiarism can now be seen as a kind of alteration of memory akin to amnesia,[131] and the anti-canonical stances of postmodernism as but selective memories of its own lack of subject. As the richness and explosion of all art forms of Western Renaissance pre-modernity up to its legalization of 'official' writing in 1767 exemplifies, imitative canonical writing is always at some level anti-canonical, for canons are upheld by the very diversity they also incorporate.[132] If Renaissance art reacted to the officialdoms of the Church, Greek and Latin as canonical languages and texts, and rhetoric as jurisprudence,[133] its vernacular experiments with their forms and models were the way to find a new voice. As feminist and postcolonial writing has rediscovered, canon especially in its aural/oral traditions can be mined, not necessarily for the memory of some ready-made self, but for one half-forgotten yet half-remembered in the cultural fabric.

★　　★　　★

Via evolution and what seemed opposite poles within post-structuralist anthropologies and of Hebrew *Urzeit*, imitation thus returns us to highly active human modelling processes, generating variegated and changing cultural forms. Western mimesis and all its progeny as exemplified and crystallized in pre-modernity is only one kind of pattern. Western imitation as pendulum ever shows the counterbalancing shadow movement behind any visible swing in one direction, and offers ways of explaining why seemingly contradictory theories such as those treated above emerge concomitantly. Appositionally, the work of Girard, Genette and Dawkins on imitation's reflections all question late postmodern myths of progress, and allow its latest manifestations to be judged and discriminated. Genetic engineering or digital simulacra propagating xenophobia come dangerously close to materializing the monsters of myth and revealing the evil genies in the bottle.[134] It is by holding up others' traditions and canons as ways of measuring cultural value that are not quantitative but qualitative, and therefore beyond interpersonal frames of fashion, taste or economics, that imitation can attend to sorting out, like wheat from tares, 'good' and 'bad' mimesis in the same fields. Paradoxically, then, imitation goes straight to the depths that the surfaces of the previous two chapters identified as different currents, not the same water.

Western imitation is then the trope of paradox within its structures and double paradox, a helix of Greek and Hebrew morphologies. Perhaps it is to the latter's longevity that post-postmodernity can turn in order to extricate itself from the exponential multiplicities of postmodernity and its prestidigitations. This cannot magic away the delusions of its pre-modern, and especially modernist past, founded itself on paradoxes which Compagnon names as superstition in the new, a religion of the future, theory mania, appeal to massification of culture, and a passion for denial.[135] As scientology or astrology, such 'New Age cults' equally mirror science and return some of the oldest taproots of all behind *scientia*, magic, alchemy and things hidden before the foundation of the modern world. It is the connective and collective stories and their imitations in stones and bones in today's language as evolution and anthropology that will continue to guarantee imitation's place beyond intertextuality.

Good imitation, then, is appositional complement to the positive form of influence in chapter 2. Its future in postmodernity already has its models. Like Dawkins's *replicator* gene, it will have memory (longevity), vitality (fecundity) and discernment of these (copying-fidelity). Like the successful buffaloes, each good imitation is unique, and one can gauge its success only by the frequency of its reappearances in other forms in future generations. What this chapter has everywhere discovered is that imitation is a key term that is as important for twenty-first-century genetics and science as for the arts in all their forms. Its health warning has already, however, been intimated by Girard. To ever mimic trees of knowledge – encyclopaedias, hypertext, dictionaries – is not to have learned the lessons of history. It is to imitation as adaptation of the 'always already' that we will next turn to find out more about such learning processes.

4

Quotation

The previous chapters have opened a succession of windows to illuminate the debates and contexts of intertextuality, influence and imitation and to reveal some of their internalized and externalized shadowlands. Rather than examining a fourth expansive concept, however, this chapter addresses a very precise term, quotation. Despite very different emphases, intertextuality, influence and imitation all include it within their aegis and agree on its identification. Where other kinds of cultural reference such as allusion, reminiscence, indirect quotation, paraphrase, pastiche or adaptation may go unnoticed, quotation marks placed around any utterance highlight, separate and distinguish it from surrounding phrases. Quotation, therefore, is both extraneous ornament and reference of the most overt and saturated kind. It can be a homage, an authority or a complex shorthand which also counters authenticating functions by means of parody, counter-example or ironic questioning (its preferred postmodern usage). Quotation, then, is foreign and integrally familiar matter, like sand in the oyster that forms the pearl. It marks identifications and distinctiveness in national and temporal frames. Like the pearl, these are accretions, layering the previous as similar and variant, part of (or for) the whole, and hence for a process of continual comparison and contrast. Contrary to plagiarism's primary intention to deceive, quotation openly states and acknowledges its status as borrower and borrowing.

If intertextuality, influence and imitation rely on contradiction or are too all-encompassing, the precisions that quotation affords ought to determine its central place in cultural criticism. Yet, the insignificance and marginality of quotation in current critical debates are resounding.[1] Is this because, as pre-given, its remit is assumed or bypassed for more pressing and complex critical issues? As verbal and textual term, is quotation dépassé, surpassed by electronic citation as the cut-copy-paste facility or postmodernism's protean and mixed-media bytes?

While electronic citation is paradoxically closer to the use of others' words in antiquity – attribution was integral or dismissed altogether by anonymous or collaborative authorship – unlike these precursors, electronic text producers are unwilling that their bytes remain anonymous. Plagiarism as outcome of copyright in print culture is responsible for marking ownership of words, but printing also determined the conventions and standardizations of punctuation and signs of attribution such as speech marks. Quotation, however, is about much more than its markers, as this chapter will argue. Its strongly proactive part in cultural production, including the most contemporary, will be apparent once it is unfettered from fixed definitions and critical prejudice. As with influence as source-hunting in chapter 2, quotation has been branded as the preserve of high culture and its erudite scholars and *hommes de lettres* [*sic*], such as Walter Benjamin with his quotation collections.[2] That quotation is as alive in recent popular forms as in epochs where excellence in forms of oral recitation also distinguished social levels rests its case. Something of its innate characteristics locates it with the recall techniques of recitation used by chroniclers and other oral storytellers. External aids to memory – notched sticks, beads, *incipits*, prologues – act like the speech marks, but these are only the first step to the more important re-creation process for the words in their new circumstances, and for another audience. The electronic citation superstore of concordances and databases as electronic word-search facilities have not changed the 'tag' process that quotation epitomizes. Like the point that focused the power of the Big Bang, quotation is less Copernican than Einsteinian. It is in its pulsations that it is recognized, rather than its 'original' format. Quotation, therefore, is far from a neatly circumscribed sub-set of our three previous window concepts, intertextuality, influence or imitation. Like a hologram, quotation constantly and openly moves between foreground and background. Hence, of itself or within these three more global terms, it names no single 'authority' as some static, even deadening, verifier.[3] Outer and uppermost, or the link between the three as intersecting sets, quotation is potentially their clarification, since it concerns multi-vocal reproduction that does not prioritize writing over speech or speech over writing. Thus, this chapter goes back to, and fronts, the theories of Kristeva, Bloom, Genette in superimposition. En route, it will also revisit issues such as mimesis, authenticity and individuation, interdisciplinarity and deconstruction by reiterating quotation's constant 'dual nationality' (as opposed to double identity as uncovered in imitation). As particle and wave, grit and pearl, its highly complex and sophisticated modes will be elaborated from three inter-related angles on the same question: what does it mean to re-create in the same but other words?

Quotation in context: dictionary or postmodern definitions?

What is a quotation, let alone a quotable quote? These knotty questions are opened up precisely in the place of definition, the dictionary. In the *OED*, the first entry for quotation is 'a (marginal) reference to a passage in a book', yet such 'marginalia' are used throughout as a key method to underpin definitions of other words. A further knot is Latin etymology. Shifting between *quotatio* and *citatio* (as various European languages illustrate), quotation has both apportioning and legal frames. Copy and repetition that is verifiable as in a court of law give it a status tantamount to the later 'copyright', or, as medieval theologians upheld, quotation is like the Bible as directly dictated to humanity in its entirety, and hence every word was true. It is not in fact the bookish base, but this seemingly preposterous idea of direct dictation that helps to clarify what quotation is. The 'Thus sayeth the Lord' of prophecy comes much closer to quotation than the now archaic 'quoth' and 'quotha' (with very similar roots across European languages in their old high forms). Here, it is the saying (utterance and act of uttering) that is foremost, but in interestingly pre- and postmodern forms. 'Quoth' is attributive – the segment which comes before or after the speech marks in stories, such as 'said the tortoise to the hare' – while 'quotha' is the potentially contemptuous or sarcastic use of another's words by repetition, 'said he (indeed!)'. Thus, quotation is about making belief or disbelief, such that, to return to imitation and counterfeit in the last chapter, the Devil is also a quoter but not a giver of Scripture. Therefore, it is not what is repeated, or indeed who repeats, that is intrinsic to quotation, but the how and why of its repetition.[4]

The better question is then what makes a quotable quote. Brevity, obviously, is essential, but qualified by pithiness: shortness in length is nothing without distillation of sentiment.[5] Aptness to the host context is a further criterion. Expression that is to the point must also have a point, or draw attention to how it is framed, as do conceits and the so-called redundant or decorative uses of quotation.[6] Quotation does not replicate or assimilate the embedding sentence, since this would only repeat or generalize it.[7] Rather, the quoted extract draws out the relative paucities of both the old and new quoting contexts. Quotation is therefore the most condensed form of paradigm shift, transmuting the context, form and meaning of the items both inside and outside the quotation marks. It is always enrichment by inclusion, integration and proclamation of otherness, a dialogue not a monologue. As both work of distillation and accretive multiplicity of viewpoints and shared experience, a 'perspectival montage or ambiguity',[8] quotation singles out in one short encapsulation a reference combining many. Mottoes, adages, apophthegms, axioms, proverbs, epigrams, maxims or modern slogans are all forms of this commonality in memorable form. Often without known authorship or necessity for quotation marks, these operate like a time capsule across epochs and national boundary.[9] It is more singular or striking catchphrases which normally assume diacritical markers, since author or textual source are known. 'To be or not to be', for example, is unequivocally Shakespeare, but is not limited to *Hamlet* or Hamlet, since the highly memorable form has made it meat for bowdlerization and parody. As multiple expressions in singular form, therefore, quotations invite onward transmission, whereas the new context, although often particular to accommodate it, will rarely make 'quotable quote' status itself. The host is the carrier pigeon, rarely the new message.

In recent history of quotation, especially its deconstructive postmodern stage based on Saussurian linguistics, the *citation* potential of all language has displaced quotation *per se*. All words are 'traces' (Derrida), or, as Kellett put it in 1933, 'In one sense *all*, or practically all, our writing is quotation.'[10] The very fabric of texts constitutes the anxiety of quotation, and authority itself. Thus, postmodernist critics (as modernist ones) have concentrated on quotation and authority as two key problems. We investigated Bloom's 'anxiety of influence' in chapter 2, but how does one deal with unrecognized and unrecognizable quotations, allusions or other cultural references? As we saw in chapter 1, Riffaterre called such items 'ungrammaticalities' and, as super-reader, revelled in such knots in textual unfurling. The more usual postmodern response is to redirect by renaming, as illustrated in chapter 3 by Genette's dismissal of quotation and allusion in *Palimpsestes* as 'intertextuality' concomitantly to downgrade Kristeva's term. Renaming then deflects attention from meanings and from serious attention either to 'recondite' particularities that sum up high-cultural texts or to 'transient' buzzwords in popular cultural forms. It also manoeuvres round the second problem, priority, that some elements in the language system have weightiness or precedence over others. Conflation of anterior or posterior status of quotation or allusion as linguistic[11] then makes citation 'excess',[12] the Derridean 'supplement'.[13] Quotations from (high-cultural) pre-modernity then have prior status erased by ironic reinscription (often using quotation marks), while those from modernity are lauded for their unstable and fickle playfulness. Among the few critics who have devoted monographs to quotation, the perennially awkward questions of authorial property and intention are conveniently elided and occluded by chronology debates. Compagnon names three stages, the 'gloss' of antiquity, the subversive 'emblem' of the Renaissance and the author's 'seal' in modernity, whereas Kellett proposes two, pre- and post-copyright.[14] Anonymous but deeply embedded phrases such as 'Once upon a time' are thus easily consigned to nebulous 'tradition' or defined as cliché, while authorial intention can be removed by denying the author exists (Barthes), by situating meanings with the reader not the author (Riffaterre), or by claiming that all language usage is incidental since it has always already been spoken or written (Derrida).

Arguments about elitism and correct attributions, or for cerebral or erotic play in the postmodern word game, cannot explain particular or persistent linguistic vibrancy that marks out certain words. What makes the neologism *différance* stand out, let alone quotable? It is this question that quotation, not citation, blows open from the very inside of the Saussurian language 'system' of signifier and signified. Quotation is its doubly denied 'other' as both referent and reference-making mode. A pithy aphorism within deconstruction is only a clever linguistic turn, yet as quoted catchphrase elsewhere it may provoke wit and satire and offer an important political rallying call. The gag is now off postmodern quotation as tantamount to ambivalence or irony. Is quotation insignificant and marginal for postmodernism and deconstruction precisely because it is too significant and central to their unmasking?

To understand and redefine quotation as shadowland term and map its rich geographies, including its manifestations in critical theory, the familiar deconstruction lenses in the critical spectacles will need to be replaced in this last chapter by bifocals which bring the blind spots into focus. Quotation itself disallows binaristic thinking or the adoption of syncretic or synthetic alternatives. Indeed, as reference point and referential process, quotation in this chapter will be shown for its singular ability to merge or conjoin the previously separate for mutual and future enhancement. This book has already considered what seem similar forces for transmitting cultural production as linguistic quantum theory (Kristevan intertextuality), counter-reaction (influence) or pendulum swing (imitation). A danger might be to correlate them with quotation as the hub in too spoke-like and monolinear, or too neatly concentric, a fashion. Quotation in this chapter will reveal its altogether more overt and illusive energies that combine the perceived malleability of intertextuality, touchstone qualities of imitation and relational processes of influence. Quotation will prove no keep of the cultural castle, but richly the place of its outside as bailey depends on motte. As the process of beating cultural bounds, quotation will be found to circle, not polarize, the recondite and the commonplace. Seen then as an engagement that actively espouses difference, how and why can quotation energize the future of a very old script to say again the same, yet other, words?

To answer this and the question of this book about the longer-term relevance of intertextuality itself, three inter-related yet distinct manifestations of quotation's energies will be clarified and informed by the three key elements already identified as quintessential to quotation: pithiness, aptness, extraction. The first part of the chapter deals with quotation's powers of concentration or crystallization. As sum of its repetitions as insertions or excerpts, it is highly illustrative. While illustration is associated primarily with picture-making, quotations frequently create such concise 'word pictures' or verbal images. Thus, quotation in its most icon-like form will be elucidated through its closest relatives, indirect quotation, self-quotation and allusion, for the ways in which they all reduce or concentrate ideas in few other words.

Quotation also re-energizes and effects what borders on the marked segment (in literal or metaphorical speech marks) in both quoted and quoting contexts. It is in the latter especially that the negotiation process that constitutes aptness is worked out. Quotation therefore names an aptitude in selecting and rejecting sites and configurations to make the old and new fit together. As dynamic strategy to harmonize affinity and repulsion, provocation and re-vocalization in both host frames, quotation is the locus of a simultaneously magnetic (centripetal) and counter-magnetic (centrifugal) force. While recalling the mimetic impulses of chapter 3 – Genette's use of figures, theatrical re-embodiment of words and personas, Dawkins's 'selfish gene' – quotation will be seen in the second part of this chapter as a different kind of engineering. As shorthand or abridgement, quotation is also the bridge which surmounts an obstacle or connects two previously separated entities. Moreover, quotation can be imagined here like the bridge of a stringed instrument. It is the all-important but forgotten support (fret) that transmits vibrations to the sounding board. Thus, quotation as bridging device will be investigated as vehicle that both spans and extends what were previously replete or separate cultural banks. Its multifarious amplifications, agglomerations and adaptations will also return this part of the chapter to recycling, but in rather different form to bricolage, or postmodern mosaic of fragmented artefacts, discussed in chapter 1. It is quotation's facility to extend by strengthening that makes it like highly tensile steel wire, extremely pliable, yet intensely strong as reworkings of itself, like the cables of a suspension bridge. The various forms of quotation that exemplify these processes, such as recitations and commentaries, will conclude the many ways that quotation can say the same again, but in a strategically controlled span of other words.

Quotation has been too often equated with the quoted as entity, fixed piece or final authority. The metaphor above of the fret, however, allows the rather forgotten because invisible agency of quotation to be reconsidered. Where intention was given another hearing in chapter 2 to recuperate it from postmodern vilification of authors or authorities, similar rethinking of agency will be addressed in the third part of this chapter. Here, quotation will be considered primarily as extraction in the sense of re-expenditure of resource. To use a further corporeal metaphor to develop the capacity of span (itself the measure of an outstretched hand), quotation forms the sinews or tendons of cultural re-embodiment. Unlike prominently placed quotations such as ornaments, decorations or details to catch the eye as epitomized in epigraphs, this variety names the all-important yet deeply hidden connective tissue that links cultural bone to muscle. In animals and humans, tendons provide strength and power for both weight-bearing (growth) and movement (survival) and are intrinsic to life force. Where we examined Dawkins's prescription of copying-fidelity, longevity and fecundity as essential for successful memes in chapter 3, quotation names the formative not as copying ability but as constant flexing to maintain fitness and suppleness and to prevent wastage. It is quotation's creative exercising or circulatory process that will be highlighted to reveal some of the hidden energies that make quotation a driver of cultural transmission and transformation. Usually devoid of speech marks, such quotation loses nothing of its authority as message bearer. As deliverer and delivery of messages, its intrinsically intermediary functions will bring its 'telling' nature back into play. From prophet to oral storyteller, to the interpreters and translators of other tongues, 'direct' quotation will be seen to return to the seemingly preposterous extractions above of God's words by 'dictation'. The seeming repetition in many other words that is quotation as translation proves the flexibility and strength of language and cultural representation ever to extend itself.

By coming full circle to the importance of translations or their lack for the dissemination of Kristeva's version of intertextuality in chapter 1, quotation's place in meaning-making are also returned. Quotation everywhere proves that it is as much imparting as importing word, metaphorical and transformative at the same time. The overt reliance throughout this chapter on metaphor to rethink quotation also moves it to its coda, the work of one further theorist, and contemporary of the others already considered, Paul Ricoeur. His constant bridging of narrative and exegesis demonstrates the interpretative conjoining of what are the usually separated arts of interpretation from religion, philosophy, literature and science. This interdisciplinarity is then the hermeneutical response to postmodernity's version, but as different harmony rather than strident discord.

The notion, then, that quotation is a verbatim replication is as rigid as the fixity of typesetting. Quotation is not the honed artefact between its speech marks, but the effects of its refashioning. It is only by removing the speech marks, which allegedly give quotation its definitive (authority) status, that its unrestricting pertinence and protean forms can become apparent in what ensues. As a concentrate of renewable energy, encapsulating all time frames, cultures and media, yet eminently economical in form, quotation will be considered primarily as an agent for change. More concise and precise than influence, it highlights the place and complexity of negotiation between multiple contexts to instigate apt and targeted communication. If quotation ultimately epitomizes interconnective and referential processes, where does this leave intertextuality, influence and imitation for the twenty-first century?

Quotation's crystallizations: illustration in few other words

Where unmarking citation in deconstruction moves language towards deferral of meanings, unmarking quotation proposes meaningfulness. The rather forgotten indirect quotation makes the point. If '[d]irect speech is the repetition of the *form* in which the original speaker expressed certain ideas [. . .] indirect speech is the expression by the hearer of these *ideas*.'[15] Whether this hearer is another character, the narrator or the reader, such reported speech takes nothing away from the 'authority' of the words attributed to a given speaker. Free indirect speech is a further refinement of this process. By cutting expression loose from specificity, reverberation of the particularities and importance of the words themselves is released beyond their speaker, time frame or context.

Yet reverberation of quotation's meaningfulness neither diffuses it too widely nor delimits it too narrowly. Indirect quotation's related form, self-quotation, as allegedly maximal authority and closest form to truth-telling, amply demonstrates this. As the confession or autobiography show, self-quotation can also be the most enfolded form of lying or self-delusion. It is on the development of these breakdowns of quotation as definitive truth statement that postmodern self-citation (intratextuality) most capitalizes. As the 'autobiographical' *nouveau roman* or Derrida's ruminations on the signature expound, repetition of the writer's words best denies and invalidates the notion of a fixed self, identity or subject.[16] The second chapter has already pinpointed the no less authoritative thrust of such (non-)positions. From quotation's premise of referentiality, however, lack of meaning or meaningfulness is only another kind of meaningfulness prefaced on absence and aporia, not presence and the symbolic. Arch and ironic postmodern self-quotation (use of speech marks) also sits on the most saturated signification of all, the unrepresentable 'I am that I am', approachable only through language. Thus, where Girard's *scandalon* in the previous chapter uncovered imitation's re-presentations through Christ as ultimate scapegoat, self-quotation covers and uncovers the represencing of all quotation as form of self-substantiation. Quotation's form of forms is self-transubstantiation.[17] As embodied and transfigured Logos, Jesus realized the word spoken by the prophets of himself, yet transfigured it beyond a moment in a human lifetime, to release its spirit, the eternally Living Word.[18] The use of self-referential language to furnish arguments for the authority of the Bible and other holy writings such as the Koran lie outside this study, not least because self-fulfilling prophecy is proved from the same arguments.[19] The point is not authority at all, but how all quotation makes belief or unbelief.[20]

Indeed, quotation's non-religious self-transubstantiations only further endorse this. In logic, a similar paradigm shift occurs to transmute the meaning of meaning in special cases of syllogism and certain paradoxes, such as the Cretan Liar.[21] Saussure's lifelong fascination with anagrams as the conundrum inside his system of signifier and signified is a further example of verbal transubstantiation of a word from the substance of its letters. Self-quotation in all these guises, then, is epitome of the meaning-making economy as self-representation and self-creation of renewed substance. Whether as sacred Logos or as secular anagram of 'scared' from 'sacred', self-quotation shows up the necessity for all quotation to transcend its moment of entry into language if it is to undergo various reformations and carry forth into longevity.

Allusion

If indirect and self-quotation reveal the intensity and substance of quotation's referential energies, they also show how close quotation is to another unmarked and shorthand form of reference, allusion. As cameo designation of complex cultural configurations such as 1789, Rome, *Don Quixote*, allusion has perhaps caused deconstruction more headaches than quotation. Like any signifier, allusion is not self-referential as it points beyond itself. However, allusion does not disperse or defer meanings either. Like quotation, it intensifies meaningfulness, but extensively rather than intensively. Allusion gathers up the many inferences of the referent as if by the way, to navigate meanings to another port.[22] A point of origination is then inferred: 'You can only allude to what preexists. An allusion *in vacuo* is impossible. Allusion is parasitic.'[23] Yet allusion eschews simple before–after hierarchies, for it is neither an original, a copy, a plenitude, nor the part for the whole, but connected parallels that take meaningfulness forward, and differently. Like an echo, it depends on the noise that makes it, but is no less a presence that resounds, reverberates, distorts, mocks or amplifies.[24] Allusion therefore extrapolates beyond its attribution to create 'a new entity greater than any of its constituent parts'.[25] Thus, if allusion as shorthand frequently overlaps with proper nouns, it does not designate ties to individual ownership. An allusion, for example, to *Don Quixote*, as its adjectival reformulation 'quixotic' indicates, distances yet re-energizes the reach of Cervantes's work, whether by re-embodiment in another cultural frame or by parodic reinvestment. Allusion therefore is animation by launching and passing on, not taking and plundering.[26] Its energy is towards a collective spatio-temporal elsewhere within and outside its origin or heritage.[27]

As complex illustrations, quotation and allusion are less about fixing image within image (*mise en abyme*),[28] or about layering like enamelling, and more about dynamic reconcentration of cultural meaningfulness. As non-identical twins, they filter and infiltrate more complex cultural patterns to recirculate ideas. While quotation and allusion are tied to no genre in particular, the crucial distinction remains that quotation can self-refer, and even make a larger form of itself, as the cento for example.[29] Allusion on the other hand cannot self-allude – grammar covers this in conjugation of verbs – yet its position as always at one remove from its referent is no less freighted: it suffuses and extends meaning by alliance.[30] So how then does allusion become a 'new entity greater than'? Does it have a form, or is it outside form and genre altogether? Is it enough to say, as Allan Pasco has insightfully suggested, that allusion is what it is not?

> Plagiarism [. . .] does not satisfy the requirements of allusion [. . .] Nor is acknowledged paraphrase allusion. In paraphrase, the attempt is to remain faithful to the meat of the source, while rendering it in a somewhat different way. It involves stylistic changes. [. . .] Parody differs in that its two or more terms are different, the one constantly holding the other up to ridicule and judgment [. . .] Metaphoric integration is violently resisted. Source, as well, falls outside the real of allusion. Although a source may be turned into an allusion, in itself it does not suggest the combination with another image (or text) that will permit the metaphorical relationship. The source is merely the material of which the fiction is created. [. . .] Allegory [. . .] also resists integration of the two terms. [. . .] Nor does allusion fall into the category of models. [. . .] References, on the other hand, normally do expand the text into something more, and thus have the potential for use in constructing allusion.[31]

Consideration of quotation and allusion in extended form will now rediscover something of their dual part in generic enhancement itself. Is allusion, beyond what Pasco suggests here as also not parable, some 'not-as-yet genre' that postmodern conflation of genres counterfeits?

Quotation's aptness: adeptness in other words

If equating quotation with fusion and allusion with fission divorces understanding of them both as concentrates of reference-marking and -making, the same applies to imagining their extended forms. A pre-type-set mentality of quotation as 'quoth' recalls recitation not as verbatim repetition, but as creative paraphrase.[32] The use of set formulae, conventions of form and episodic rather than chronological links provides signposts and recognizable shape for speaker and audience. Interpretation, instruction and entertainment were of equal importance:[33] priority of the pleasure of text occurs only with the leisure of a literate readership.[34] In tales, songs, poems, parables, allegories and longer epics, legends, myths and romances, whether oral or chirographic, grafting and crafting therefore go together. Repetitions and clichés are not redundancies, but enable new detail and comment to be apprehended. These familiar and marked shifters operate as abridgements whence the knowledge-base could then extend. Indeed, it was deemed the responsibility of priests, teachers, poets and storytellers to amass, copy and pass on others' words in their own. Plagiarism is therefore an unknown. As with indirect quotation, authority came not from ownership of specific words, but from the status of the teller as wordsmith and the quality and public effect of the delivery of the retelling.

Abridgement as allegory and parable

Clearly, quotation as one-on-one structure of meaning and allusion as reference at one remove are both motors in all extended narrative forms. The mistake would be too readily to classify parable and allegory as forms of allusion, not as extended forms of quotation, since they seem to point beyond. The 'higher' meaning in allegory, however, comes from a carefully constructed hierarchy (of the world or worlds, of social and semantic orders) with a one-on-one correlation of similarity and difference.[35] What 'really' is, and belief that this is so, is authorized by the directive (didactic) narrative viewpoint into which the listener is drawn.[36] While chirographic developments probably enhanced mental visualization sustained at length on two meaning levels, as Ong argues,[37] the analogical must also convince the public ear of the imagination. Allegory, then, shares similar one-on-one meaning structures with the epic, classical tragedy and mystery plays, where the gods are at odds with, yet superior versions of, elite and common humanity. Dronke argues that similar correlations of levels of significance were in operation in the instructive romance: dream visions, the sensual, the wondrous, the scientific, the arcane, delectation in linguistic virtuosity all intimate the supernatural.[38] From allegory's religious and moral functions as homily or apologetics, political allegory in modernity has been equally effective in times of oppressive (hierarchical) regimes to recount the unsaid significance of abstractions from the concrete world of what the hearer already knows.[39]

If much ink has been spilled in distinguishing allegory from parable,[40] religious parable is a tautology, even though its stock, as Ricoeur remarks, is paradoxically and 'radically profane'.[41] In diametrical opposition to allegory and fantastic tales which push meanings to the extraordinary, parable narrates the extra-ordinary as the sublimely ubiquitous. What makes this unpromisingly quotidian matter spiritual, moral and political lies in the coda, the explanation and interpretation of other significance. The teller is the authority of this interpretation, speaking from a standpoint of testamentary experience so that age-old stock turns into new wisdom. It is the fact that Jesus tells and interprets their codas that gives the parables a significance that they might not otherwise have. Parable is therefore a direct extension of self-quotation in its immanent form above. Witnessing and wisdom in the natural and supernatural allow a viewpoint on what the Kingdom of God is 'like'. Again this 'like' is not allusion, but simile and analogy combined self-referentially and transubstantiated. The jolt for the listener is the leap that similarly exists in wisdom's most pithy sayings, proverbs, especially those built round paradoxical axioms such as losing life to find it. If parables are then read together, as Ricoeur suggests, their antithetical intensities all converge as the same 'intersignification': meaning as revelation of the moment is reinterpreted as transfiguring Event.[42] Such conceptual profundities are, however, built on their ultimate paradox. Profound simplicity and refusal of all but the most ordinary subject matter, events and language makes them the acme of non-discriminatory narrative form, accessible, comprehensible, quintessentially popular.

Parable can thus be distinguished from two related forms of extended quotation. The first is story in densely symbolic or hermetic language, exceeding even metaphysical poetry. If this is epitomized in the Revelation of St John, it occurs also in founding myths, and in shamanistic narrative induced by drugs, fasting and repetitive chants, drumming or dance. Testament is again the over-riding viewpoint and arbiter of the meanings of the experience or trip. The second form combines the stuff of moral tales or fables with a particularized religious-ethical setting akin to parable, the Jewish *mashal*. The *mashal lemelekh*, or king parable, is its most conventional form. Meshalim often form a single collection, anthropomorphizing various attributes of God, the community of Israel, the covenant.[43] Like literary-rhetorical narratives such as fable and moral tales, they are designed to persuade the audience of certain truths which it must grasp for itself as it perceives the ulterior message. Unlike the case of fable or parable, these truths are contained within an external monotheistic theological frame, and the didactic purpose is also bounded by the teachings of Jewish Law.[44] Contrary to expectation, this does not close down meaning, but releases reinterpretations, not least because the 'explanation' of mashal is a matching narrative, the *nimshal*. By embedding the 'moral' in a further narrative rather than a one-liner, epiphany or epimythium, the insufficiencies of these kinds of saturated meaning statements are revealed.[45] The teller or implied interpreter in each part of the story is not the ultimate authority of its interpretation (as against New Testament parable), but the authorizer of interpretations created endlessly by suggestive links (as opposed to gaps) in the interconnecting narratives. The practice of mashal-nimshal narrative provokes in miniature the same results as the tradition of Jewish midrash and biblical exegesis more widely, as homily and instruction for apologetic or exhortative ends.

Unlike written aggadah or halakhah (both amplificatory forms of biblical exegesis), the mashal, like parable, requires no specialist scholarly expertise or language of its audience.[46] It is transparent and exoteric in its plain use of words. These do not, however, hide the tenor of end things, consequences or ultimate choice regarding eternal life, as Shahrazad similarly discovered for her ephemeral survival.[47] Not to tell on is to die.

Bridging as cycle and cyclification

If abridgement and miniaturizing further condense the import of quotation's extended narrative forms to guarantee onward survival by recasting, this energy pertains equally to the form itself. Collections, cycles and cyclification of songs, parables, fables, tales, poems greatly increase their 'intersignification', as Ricoeur termed it, but also assure a formal longevity through recognizable pattern and its adaptability. Serialization as a later variant more closely linked to print, film or other taped media shares much of the formulaic, yet revivifying, nature of older oral forms. In what Ong calls secondary orality,[48] radio and television soap operas are modern descendants of the epic and romance, with their success or failure as dependent on audience appeal and how 'relevant' issues can be integrated, adapted and arranged to fit audience expectation.[49] It is therefore only when collections of a form have become so familiar and ingrained in their cultures that the main constituents and parameters, such as key narrative formulae, integral meanings, stock characters, can be mocked or parodied for comic or critical effect. Parody and meta-commentary of the generic form of telling itself comes even later, but replicates the process of necessary generic stability and adaptation, but as shrinkage: the baggage that would determine obsolescence needs to be discarded as a sloughed-off skin so that renewal can begin afresh.[50]

Cyclification is therefore the crucial turning or bridging point of cultural forms, for it marks the apotheosis of adaptation and adeptness concerning a genre's quota of (quotable) elements, its form as generic receptacle, and the synthesis of two seemingly contradictory energies, expansion by reduction and extension by transformation. As Besamusca et al. note:

> The development of narrative cycles is a characteristic aspect of medieval literature. A cycle can be the end product of a gradual process of expansion as a result of which an original tale or romance is preceded by stories telling of previous events, or continued by

sequels or continuations treating later developments. It can also be the product or a compiler who arranges or combines existing works into a comprehensive structure. A cycle is distinguishable from a mere collection of works by the fact that events are presented in a linear sequence, that the principal characters throughout the cycle are identical or related to each other, and that the cohesion between the constituent works is made clear by external or internal references.[51]

While the emphasis here is on the greater potential for plot, sub-plot and character development as diachronic progression, the oral undertow continues to draw out processes of synchronic recycling such as digression and recapitulation.[52] Undertow currents emerge not only in internal narrative returns or recuperations, or agglomerative synthesis of the works of a number of often anonymous authors, but also in *contrefacture*, the reworking in prose of verse cycles.[53] For Vinaver, the rise and insertion of vernacular romance into epic or chivalric verse narratives marks a division of narrative forms and romance's novelty.[54] Expansion by incorporation seems, however, more in keeping with the rhythms of narrative cycle itself. As cycle of cycles, the romance is then protogeneric or, as Douglas Kelly argues, 'does not know genre'.[55] It is then unsurprising that Kristeva holds up the novel as exemplar of inter*text*uality, but by incorporating Bakhtin's intersubjective (oral) slant on it, as apotheosis of *polyphonic* and *dialogic* form. Medievalists will emphasize what should now be obvious, that the romance foreshadows the novel as inter-generic or 'supergenre' in both its modern and post-postmodern forms: 'Our modern novel corresponds to our present, very limited range, while the thirteenth-century cyclic novel leaves us far behind [. . .] It is not a question of bulk or length, but of arrangement.'[56] With its interlinkings of previously separate texts and their genres, hypertext in various media including the aural is again only following the formal precedent of the richly agglomerative oral and textual romance.

Recollection and recycling in its pre-modern sense illustrate the double energy of attractions and counter-propulsions, without these necessarily resulting in parody. With syntheses and agglomerations of romance come reversals and contrary offshoots, which may in turn spawn another form. From the romance containing elements of chronological story as history (legend), and topoi with nationally recognizable resonance (epic), came the release of prose chronicle combining these overtly and more substantially.[57] Again audience response was vital to stabilize the new form. Rising interest in history corresponded to a period when various cultures were exploring vernacular modes of expression and self-expression outside 'authorities' of the classics or the Bible. Cyclification thus defines harmonization on the one hand with potential for disaggregation on the other. As Hebrew mashal cycles and their wider midrashic tradition clarify, cyclification may restructure oppositional movements as a double helix – pulling out one loop links it more firmly with the others in the strand – or as further amplification of the one authority under-girding all their forms. All varieties of this inter-narrative are then endlessly secured, unless the whole is drowned out by radically other authorities. In the West, reformation in both its upper- and lower-case meaning upholds patterns of burgeoning generated by separa-tion and subdivision of authority (of Scripture, of the classics) as plural. Quotation's tacit marking of belief or unbelief systems thus remains the underlying authorization that will determine how cul-tural productions are sustained, maintained and renewed within a heritage. It is to the constant modes of this authorization that quotation's abridgements and cyclical bridging return, the span of its operations.

Span and interpretation

In all its manifestations and extensions, quotation supplies the autho-rization and interpretation of its two conjoined sites, the source text on the one hand and its ensuing reformulations within and contrary to its aegis on the other.

> History and literature as discourse are *always* being questioned in the Middle Ages; they are always *at stake*. Their status is not yet a given, especially in the vernacular, but is continually being called into ques-tion by the existence of authoritative models, both classical and scrip-tural. But at the same time, these authoritative pretexts *authorize* as well as contest their emergent epigones.[58]

This summary of medieval authority structures, which appears to inform Western (patriarchal) cultural models and rebellions against them, such as in Romanticism, deconstruction and feminism, has another heritage, interpretation as process between any 'authority' and its reformulation. Rather than regarding authority as a mono-lithic and monumental given (the items inside the speech marks), quotation's span as 'motte and bailey' offers a more dynamic model of authority's exchanges and interchanges. The third part of the chapter will return to specifically interlingual dimensions of this arrangement. For now, two vital elements of this dynamically autho-rizing span need to be elucidated. To recall the metaphor of the sus-pension bridge, its strength and flexibility come with the substance

of the twinning and twining of its steel cables. In this light, authority understood as medieval and post-modern can be revised: as
Minnis avers, *auctoritas* was 'a quotation or an extract from the work
of an *auctor* [. . .] a profound saying worthy of imitation or implementation'.[59] In the abstract sense *auctoritas* is the span of veracity
as sagacity, authenticity and authentication of proofs.

As twin cable with imaginative narrative forms, the exegetic
tradition often associated with medieval scholasticism offers similar
cultural fuel in gloss and commentary.[60] Chapter 1 investigated the
rich tradition of oral criticism, critique and scroll-based records, and
collections produced *summa* texts (as the *Deipnosophistae*). *Codices* in
the medieval period, or the more ancient Hebrew Scriptures (the Old
Testament) and rich tradition of exegesis, including midrash
(halakhot and aggadot),[61] operate the same span of interpretative
strategies aimed at searching out truth.[62] The surprising openness
shared by Hebrew, Greek and medieval Christian exegesis and commentary is perhaps exemplified by Hebrew scholarship. As Fishbane
explains, interpretation of scriptural meaning is fourfold: it combines
plain sense, hermeneutical context (ideological and social), discovery of new symbolic and hidden meanings and uncovering of
transcendent dimensions.[63] To arrive at this multidisciplinary
understanding, which includes 'poetic' appreciation of harmonies of
the language itself, the sediments of prior understandings had to be
'sifted, blended, and refocused, and countless teachings were scrutinized, supplemented, and winnowed.'[64] Clearly, no single, or earlier,
'authority' could pertain.[65] Conflicting or unresolved arguments
between interpretations would obviously emerge, but this was the
spur to a further text, or to lateral thinking.[66] It was therefore to the
interpretative authority of the tradition of 'the talent of individual
interpreters, but without "the individual talent", without, that is,
myths of private genius', that the scholar returned.[67] Constant recir-
culation and reintegration of written and oral reinterpretation thus
offers a richly unfinished, accumulative, multiple and transformational 'knowledge bank' in all exegetical traditions. Furthermore,
because retelling works from and through the already known in
tradition, the anticipatory character of exegesis is also ethical: it con-
strains action as the present of interpretation.[68] If Hebrew exegesis
knows no divisions in its authority, and Western authority is plural
in splitting law, theology, philosophy and science, the spirit of inquiry
and interpretation remains the same.

As constantly open to question, exegesis would seem to be the
most synthetic form of interpretation, and inclusive of rewritings of
history and literature that were seen to be 'at stake' above. Yet the
steel wires of all exegetical traditions that would bridge science and

the immanent, commentary and narrative, rule with a rod of very exclusive measure or span. This has no bearing on the texts or the interpretative strategies themselves, sacred or secular. Whether in Hebrew, Greek, Latin or Chinese, the fact that recording and retransmitting occurs only in a specialist *written* form of the language made all exegesis available only to an elite, educated and privileged few. This limitation of access was more usually gender- than class-based. If history and literature in the vernacular are awaiting fuller authorization in medieval times, is this because these variants are largely the preserve of male writers, or because superlative female 'pensmanship' in the period is complicating their acceptability? Much feminist re-reading of medieval works has not only indicated the importance of the *lais* of Marie de France, but also rediscovered other 'anonymous' but highly educated women writers. Exegesis may then have flourished because the intricate weavings of another similarly combinatory and oral-based interpretative forms were forced underground. The evolutionary and revolutionary missing links in vernacular cultural heritage, its tellers and its transmissions are no less abridgements, bridging and span, but may have used stepping stones at the same crossing places. Accepted critical verities about the so-called feminization of certain prose forms therefore need serious revision, as do accounts of culture and criticism, which only go by the official channels.[69] Feminist research of various hues has sought 'text mothers', for example, to redress the balance, but this may prove a less fruitful avenue than a search for 'song mothers'.[70] Given that rhapsody as *Urversion* of intertextuality means to stitch songs together,[71] African feminist work has made a head start for such recuperations. 'African feminist literature has a spiritual and physical mothercenter Motherhood as "membrance" [. . .] It is a theme that not only asserts the ability to create life, but a principle that emerges as central to feminine *potentia* in religion, politics, economics and social spheres.'[72] These spheres were not necessarily the marketplace, although in many civilizations it is women not men who barter and sell, but 'domestic' arts of herbalism and healing, recipes and potions, stitching and quilting. Against Hebrew aggadah as 'lore' (story as opposed to the Law), 'lore' in its often pejorative Western sense of 'old wives tales' shares much with other, 'secret' wisdom traditions, the 'unofficial' oral cultures which were ruthlessly censored by officialdom and its writings. Jazz and blues, hip-hop or Lurian Kabbalah, as chapter 2 uncovered, are all other voices of creative criticism, understanding and story that speak of gender and racial oppression and ways of encountering it, by countercultures.[73]

If medieval scholasticism is not an altogether unique intellectual movement, are there elements that mark it off from both antecedents and successors? Commentary and gloss, although not new, find a flowering that proved unprecedented in various inter-related ways. The first was the understanding of both of these procedures as *illumination* in substance and medium. Where paraphrase and annotation frequently appeared in interlinear or marginal reworkings on the manuscript or scroll itself, so that such 'marginalia' then found incorporation within the main body of the recopied and retransmitted manuscript, illuminated lettering in the most precious works had a similar decentring and recentring role. Illuminations were the analogous 'colours' – of composition, of rhetoric, of nature – self-contained yet also potentially allegorical, denoting the order of micro- and macrocosm held together by the word. Both word and image harmonized viewpoint (literal and figural) to emphasize balance of the tensions of orthodoxy, inherited wisdom and ongoing exegesis of the text in question, especially if it was the Bible. Composition as illuminated manuscript synthesized and transfigured the best of oral (gloss) and chirographic (commentary) forms to show the intertwining convolutions of episode and detail, moment and eternity.[74] To be an *illuminator* meant that one was no mere copyist, *glossator*, *compilator* or commentator, but a co-recreator in the world of the Book and of nature.[75] An illuminated letter might then be compared to the interlace of the romance genre of the period.[76] Illumination can be seen also as a cameo of medieval understanding of the power of the letter and the word in a higher scheme of things tied together. Papal encyclicals, letters at their most authoritative on worldly and otherworldly matters, circulate as the matching 'serious' form of cyclification. The arts of the letter, calligraphy and manuscript illumination, would come under serious threat with the advent of the letter forme or printing press. Only then would the borrowings, reworkings and enhancements that manuscript took for granted as its very substance become the problem of intertextuality.

The period of flowering of medieval commentary also coincides exactly with the founding of universities, and a curriculum in which commentary techniques applied to sacred and secular texts played a central role. Scholasticism and humanism fed off one another, often positively.[77] In this is a second distinction from schools like those in Alexandria in the third century AD where, if Greek was the scholarly script, its living, oral, dimensions percolated much more substantially into the arts of discoursing and debating. As fossil of oral heritage, Latin was primarily the written tongue of the medieval schools, making it more remote and abstract. As Ong notes, 'Modern science grew in Latin soil, for philosophers and scientists through the time of Sir Isaac Newton commonly wrote and did their abstract thinking in Latin.'[78] Thus, the arts of abstraction as *scientia* in all domains could be taken to new limits. The enormous range of past authorities could be epitomized, collected and reorganized to produce an amalgam (*compilatio*) that was highly codified. Recycling, the narrative cycle, encyclicals were all part of an encyclopaedic movement, although it was not to be named as such, which predates the great secular efforts of Chambers and Diderot in the Enlightenment. 'Medieval ideas [derive] principally from the commonplace attempt to gather strands of learning together into an enormous Text, an encyclopaedia or summa, that would mirror the historical and transcendental orders just as the Book of God's Word (the Bible) was a speculum of the Book of his Work (nature).'[79] The specimen text was a similar 'pattern-book', but on the art of poetic composition from which specifics could be extrapolated from models.[80] Given that only God could create – the paradigm *opus* was both Nature and the Great Book – medieval scholars and writers, like their Hebrew midrashic counterparts, were free not only of 'the anxiety of influence' but, more importantly, of the anxiety of authority.[81]

Latin gave a further freedom, however. Both scriptural and non-scriptural works in their divergences could be merged and harmonized through allegory, literalization or moralization. As with cyclification, which energized chronicle to spin off from it, this inclusive Latinate *summa* would cast off increasingly secularized elements from its epicentre. Astronomy and science would diverge from theology, while the gathering empowerment of romance vernaculars would slough off Latin authorization (the Bible and the classics) for its poetics. In due course, the micro-macrocosmic medieval worldview of man and earth as centre of a concentric God-ordained universe would be challenged and changed forever by Galileo and Dante respectively.[82] Since its split with Eastern Orthodoxy, the Catholic Church by the Middle Ages, like the *summa* and cyclification, embodied comprehension and comprehensiveness. It would be forced to discover its lower-case significance as the next generation, the Reformation, challenged its very authority, sole interpretation of the Book.

Medieval scholarship was therefore already intensely aware that many paths led to a fuller understanding of Scripture as authority on matters of faith and conduct, and hence that exegesis was itself made problematic by its parts. One key problem was establishing 'the Text', what constituted 'the Bible' and which were the books of the *Apocrypha*. This major issue aside, interpretations of the Authorized Version in the Middle Ages were as ideological as they were theological.[83] The various exegetical and critical interconnections between words and the Word central to medieval debate and later secular reappraisals of canonicity and authority would continue, however veiled. Postmodernism, especially by its use of the word 'text', can find no other for omni-definitional 'authority'.[84] Rather than recast the debates between secular and scriptural word here, it is medieval appreciation distinguished as *sui generis* that is relevant, and in ways which reinscribe previous discussion. If the medieval populace was denied direct access to the Book, although it was read aloud and oral exegesis ensued, the barriers of Latin were overcome by the compositional *opus* in stone before their eyes. The great cathedral-building movements across Latin Europe in the Middle Ages have never been rivalled. They brought together the manual skills of scholars (copyist and illuminator) and artisans (the master stone mason and carpenter, goldsmith and silversmith), but to transcend craftsmanship or its collaborative orchestration. Gargoyle and angel co-existed with flying buttress and fan vaulting, choir stall and monstrance in one edifice to bring together the disparate as harmony. As feat of engineering, the cathedral exemplifies in stone what the work of quotation operates in exegesis: precision, strength and the all-important balance of the harmonizing span as figure of what the true *oeuvre* (opus) should aspire to. Proust was unerring in his choice of the cathedral as metaphor for the acme of composition.[85] Harmony is the opposite of the uniform.

As abridgment and span, bridging and cathedral, quotation in its short and extended forms seems to have ousted allusion completely. Yet allusions in more extended literary and cultural forms turn up in the many key genres of quotation already visited, not as re-enactment centre stage, but as all-important *voice off* from the wings. A brief collection of some samples will allow assessment of their potential as future cultural generators for post-postmodernism. Not unsurprisingly, their manifestations are central in complex oral genres.

One of the clearest examples is provided by drama and essential in ancient Greek, Classical French or Shakespearian tragedy, among others, the *peripeteia*. Without this hiatus in the momentum in the plot, without this 'reversal' of action, the dénouement would not have its full impact.[86] Usually in the fourth act, *peripeteia* plays on the unexpected within the expected, and with suspense and suspension, in ways which connections between sub-plot and main plot do not. Micawber-like, recoil enables some future action. Allusion to the past proves a constant dynamic for the present or future, even though it will not be *exact* outworking or replication of the previously known.

A second example is *petihta*, a vital component in Hebrew midrash. The *petihta* or proem is not the connection between two previously unconnected verses, but the enabling of an opening of meaning previously unavailable in either.[87] An analogy might be the crossing of the Red Sea, which opened before the Israelites where there seemed no escape route from their advancing enemies. Contrary to the *peripeteia*, this interim passage appears near the beginning of a text, energizing substantive new interpretative movement on materials that may already be well known. Thus allusion is akin to the place of revelation, the white space awaiting fuller meaning, which will have vast implications when opened to the known. Cohen does not name *petihta* as such, but has likened this opening space to the peristyle of a palace.[88] Greek tragedies site the tensions of the ensuing drama in exactly such interconnecting architectural spaces.

Allusion as almost end or almost beginning can be both at the one time, as demonstrated by medieval romance. We saw how this form incorporated the climaxing of mature cycles while, simultaneously, providing a spawning ground for new and as yet untried formulations. *Conjointure* names this interim place where caterpiller is pupa but not yet butterfly. Vinaver attests to Chrétien de Troye's innovative use of *conjointure*, its coinage and etymology: '*Conjoindre* meant "to link", "to make a whole out of several parts". The noun formed from this verb would presumably mean "a whole made out of several parts" or simply "arrangement".'[89] Where *petihta* determined a new passageway through old understanding, *conjointure* stresses compositional innovation determined by fully wrought materials. At its maximum extension, *conjointure* is even a 'bridge work' in the medieval *opus*, in the space between sophisticated Latin and vernacular composition.[90] It is a short step from this to the importance of vernacular translation, to be discussed in the following part of the chapter. Like an allusion to a fictional proper name, *peripeteia*, *petihta* and *conjointure* find new conceptual avenues of *lateral* thinking: contiguity or sidestep, not least in parallel vernacular tongue, is almost more important than continuity.[91] Is it then an accident that all three are embedded in some of the most long-lived forms of oral transmission? This has at least two implications. The first is that similar oral 'bridge work' may indeed galvanize postmodernity. Should 'mixed' sub-genres of the novel including autobiography then be understood less as hybrids than as contingencies?[92] The second implication is hope for cultural production after the wake of postmodernity's 'crypts', its nihilist aporias and textual crazy pavements, or desacralization of the artwork by electronic automation of text as story of the 'fetishization of technology'.[93] Quotation may transubstantiate, but allusion is no less powerful as *voice off* and enabling as pass-over.

Quotation as extraction: recirculation and exchanges in so many other words

Although he is now rarely cited by critical theorists, McLuhan's 'medium is the message' resonates through postmodern culture, with its unprecedented development of advertising and visual media – photography, film, television, computer screens, video – constantly bombarding the viewer with image and text.[94] In the 1960s and early 1970s McLuhan's concern was with the unrelenting legacy of the 'Gutenberg Galaxy', exponential massification of image culture, on the one hand, and the deeper thrall of maintaining the illusion with ever more inventiveness, on the other. The previous chapter investigated the increased speed and pictal precision of the copy as mimesis taken to new limits, while the first chapter demonstrated that hypermedia plethora, user or viewer choice and control of links, as well as the on-off button, were far from free. If news broadcasting provides the paradigm of postmodern tenets – immediacy, the latest information, omni-available access to global village reality within seconds of major catastrophe, disaster or triumph – its sanitized distancing, desensitization and repackaging of the shocks of real experience as if they were virtual reality are no less designed. The audience is arrested, but only inactively, to suppress the real shock of reaction and maintain dependency on the medium and its transmission of messages. Electronic news transmission and its newscasters are then no different from their precursor human media, the shaman or seer, before their captive audiences, tellers of reports from another world. Formulae to make the words acceptable, authentic and recognizable as announcement overlay the hidden 'script'. As inscrutable as the oracles or gods of old is the actual knowledge source behind the talking head. What is broadcast is taken largely as read.

If such deliberate comparison shocks, such a strongly reactive mode is one of art's methods to uncover gullibility and inertia, provoke response and self-criticism, or enable profound relief and thanksgiving. The adoption of human metaphor for mediums of cultural transmission in what follows will develop the transporting but 'engineered' concepts above of span, bridge and intermediary passage to review the anodyne 'media' of the electronic age. Shock of itself cannot be superficial or virtual, except as secondary effect. Immediate and often physiological expression, it precedes language rather than being measured cerebral-linguistic response. It excites, agitates, appals, disgusts, nauseates, numbs, consternates, stupefies, traumatizes, upsets, prostrates, distresses, stuns, paralyzes. Outrage and exuberant rejoicing are its public manifestations. Quotation as the very sinews or tendons of cultural re-embodiment will be seen to be such a locus of irrevocable transformation of cultural viewpoint in two hidden but highly developed and specialized forms. It is prophecy and translation, often confused as word-for-word utterances, and words as much as persons that allow cultural agency for change to be rethought.

Prophecy

Theology, let alone linguistics, rarely acknowledges the special nature of prophecy. Prophetic pronouncement is usually understood as words in 'meta-quotation marks', so that prophets, mediums, oracles, griots and soothsayers are seen interchangeably as conduits to supernatural sources, intermediaries enacting or transmigrating other forms such as shamans and Hindu avatars, or purveyors of messages about future events. The affirmation and fulfilment of the message constitutes the test of any medium's powers and the public validation of their function.[95] To be a prophet, then, is to have a particular command of imperative, the authority to pronounce, tell, warn, encourage or rebuke. Occasionally poets or philosophers pass muster as such inspired or special imparters of cultural woe or sublime expression. Marx, Nietzsche, Freud and Romantic poets have all been cast as secular prophets or seers.[96] It is the special state and status of the medium, whether through trance, dreams, trips (via drugs, dance or drumming) or possession and inspiration by a Muse,[97] a demon or nature, that distinguishes from commoners figures such as shamans, oracles, witches, the possessed, followers of mystery cults, or poets. Consequently, their messages as mediums are in distinctive, imagistic and esoteric language, ranging from babble to sublime poetry.

If the prophet is no less an intermediary, this function is quite distinct from those of the medium on several counts. As with oral storytelling, prophetic pronouncement is not necessarily verbatim or passive channel of recitation. In Old Testament accounts, for example, a figural enactment often accompanied the words. Prophets had to sit in holes, grow beards, buy fields, to demonstrate and illustrate the verbal message bodily. They also played on the etymology or etiology of names in an ultra-serious punning to bring out the import of words. Such prophetic 'translation' thus leaves considerable scope for recognizably personalized transmission – the words or acts of Ezekiel cannot be confused with those of Isaiah – but both embody timeless prophetic conventions. These are less authorizing forms of words such as 'Thus sayeth the Lord' than acts of profound and freely chosen obedience, service and faithfulness to the delivery of the message to its stipulated audience.

Contrary to the words of an oracle, clairvoyant or poet, the prophet's message is rarely in code, but maximizes ordinary language. As extremely plain speaking, the message often addresses extreme situations, to restore with words of reminder or remembrance as much as of rebuke or exhortation. The transgressive in the prophetic word is therefore its intensely arresting, logical, yet transcendent shock-value, to jolt from world-orientated complacency, self-absorption or waywardness. Even if it contains hope, message and messenger will thus rarely be popular with their audience. Indeed, the directness of the message constitutes endorsement of its contents and the person of the messenger, but consequently makes the bearer often an offence to the receivers. An indicator between true and false prophet is that the latter will usually invoke what the audience wishes to hear, to pacify, mollify or soothe by offering superficial optimism or a state of affairs that remains very much unchanged.[98]

Such reporters of the status quo, as prophets of rebellion, are very different from prophet-envoys who might prefer not to have been publicly appointed.[99] The modern prophet is, however, self-styled, speaking reinterpretation as dissent and in 'unacceptable' modes against official authorities or art forms.[100] In short, mediums and self-styled 'prophets' may be interpreters of messages as much as their transmitters, and thus re-enactments of Hermes' various functions, not least the 'patron of hermeneutics [. . .] numen of boundaries, an agent of monetary exchange, and even a frequent visitor to the netherworld of the dead'.[101] On the contrary, the prophet of reluctance is a very human messenger elect, not an interpreter or ecstatic,[102] with a message of such severity that the prophet trembles before it, as the medieval exegete or translator before the Bible. Service to the Word and to the authority of the Word as appointed and anointed office likens the prophet to the preacher, spokesman or intercessor.[103] Delivery is the prophet's all-consuming and lifelong task and may even lead to death.[104] Bad reception is then almost guaranteed, because the interpretation and implementation of the message lie with the recipients, not the messenger.

If soothsayers or augurs claim direct grasp of future events, prophets convey future consequences. Prophets are only visionaries by first being intimately aware of the past and redeeming present of faith in an unchanging God who could translate circumstance beyond the present moment of crisis. Like shock, this hope is another subversive facet of prophecy. It refuses to take the present as reality, as the best there is, but seeks real change for the future. Thus, the prophet stands in the gap between message and deliverance. Through embodying painful waiting, isolation or struggling obedience as they rail with God and against a 'stiff-necked' people, prophets enact future implications for the recipients if they remain stubborn and deaf to the message for change.[105] This embodied verbal presence and revelation of hope, like *petihta*, enters into time and space in a crisis gap in history. Prophecy is then the enactment not of direct quotation, but of allusion as interim passage, as *conjointure*, as the call in the literal or figurative wilderness at one step removed from the living God and the values of the metropolis.[106]

Like oral forms of narration, mediums have not been made defunct, but return via electronic media as weather forecasting, newscasting, sports and economic predictions. Email and mobile phone text-messaging are but the most recent manifestations of oral or written message and messenger system. In spite of its global advances and speed in delivery time, it shares all the same old problems of interference and unfailsafe reception. Neither is the work of Old and New Testament prophets among the people and *extra muros* finished to speak radical reform to the roots of injustice – 'radix' is a root – in shocking, polemical, even ludicrous ways.[107] Radical reformers know that the power and authority of temple, palace, city, law court, university or bank and their orderlies that block change and renewal for the poor, uneducated, downtrodden or rejected can be overturned only by open letter, petition or pamphlet. These reprises of the oral forms of prophecy find the same groundswells of agency, determination and self-determination as also the misunderstandings and rejections of communication in the gap of understanding. We have just forgotten that the ear is the best test of words for their veracity and appropriateness, and the measure of their worth to be translated into actions.

Prophecy, therefore, stirs profound reactions from the depths of acculturated norms and their recorded, fixed ('stiff-necked') forms. It can be tested only by the transformations that take place and their duration. Prophecy as subcutaneous articulation will always ultimately (*contra* Derrida) defy print or any fixed *medium* of communication. Where prophecy as meta-quotation ceases is the point of translation's intra- and interlingual gain. It is only here that faithful rendition in other words can begin. The translator takes on something of the mantle of the prophet by attempting to be faithful to the spirit and the letter, whereas the plagiarist is the false prophet's successor, operating under a borrowed cloak of others' words verbatim, until defrocked.

Translation

The subject of translation returns us full circle to the first chapter. Kristeva's use of the metaphor of translation made intertextuality a translingual connection in a number of ways. Yet, for want of translators, *Semeiotikè* has rarely been studied in its entirety, unlike the *corpora* of Barthes or Derrida, whose extensive reception has in no small part been due to translation. Translation raises exactly those difficult questions that fuelled the debates in all the previous chapters. What happens, for example, to *meaning* when texts are reworded intra- or interlingually (intertextuality)? How does one negotiate *intention*, which, while blatant in satires, comedies or caricatures, may be inherent in all utterance (influence)? Should the target text be an exact copy or improvisation of the source text (imitation) and, if so, how can *faithfulness* or *appropriateness* of the copy be measured? And why, finally, has translation been so maligned when compared to creative writing or, more crucially, criticism? Can the ostracizing of the prophet reveal something about what or whom current critical theories would keep outside their academy?

The introductory survey of recent studies and readers on intertextuality found a striking monolingualism and dependency on translations.[108] None mentions translation itself as intertextual generator.[109] There is also overt critical inattention to the early Barthes and Derrida, whose first undertakings were as translators. Their over-riding concern to oust authorship and signature passes off any near plagiarisms with the notion that language is completely public property, particularly in print. 'Text' as generic of all cultural productions thus conveniently slides translation into the folds of target language output. The translator who enables increase of any monolingual cultural wordbank is inexistent or too menial (and hence without 'intention'), or as amanuensis too 'feminized' (in a Lacanian view of language). As Derrida undoubtedly discovered, translations do not spontaneously combust, or emerge at the touch of a button, whatever machine translation would claim to the contrary. However hidden, the translator is a human agent, the embodiment of the interim passage of text, whether from older to modern form of the same language or from one language to another.[110] Without persons, languages and texts remain dead. 'Dead' or living languages can ever be resuscitated and rearticulated through retranslation, for rewording instils new life.

The translator is therefore strategic in the transmission and transformation processes of cultural development and change for both source and target language. As first expositors, translators, like their medieval exegete predecessors, play an intrinsic role as commentators. As articulators of current usage of source and target languages, translators also stand in the gap of past and future expression as active intermediary. Like that of the prophet proper, this place allows a personal stamp to be put on what is communicated because the constraints on the words to be translated, the target audience or the pliability or not of the target language need particularizing mediations. Re-presentation via the body of the translator is not clone copy, but revivification in other, now very different, words to enrich meaning and expression. Latin and its literature might never have been so rich had not Greek language and culture forced out its ingenuities of expression.[111] Similarly, the classics provided a platform turned springboard for vernaculars to find their own levels and heights. While writers performed such rewriting by imitating canonical works, translators were as vital in the process of circulating works from outside known frames, thus enlarging the cultural stock. How different might the development of prose forms have been without Antoine Galland's translation three centuries ago of *The Thousand and One Nights*?

The reshaping of any utterance occurs not only in a semiotic dimension between signs and discursive systems (intertextuality). Sign systems are always prefaced by oral, face-to-face communication, which is what Ricoeur calls not 'parole', but discourse.[112]

> [D]iscourse is *the* event of language [. . .] An act of discourse is not merely transitory and vanishing, however. It may be identified and reidentified as the same so that we may say it again or in other words. We may even say it in another language or translate it from one language into another. Through all these transformations it preserves an identity of its own which can be called the propositional content, the 'said as such.'[113]

As George Steiner has remarked, 'The theory of translation is not, therefore, an applied linguistics.'[114] Translation insists on the semantic, on comprehension as the most basic kind of word processing between interlocutors. For the translator, a semiotic method (word-for-word or sentence-by-sentence correlations within systems) will not take the source language very far for the non-speaker. Much larger and more nebulous 'units' than word strings governed by recognizable rules determine any meaning cluster, whether conversation or extended metaphor and poetry. The translator's difficult task is to be the perfect interlocutor between such 'unit' combinations of words, grammar, syntax, register, context, speaker intention, addressee expectation, imagery and so on. The medieval exegete

working on Latin translations of the Bible and other classics provides
an exemplar. While representing and serving the source text, interpretation is less important than reworking in one's own words the
sum of what others have said.[115] The interlinear commentary is then
equivalent to word-for-word rephrasing, paraphrasing and adapting
meaning for comprehension, while the connective levels of understanding beyond immediate sense are often like the marginal anno-
tations. A translator, like the exegete, must balance both text and
gloss, but withdraws visible presence in the production of new interpretations. While this dimension becomes the realm of the modern
secular critic, it presupposes stability of the source text to mine it for
meanings. Yet it was not unusual for premodern translation itself to
aerate a text and attain this level of critical interpretation. Renaissance redefinition of the classics was derived through vernacular
translations to 'modernize' them.[116] Our modern obsessions with the
contemporary, novelty, functionality, application or usefulness substantially stem from the Renaissance bid to translate for and into
living idiom. It seems then no accident that scriptural exegesis was
increasingly replaced by a focus on the essayistic spirit,[117] a trying
out of old ideas transplanted into a vernacular (whether as original
quotations, allusions or translation proper) and interlaced in specifically modernizing and self-referential ways.

As Riffaterre realized, to ignore the references in culture, the
'ungrammaticalities' or traces that disrupt smooth reading or translation of words, is to ignore the ways in which text retranslates itself
over time. Where deconstruction and semiotics ground this retranslation in writing, Ricoeur pinpoints what is not translated: 'Writing
may rescue the instance of discourse because what writing actually
does fix is not the event of the speaking, but the "said" of speaking
[. . .] What we write [. . .] is the *noema* of the act of speaking, the
meaning of the speech event, not the event of the event.'[118] If Derrida
circumnavigates this place and non-place variously as *Shibboleth* (day
of circumcision),[119] it is, with Benjamin's Gnostic pessimism, to tear
words (knowingly) out of place and context.[120] Such exclusive refusal
of common and common-sense language is diametrically opposed to
translation's intimate awareness of the varied resources of one's
mother and other tongues as the transforming place for expression
within community.[121] It is of this 'fit between' that the literary translator is especially mindful. As with all language use and cultural
expression, borrowing and remaking in new contexts prevent ossification and obsolescence, on the one hand, and enable rediscovery of
previously concealed elements, on the other. It is the prospect and
challenge that the untranslatable will find expression that keeps language and its translations in all forms constantly exercising and cir-

culating. Proverbs, clichés, dead and living metaphors are then moulds of glibness or creativity, not of themselves, but through reusage, context or intention. Translation is among their most serious reactivation. Paradoxically, where translation is especially challenged is bridging two tongues at their most vernacular and contemporaneous. Simultaneous translation of current slang or jokes is among the most difficult of tasks, for polysemy is at its most unsettled, abstruse or volatile. Successful translation can be tested only in the ear of the other, whether it jars or 'disappears' as if in the (m)other tongue.[122]

In chapters 2 and 3 of this book, authors and texts were seen to be grappling with notions of belatedness in modernity and postmodernity, or questions of authenticity as derivative copy or adaptation. Translation seems the magnification and synthesis of being secondary. Steiner's *After Babel: Aspects of Language and Translation* (1975) was among the first serious attempts to restore its fortunes and provide a history for its Western (both Greek and Jewish) manifestations. Through it and the growing field of literary translation studies thereafter,[123] much of the rich interconnectedness and rejuvenation of individual national cultural heritages is now recognized to be in part the cross-fertilizations between languages and foreign texts in translation. In a number of highly sophisticated ways, literary translation studies revisit comparative literature and influence, gender studies and postcolonial criticism, for 'New worlds are born between the lines' and 'Every different tongue offers its own denial of determinism. "The world", it says, "can be other".'[124] Steiner's choice of Babel as his central metaphor, however, nevertheless traps translation in the double bind of both Western metaphysics and Jewish midrash. Languages are all derivative of an originating *Ursprache* or transcendent tongue scattered by God. Translation is then an attempt to restore the notion of a pristine Edenic unity of language and meaning, interpretation and signification, or make theoretically possible such restitution in a family tree of languages. Translation is always a 'Fall' and, for Steiner, that of Babel is more terrible than that of Eden.[125] Translation studies and theories ever divide over translation as 'loss' or 'gain'.[126] If gains are noted, in the main it is avoidance of loss – semantic, grammatical, phonetic, poetic, metrical, ideological, allusive – that centrally and constantly preoccupies translator and translation. In a word, the task of the translator is viable only because the 'original', like Cordelia, cannot speak again unless 'silence' is granted another living tongue.

Translation need not be the problem of Babel, but rather the problem of plethora. Because of its position always as response, not initial call, it can enjoy some of what we have uncovered as the freedoms of allusion. It can revel in the delimitations of fixity as quotation from its own or another language. Translation, like prophecy, is innately connective and potentially restorative as it is re-creative. It can shatter ideological chains and conceptual structures by harmonizing diversity or drawing deeper upon heterogeneity to refresh wording. Translation is then not a mode (like irony) of the 'translatability' of languages, as Benjamin suggests,[127] or a medium of transmission (semantic, textual or cultural). Rather, its one-step remove (its linguistic creativity) allies it to the freedoms of its target and source languages to experiment, explore, widen and deepen versions of non- and interconnection. Benjamin calls it an echo or reverberation, so that translation remains derivative, always an emptying of the greater sound.[128] Translation, surely, is always as much a *new* voice, where previously there was no voice to make dialogue, or, for the non-speaker, the harmonization into recognizable sound-structures where before there was only cacophony. Any translation of such a place must then be gain, a place for provision within the provisional. It is translation that enhances the lateral mobility of the fixed 'source' to *dismantle* its stiff structures and reveal its still vibrant adaptability. Inevitably, like allusion, it will loose former coherence and unity (like our example above of Don Quixote). The gain is the discovery of unfathomable reverberations of itself in later *translinguistic* transmutations and transformations. It is not only creative reproduction of previous text that emerges as butterfly from its chrysalis. With their prioritization of the enhancement of its own cultural depths by integrating the other, Chinese and Japanese views of translation, often using free adaptation or loose paraphrase, are much closer to this metaphor of transformed articulations than Western views of faithfulness and adherence to the fixities and authority of the source text.[129]

A (psycho-)semiotics of translation (Kristeva, Lacan), hermeneutics of translation (Steiner, Benjamin) or history of translation (Steiner) are then only part of its story. As extension of the intensely connective forms of allusion inherent in every language, translation enlarges the place named by *peripeteia, petihta, conjointure* and even a 'prophetic' verbal standing in the gaps of the present to bring past and future language into being. Among 'those things hidden since the foundation of the world', translations as living language are clearly sensible to the ears long before the eyes. My allusion to Girard's title also revisits the imitative nature of translation of its source text. Semantically, it remains tangentially imitative (connected) but, as expression, it is richly improvisational, even spontaneous in creative ways both dramatic performance and prophecy share, a place of very open interpretation. Prophecy and translation therefore constitute two very different, but equally overlooked and downgraded, forms of cultural renewal. They have been overlooked because they are allegedly at once too deeply or superficially preoccupied with 'creative' language. They have been downgraded because they are outmoded or a mode of linguistic transfer. More to the point which both uncover, they pronounce shock and joy in exuberance (*copia*) which systems of language, ideologies or creeds cannot contain, only control by damage limitation – marginalization, subordination or complete ostracism. These three equate with the cultural position of women in East and West. Unconceivable as a set of fixed language rules, or even intellectual games, both prophecy and translation find strong analogies with revelation and hence offer to past heritage and to post-postmodernity their most ancient and futuristic gift, aurality and the literal.

Coda: the return of reference and the work of Paul Ricoeur

The three main sections of this chapter have put quotation and allusion squarely in the fray of intertextual debate. At the same time, they have recirculated the pivotal issues of previous chapters and their sub-sections. The mappings of this chapter against Genette's quandary of chapter 3 – whether architectural or bodily models offer the best meta-functional description for cultural renewal and mimesis – have taken his many contributions to 'intertextuality' into a number of different dimensions as 'bridging' and 'tendons'. While these have been redirected towards hermeneutics as opposed to semiotics, they recuperate precisely those aspects of *Seuils* (1987) that Genette named as *outside* his study: illustration, serialization (cyclification) and translation. Throughout this chapter, each has in turn supported a sub-section, and also returned intravenous or vital articulations in the cultural body, the holding, supporting and extending qualities of cultural span in its wider history. Less prominently, illustration, serialization and translation have remembered a mainly forgotten audience of culture, the *populus*. As image, episode, vernacular, all three present complex meaning in commonly and immediately understandable linguistic and conceptual form. Postmodernism, for all its so-called levelling of high-cultural forms or mix of popular ones, pursues a highly obfuscating cultural agenda which remains inordinately *text*-based. Witness its often dense and impenetrable *writing* and critical vocabularies, even in translation. Reams of critical gloss have subsequently provided these with a highly sophisticated overmantle, masquerading as explanation.[130] By setting out to overwrite sources, postmodernism and deconstruction by comparison with earlier eras have revealed themselves to be negative forms of scholastic medievalism, and pseudo-Renaissance iconoclasms. By variously construing language as meta-model – primarily as grammar and syntax – these critical theories have only reiterated what rhetoric had staged in pre-modernism.[131] For all its anti-metaphysical cleansing tactics on simile and metonymy, postmodernism's unavoidable dependence on text belies the heuristic 'non-metaphor' it lives by.

Language is at once literal and figurative, and hence intrinsically metaphorical, as living languages demonstrate. Throughout this chapter, quotation and allusion in all their short and extended forms demonstrate that reference and inter-referential transformation through interconnections of text, image and their translations are all very much alive as ways of interpreting the world and words. A key metaphor that will undoubtedly be recorded for the twentieth century in the world history of metaphor (which, as Steiner notes, is yet unwritten)[132] is space. In an epoch marked by the space race, manned and unmanned explorations of outer space, astronomy discovered black holes where deconstruction found aporia. Similarly, 'intertextuality' names the 'shuttle space' between texts in a universe where the outside of the text, as God and authors, is supposedly dead.[133] As Ricoeur pertinently asks, 'Everybody knows the famous saying "God is dead" from *Die fröhliche Wissenschaft*. But which god is dead? Who killed him (since his death is a murder)? And what kind of authority belongs to the word that proclaims his death?'[134] One can seek not to find, as much as to find. As chapter 2 discovered, Bloom and Derrida are key figures of such critical hide and seek in worlds deeply informed by Jewish Kabbalah and midrash respectively.[135] While Derrida, Kristeva, Irigaray and others have found much to say more recently about religion, such subjects are part of their continued disengagement with hermeneutics and noncommunication with theology.[136] Their texts emerge as new variants of unbelief statements about the space of culture as other '-isms' before them, atheism, deism, pantheism, agnosticism, hedonism, cynicism or nihilism. Contrarily, René Girard has testified overtly to finding, but outside philosophy. His anthropological and textual criticism puts faith rather than theology on the critical agenda. He represents the radical other to Bloom's negative theology and Derrida's 'hermeneutics of suspicion' in contents and style.[137] Any embarrassment regarding Girard's foregrounding of faith has nothing to do with his extremely clear and logical style of writing. As with the prophetic, embarrassment and rejection belong with the audience.

Equally contrary to the voluble and visible philosophers associated with post-structuralism and deconstruction, such as Derrida and Foucault, are Hans-Georg Gadamer, Emmanuel Levinas and Paul

Ricoeur, who have more systematically and unobtrusively amassed *oeuvres* which ask of philosophy a hermeneutics of action and an ethics of language outside critical fashion.[138] They also reply to the hegemony of 'text' by returning to the etymology of *oeuvre* in the manner of the medieval *opus* as a window on the *opus* of God:

> Text implies texture, that is complexity of composition. Text also implies work, that is, labour in forming language. Finally, text implies inscription, in a durable monument of language, of an experience to which it bears testimony. By all of these features, the notion of text prepares itself for analogical extension to phenomena not specifically limited to writing, nor even to discourse.[139]

A window is no less a space, but of light, not darkness. It is also the framing medium of sight and insight between outside and inside at once, that dual perspective which translates afresh the medieval micro-macrocosm.[140] From the inside, a panorama is opened out: from the outside an interior is magnified as point. Space and matter together are important, and it is interpretation which distinguishes, explores and combines both viewpoints. Dialogic imagination is then the richer when it actively engages with its other as equal (or, in Levinas's case, 'autrui' as prior), rather than cutting the other out or actively disengaging with otherness as the only way to maintain the self-eye view. As Benjamin has noted wryly, 'There is no muse of philosophy, nor is there one of translation.'[141]

It would principally be with the word 'muse' that hermeneutical critics would disagree, for their framework of engagement is neither as recipients of some direct source of inspiration or knowledge nor as Promethean forgers. Acting as interpreters of complex meanings in various media (languages, forms of representation, authorities), the approach and method of Gadamer, Levinas and Ricoeur is one similar to the translator or medieval and midrashic exegete, with open, highly informed and trained minds before the text. Paul Ricoeur's work and method exemplifies such anciently modern hermeneutics in ways which have much to say to intertextuality, influence, imitation and quotation.[142] So many of Ricoeur's key concerns about narrative and time, metaphor and revelation, interpretation and social discourse provide a final circle round the issues of this chapter and preceding ones. He fittingly provides a culmination point and opening for more general remarks in the conclusion.

Ricoeur has often been found difficult to read, for his method is the slow and careful piecing together of argument and counter-argument as stepping stones. These then take the argument itself to a higher plane so that the central issues can be seen more clearly, and the rethinking process itself can gather energy and speed for its revised resolution. Ricoeur also returns to previous work to develop it at a later point in his own explorative, open and configurative understanding.[143] To follow him is not the mental headache of the equally 'difficult' reading which is tackling the abstruse or abstract in deconstruction. Rather, to understand Ricoeur's method is to see it as similar to the medieval narrative cycle and cyclification. While apparently digressive, it is an ordered marshalling of viewpoints and reprise. The 'logic' or intrigue may be as much episodic as diachronic.[144] Similarly, the obstacles and adversaries along the route are often retrospectively the moments of greatest challenge and change for the central protagonists. In a nutshell, this is how Ricoeur has always dealt with philosophical problems or adversaries. Confronting objection and difficulty to find a way through is a hallmark of his style of philosophy.[145] This may include getting to know the antagonist better.[146] At least two inter-related outcomes result. Listening and waiting, evoking not revoking, become more important than out-thinking and overcoming.[147] This waiting with the other serves the same function as narrative 'gaps' where no explanation is given. Second, impression and identification of appearance can be recognized on reflection as mistaken identity. This is because initial, simplistic or merely oppositional difference gives way to a realization of deeper complexity or similarity. On the level of events, adverse situation serves the same open end. Later narrative revelation and interpretation are therefore closely allied to philosophical illumination through reason.[148] A further parallel between Ricoeur's method of philosophical investigation and medieval narrative cycles becomes apparent. There is a move always from the familiar to the unfamiliar and, because audience reception is crucial throughout, an attempt to clarify if not resolve what is unfolding through familiarization and defamiliarization.[149] Abstraction as we saw in parable is not compromised, but enhanced by ordinary language which is both highly wrought yet moulded for a general public. Thus it is the medieval romance storyteller's expertise, craft and responsibility to material and audience that can be taken as the paradigm for Ricoeur as hermeneutical narrator.

Romance, cycle, tale and parable all point to their microcosmic cousin, metaphor. Neither quotation nor allusion, metaphor is probably among the most used but least understood of tropes. Without doubt, Ricoeur's work on metaphor has clarified and developed the important contributions of Beardsley (1958), Black (1962), McFague (1983) and Soskice (1985). Ricoeur, always cognizant of helpful forerunners, quotes Beardsley: 'Metaphor is a poem in miniature.'[150] To mesh this with Ricoeur's reconfigurations of metaphor throughout his *oeuvre* in order to bring out both the simplicity and complexity of his theorization is the subject of others' books.[151] Rather than provide another gloss, explanation or even alternative metaphor, I would pull out three characteristics which have been central preoccupations of this chapter. Ricoeurian metaphor returns us afresh to that place in language of the one-step remove, to illustration, serialization and vernacular translation, but in their crystallized form.

As icon is a miniature version of the medieval cathedral in its illustrative force as *summa*, metaphor is to the paradigmatic sentence:

> The object of semiotics – the sign – is merely virtual. Only the sentence is actual as the very event of speaking [. . .] The sentence is not a larger or more complex word, it is a new entity [. . .] A sentence is a whole irreducible to the sum of its parts. It is made up of words, but it is not a derivative function of its words. A sentence is made up of signs, but it is not itself a sign.[152]

Predication is focused by the singularity of its subject yet its multiple contexts. Sense occurs at the level of the whole as the parts are being put together. Like 'seeing' a hologram, the two are concomitant. It is the imagination that can hold any apparently jarring nonsense as sense in the making. To speak of the irrational and rational elements of metaphor, or of its play or conflict between literal (absurd) and figural meanings, goes against the spirit of Ricoeur's philosophical method, which is reflective and conceptual at the same time. Illustration connects his views of imagination, language and the real as revealed.

It is the nature of metaphor as entity and as event which makes it a 'sentence' (as process of revelation) or cyclification in the most reduced form. Metaphor combines episode and chronotope by conflating time and tense, particular and universal, but it does so by restitution and constitution, not substitution:

> My experience cannot directly become your experience [. . .] yet [. . .] something passes from me to you. Something is transferred from one sphere of life to another. This something is not the experience as experienced, but its meaning. Here is the miracle. The experience as experienced, as lived, remains private, but its sense, its meaning, becomes public. [. . .] The event is not only the experience as expressed and communicated, but also the intersubjective exchange itself, the happening in dialogue.[153]

It is in this 'discovery' or disclosure of meaning, of conceptualizing from ready-mades of often banal experience and existence, that metaphor then approaches vernacular translation as the articulation of 'another' tongue. As we saw, this is no direct correlation, but the possibility of new expression from another elsewhere. The approximate is also proximate, familiar yet defamiliarized.

> The sense of a text is not behind the text, but in front of it. It is not something hidden, but something disclosed. What has to be understood is not the initial situation of discourse, but what points towards a possible world, thanks to the non-ostensive reference of the text. Understanding has less than ever to do with the author and his situation. It seeks to grasp the world – propositions opened by the reference of the text. [. . .] The text speaks of a possible world and of a possible way of orienting oneself within it [. . .] Here showing is at the same time creating a new mode of being.[154]

The challenge that Ricoeurian metaphor poses for a renewal of critical theory by hermeneutics is then more than a return to semantics to counterbalance semiotics. It is critical approach itself which finds its most radical reversal or overturning. Ricoeur, like the translator, holds text and audience in balance. Meaning and interpretation in both are multiple, conflictual, but not irreconcilable, constantly deferring and exponential. Text-centred theories (deconstruction, post-structuralism, formalism, New Criticism) and reader-centred theories (reader response, and also feminism, postcolonialism, gay studies, Marxist criticism, psychoanalytic theories) are, however, not two halves that will form the whole. Ricoeur, like the persons of the medieval romance storyteller, the prophet, the exegete, stands in the all-important critical gap that makes potential *conjointure* possible. Only if one starts to imagine from greater wholes (metaphor) rather then signs, and from bridges over the spaces and gaps of aporia, can criticism take up the task that intertextuality so pressingly set out in the first chapter. Interdisciplinarity and our technologically interconnected world urgently require modes of thinking and interpretation which discover how science and its related critical theories have in fact made knowledge more fragmentary and marooned in information technology (gloss). Waiting in the wings as *voice off*, we have in Ricoeur no less of an interdisciplinary exegete in his hermeneutical critical approach to text as a vehicle towards recollection and rediscovery.[155] Exploration of new worlds is not their conquering and subordinating from a position of knowledge, but the discovery of how adjacent, similar and unfamiliar they are because we have at last chosen to let them speak. As long as they remain 'texts' they will never do this, not even in Kristeva's most sophisticated version of intertextuality as 'translation'. It is Ricoeur who returns and surpasses Bakhtin's insights into the dialogic and polyphonic.

[D]isclosure of new modes of being [. . .] gives to the subject a new capacity for knowing himself. [. . .] The reader is enlarged in his capacity of self-projection by receiving a new mode of being from the text itself. Appropriation [. . .] ceases to appear as a kind of possession in a way of taking hold of things; instead it implies a moment of dispossession of the egoistic and narcissistic ego. [. . .] it is the text, with its universal power of world disclosure which gives a self to the ego.[156]

This place of renewal is less the intersubjective in texts or between them and the world, and more the nexus between the fictional interpreter (narrative meaning and voice), audience interpretation (reception) and ongoing critical interpretation built on critical experience from the past. Mediators, intermediaries and intersubjective listening and speaking restore not Renaissance humanism, but post-colonializing humanism, to interdisciplinarity and intertextuality. Electronic text artists, critics and criticism thus need a more open and emptied approach to their subjects of endeavour, not to impose meaning, but as prophets and translators to find it and pass it on in their own words. Perhaps then they will, following Ricoeur, find a narrative voice which also discovers that the 'once upon a time', or the 'foundness' of words, might indeed be the best place to begin.

Conclusions

Throughout, this book has sought to realize a study of intertextuality as envisaged for the future by Clayton and Rothstein in 1991, the theorization of its literary history and the historicization of its literary theory.[1] As O'Donnell and Con Davis had stated in the late 1980s:

> [Intertextuality] is the oldest troping we know, the most ancient textual (con)figuration, though its presence as a specific form of attention may be located within the loose amalgamation of poststructuralist critical theories. [It] signals an *anxiety*, and an *indeterminacy* regarding authorial, readerly, or textual identity, the relation of present culture to the past, or the function of writing within certain historical or political frameworks.[2]

While these statements are indubitable, the trouble with this definition of intertextuality remains its imprecision regarding specific contexts or complexity of debates, a criticism already levelled in the early 1980s particularly in Germany. Inevitably, if one size fits all, compromise, pinching or bagginess will result. In contrast, the introduction and first chapter of this book differentiated the many versions of 'intertextuality' which developed out of the same seedbed as Kristeva's coinage to develop its strengths through addressing its perceived weaknesses. If Barthes, Riffaterre, Genette, and much of feminist and postcolonial criticism followed up its various poststructuralist or deconstructive turns, Angenot and Bruce returned to socio-criticism to take forward the earlier Bakhtinian emphasis behind intertextuality to re-root dialogism in the interdiscursive. Yet others, such as J.-P. Faye, eschewed the term altogether because its modelling system was deemed inappropriate. The over-riding concern behind Faye's extensive *oeuvre* is the 'totalitarian' implication of any theory of language for itself (the legacy of Aristotle) which supplants language as *act*.³ In parallel with Ricoeur's attention to words as event, Faye's work offers a radical examination of narration as economy and its potential as social transformation. Yet his terms for 'intertextual' connections, the ordinary language words 'migration' and 'circulation', are hugely ironic given that his work is rarely discussed. No migration or circulation of ideas occurs if critical fora merely rebroadcast already accepted ideas, or if critics do not read in other tongues. Unless the 'foreign' to oneself is countenanced and allowed to enter fully into critical dialogue, the ingrained intellectual dogmatism and concomitant critical nationalism, colonialism and sexism within the academy become only further entrenched and self-endorsing. The analysis of Kristeva's intertextuality proved the point in the first chapter. Similarly, unquestioned anthologizing of theories in the deconstruction camp offset by Bloom in recent guides to 'intertextuality' has slewed its representations. Throughout, this study has sought to address and redress the balance. It should now be striking that Bloom, Girard and Ricoeur engage very fully with postmodern theory, but this is not reciprocal in postmodern critical debate. The absence of properly critical dialogue and available translations have been, like the chorus in a Greek tragedy, the unifying and running threads of this book.

It was Kristeva's 'translation' of Bakhtin into French and French Saussurian linguistics as intertextuality which opened the first window of this book and the plethora of debates surrounding the coinage and subsequent colonization of her term. Only renewed attention to the specific context and full contents of *Semeiotikè*, and critique of its debates from different methodological angles, can recuperate intertextuality as properly Kristevan, and distinguish its better-known brands as important derivatives. Semblance and resemblance in chapter 1 set out a more encompassing critical problem for all four chapters of this book. Intertextuality heralded a catch-all term and methodology for the business of comparison and contrast in cultural production. The ideological frameworks its manifestations variously concealed could then be made visible only from the spectrum of a longer cultural history. While there is some correlation between the unfolding of the narrative of intertextuality in this book as the reading of a family tree from bottom to top – sibling rivals (intertextuality), parental rivals (influence), family rivals (imitation), founding rivals (quotation) – or in reverse literary-historical chronology, from postmodern intertextuality via Romanticism (influence) and the Renaissance and Enlightenment (imitation) to its pre-modern and especially medieval pre-occupations (quotation), the over-riding lessons of the third chapter make quite clear that analogy can only go so far. The moral of the fourth chapter on quotation and allusion is that there will always be other ways of ordering and reordering the narrative material for another audience. Intention and agency at some level, whether tacit or explicit, return in the shadowlands of each window. Intertextuality, like its antecedents, influence, imitation or quotation, has proved far from neutral. All have turned out to be useful, but not to the cost of the others individually or collectively. In the light of the four windows of this book, what does intertextuality then circumscribe? An answer may make more obvious a reply to the more pressing question: 'How valid is intertextuality for the future?'

As the preceding chapter clarified, intertextuality is the culminating critical term for processes of cultural interconnectivity centred on the printed text. Text production and mass-reproduction are thus epistemologically linked in variously opposing ways, as the intervening chapters have shown. Notions of originality concern copyright, genius conspires with plagiarism, and *copia* and imitation vie with copy in its most banal numerical multiplications.[4] The electronic hypermedia 'revolution' has only exacerbated, not superseded, these issues or their ethoi by adding to print a further layer, virtual text. 'Intertextuality' as the generic name for interactions of 'text' is indeed fitting and applicable to any electronic medium conceived after the closed forme of print text. Film is then 'text', as is an opera, a radio play and a television documentary, all of which can be canned. We can then be more precise about where intertextuality is inapplicable. It cannot strictly be applied to relational operations between forms before the printed book. While text refers to the substance of a manuscript to distinguish it from the illumination, the 'intertextuality' between these is more properly their illustrative, representational or referential configuration.

Second, and more essentially, intertextuality as noun with adjectival and adverbial usage has no verbal form, 'to intertextualize'. While none of the cognate languages into which it so readily fitted has discovered any grammatical way of making it a verb, it is the 'fit' that is its success. Its work is denominative and descriptive, a reagent not an agent. From the outset, its rapid success was that it labelled a huge conceptual gap, to designate a certain kind of activity of the ready-made, as it was itself. Thus, while similar to a portmanteau word – Lewis Carroll's 'slithy', for example, combines two recognizable words, 'slimy' and 'lithe' – the synthesis is a non-word or nonsense language until it is widely circulated. Intertextuality as ready-made, however, blended the existing utility of its combination with the playfulness of the portmanteau in ways which, for postmodern cultural forms, have been unprecedented. Barthesian pleasure of the inter-text thus sits equally comfortably with the Riffaterrian cerebral puzzle or the Kristevan 'translation' of cultural forms. Intertextuality is therefore an unrivalled term of denomination, and perhaps of interdenominational status, for 'high', 'low', 'popular', etc., are irrelevant. Its utility and invention combine the ends of art to please and instruct, and celebrate the inventiveness of text itself. Its undoubted appeal is extension and reaffirmation, reclassification and recombination. Gloss, however, has its limits, as analysis of Genette's exhaustive reinvestments of 'intertextuality' demonstrated in chapter 3. There are only so many variations and repetitions within systems, or combinations in a hypertext package. At the level of criticism, the only way to 'surpass' predecessors is to say similar things in more exhaustive, complex or abstruse ways.

Where intertextuality circumscribes print text and its interconnections in the world as text, coinage and neologism do not happen, but enter language in time and space and by means of coiners. While postmodern citation and Barthesian eradication of authors are deemed to displace quotation or authority in text because it is always already spoken and written, proper nouns within such systems none the less designate referential shadowlands. Influence in chapter 2 proved among the best terms available to deal with such nomenclature and the contextual *per se*, whether relations of person to person, place or time. While anxiety for some, influence was considered as much more than cause and effect, chronology and 'belatedness'. Its specific and positive relevance was to any theory concerned with cultural change and intercultural exchange. Influence therefore plays a central role in cultural histories and geographies to examine how texts or works come to be *newcomers* able in turn to empower their various heritages. Where comparative criticism began the mapping of cultural historiography and geography, gender and postcolonial criticism are hugely important successors, challengers and rejuvenators of such work. Their particular sensitivities to the many ideological issues and impacts of any overview theory provide other ways of reviewing the past. Influence proves a highly economic term for all the issues and regions of the outside of the text, including material constraints on its coming-to-being. Indeed, more needs to be done to discover how education reforms and publishing laws, access to books and public platforms, shape cultural productions, by and for whom. As the etymology of influence reminds us, it has extremely active force to get behind motives and motivation and in multiple ways, given that motives are usually mixed and power is multidimensional. Influence needs therefore to be as forcefully rein-scribed into critical theory as it was erased.[5]

The context of the text itself as stable, given or unrivalled medium is also challenged by influence study. Genetic criticism has brought a welcome return to the notebooks and draft manuscripts of an author's 'work' and complicated assumptions about the closed nature of the printed text. It also spearheads practical reappraisal of the bugbear of postmodernism, authorial intention. By highlighting authorial *attention* to the changing of words, geneticists remember that text is an *oeuvre*, the work of persons, including later editors and commentators, not textual self-generation. As Ricoeur notes, to allow agency on several counts only increases the intellectual challenge to interpretation as plural. 'If the intentional fallacy overlooks the semantic autonomy of the text, the opposite fallacy forgets that a text remains a discourse told by somebody [. . .] The authorial meaning becomes properly a dimension of the text to the extent that the author is not available for questioning.'[6] Consideration of the impor-tance of the person of the translator in the previous chapter made clear the very necessary work of persons as agents of cultural dissemination.

As the distinction was made in chapter 1 between Kristeva's inter-textuality and 'intertextuality' as popularized amalgam, like may not be alike. Intertextuality of whatever shade has no mechanism whereby it can recognize plagiarism, counterfeit or false text. It is imitation which complicates and demonstrates how ally and adver-sary or their masks are not easily told apart. Chapter 3 dug deep into the conundrums of form and reference through imitation and mimesis as representation (or not) of the real. While postmodern col-lapse of genre(s) questions the tenets and classifications of literary and cultural criticism following science as epistemological model, it cannot do without distinctions at some level, and models and metaphors.[7] Across the vastly different domains covered in chapter 3, these turned out to be largely anthropocentric. Genetics in the the-ories of Richard Dawkins revealed fewer differences than similarities with its alleged other, religion. Contributions from fields such as structural anthropology, or critics such as Irigaray and Oughourlian, join with religion and genetics to examine mimicry in ways which mimesis only shadows. Thus anthropology and the so-called primi-tive of culture challenge civilization at its most 'civilized', especially as postmodernity. Imitation demonstrated the power of the real to return where least expected. The symbolic is not eradicated either by the most sophisticated complications of copy, but is exacerbated by it. Girard's theory of the scapegoat complex and scapegoat effect demonstrates how the imitative process itself must constantly find new versions and outlets to mask the real it would constantly deflect. Imitation then brings to critical appraisal questions about evaluation and discernment. It demonstrates that relativity in postmodernism and the sciences can only go so far. The relative needs *distinctive* value to complement and endorse it. Bloom's vaunting theories at least provide such a paradigm and, as chapter 2 discovered, a viewpoint on some very similar power structures within deconstruction.

Where the watermark and copyright were other such attempts to qualify and authenticate, the fourth chapter considered print standardization on the micro-level of quotation marks, and what was between them. The radical openness of reference as allusion and quotation, particularly in more extended forms, brought out quotation's inversely proportional attention to the whole by means of the detail. Quotation then enabled exploration of oral transmissions as cultures' deeper veins. Their illustrative, episodic and bridging devices, as well as the span of their interpretative modes, allowed manuscript to be put back on display, and in play as model that hypertext has yet to realize. The unseen ear of the other and unmarked mediating tongue of the translator set intertextuality not as superior to the oral, but as its suppressor (perhaps especially in the electronics meaning of the word). Indeed, quotation reached into realms that influence only dimly perceives. Without the often nameless but essential human intermediary (messenger, prophet, storyteller or translator in the service of other authorities and beholden to their audiences), there would be no message, text or *response*. It is at this juncture that the most serious challenge of all is levelled at postmodern theories, including intertextuality. If there is no reference, no traditions, no message, where is the ground from which the critic of deconstruction or postmodern intertextuality can speak? Bloom and Derrida reach for opposition as conflict or *différance* to stand in for their conflict with the conflict of interpretations. Circumlocution of this order is rejected outright by Ricoeur. His is the harder way of the direct route of confrontation, the taking on of the argument to find another way through it. By not having to find precedents from which to speak, like the prophet, fuller investigation of the interpretation itself as well as its conflicts can proceed. Far from relativism, casuistry or partisanship, Ricoeur's careful weighing of argument and counter-argument to bring understanding is a discernment of similarities. For Ricoeur, this method spans theology *and* metaphysics, literature *and* culture, from the inside out and outside in. Grappling seriously with theology is not apology. This move moreover strikes at a key shadowland of First World critical prejudice – its assumptions that secularization is a given – whereas, in many so-called Third or Fourth World cultures, religion and the theological are at the epicentre of cultural expression.[8] Ricoeur's range is therefore at least as interdisciplinary as Derrida's, but assumes inclusion rather than exclusion of worldview, the stamps of their diametrically opposite critical spirits. To adduce is not the same as to deduce.

Having determined what intertextuality circumscribes in comparison with influence, imitation and quotation, how valid is it for the future? As primarily an appellation with interdenominational critical aegis, intertextuality will continue to play to its 'networking' strengths. Indeed, it may prove increasingly valuable to theorization and understanding of the circuitry and circulation processes of electronic texts. However, since it is applied to a range of very different jobs that critics do with text, it needs more critical use, such as the application of adjective-signatures to distinguish its many and distinct versions. Because its premises and circumference are now clarified by its shadowland terms, intertextuality will be of only marginal usefulness to critics interested precisely in the contexts of cultural production and the making of meaning. Theories of influence, imitation and quotation offer much more sophisticated tools and methodologies, as well as more precise vocabularies, to respond to this range of highly complex issues. In a global cultural economy, these will be all-important in the examination of power, control and ideological formations. Let us then make use of the long-standing range of critical methods and vocabularies visited in all four chapters, but employed appropriately and undogmatically. In the interstices that are inevitable in a study that cannot be exhaustive, may others add terms from critical traditions not covered or only touched on here. Bloom's lesson in remystifying jargons in chapter 2 and intertextuality's imprecision are object lessons for the future. As the past of all critical movements and their counter-movements has demonstrated, abstruseness, virtuosity or catch-all terminologies are too readily replaced. Informed clarity of expression has longevity, fecundity and copying-fidelity on its side.

If intertextuality with proper qualifiers is both viable and unviable for certain critical jobs, what of its part in postmodernism, and in particular the latter's alleged crisis as the twenty-first century unfolds? Intertextuality as explored throughout this study more plainly elucidates the crisis in the criticism of postmodernism. The four chapters revealed a rich number of shadowlands to intertextuality, all of which may provide threads out of the labyrinth of postmodern production. Focus on a particular cultural moment, the fifteen years from 1965–6 to 1980, to frame Kristevan intertextuality specifically, demonstrates a huge range of critical thinking and approach outside the so-called canonical intertextual theorists (upheld by readers and recycled bibliographies). The '1968 effect' in

French critical theory can thus be pressed further from two per-spectives. First, of French intellectual movements *Tel Quel* is but one, if a very vociferous and prolific, group. This book has highlighted other important work going on concomitantly within socio-criticism (Angenot, Faye), social anthropology (Oughourlian, Girard) and psy-choanalytic criticism (Kristeva, Lacan) and how various debates and issues interconnected. The insights of Élie Wiesel and Emmanuel Lévinas mentioned comparatively en route, as other critics or groups of the period, can of course be added. The unquestioned richness of such critical endeavour sets the lie to the 'crisis' in postmodernism as a whole.

The second question to ask of French critical theory of 1965–6 to 1980, epitomized by Kristeva's intertextuality, is how 'French' it really is. If language of original dissemination is the gauge, there seems little dispute regarding Kristeva, Todorov, Derrida, de Man, Riffaterre or Girard. However, all are émigrés (from Bulgaria, Algeria, Belgium, France, respectively), whereas Barthes and Genette are not. It is the very different intellectual training that Kristeva as trilingual Bulgarian émigrée writing in French brought to birth as intertextuality, her 'translation' of Bakhtin's work for a climate of French Saussurian linguistics, that the first chapter investigated and highlighted. In the history of critical theory, the truly avant-garde nature of Kristeva's contributions to what chapter 1 termed 'translin-guistics', and hence the belatedness of *Tel Quel* as intellectual move-ment when compared with the Bakhtin circle, has not been properly appreciated. The critical tools of the shadowland terms of this book will enable a more complex picture to emerge, especially regarding the pivotal influence of Russian theorists inside and outside Russian Formalism on 'French' critical theory and its 'translations' more widely. This book therefore invites further inquiry into the 'Kristeva effect' in two directions. Work by Russianists needs to take forward and complicate the received notions about intertextuality and the introduction of Bakhtin in the West as Kristeva's rather than Todorov's work. A much less francophone 'Kristeva', 'French' criti-cal theory and indeed 'Bakhtin' will result. By decentring Paris and a male *Tel Quel* as providing the canonical semioticians and critical theorists of the late 1960s and 1970s, this book then invites com-parative research into the variously intersecting schools of European semiotics of the period, Moscow, Prague, Frankfurt, Turin and Milan.[9] From these shadowlands, a richer and fuller picture of European theories of text will emerge, as also the vibrancy and plurality of postmodernisms.

The case of Kristeva in chapter 1 also epitomized the further dilutions, distortions and misrepresentations that occur through transatlantic propagations in Anglo-American translation (or its lack). When ascertaining the 'novelty' of intertextuality (as 'French' critical theory more widely) and the canon of innovators, rapid production of translations was a key but not the only criterion. If production of translations is a crucial barometer of an exclusionist or inclusive cultural and critical politics, then bilingual theorists and critics of French and English should benefit by being exempt. Riffaterre, Girard or Paul de Man as examples, however, enjoy a resounding marginality in monolingual 'readers' of intertextuality and critical theory in France and the USA. Clearly, then, critical agendas and censorship are operating at the level not of linguistic medium, but of the contents and envelope of the message. The first chapter of this book engaged with the wider politics of interdisciplinarity within the academy as disciplinarity in other guise. The importing cultural climate for 'French' critical theory in the USA (as in the UK) was mainly university departments of English perceived as avant-garde ('interdisciplinary'). These demoted and distinguished their activities from related work in feminist, gay or postcolonial studies on the doorstep to promote overtly 'foreign' critical theory, but gloss this as essentially white, male, elitist and high in other guise. De Man, who had emigrated and assimilated into this environment, fitted comfortably within such a theory-making machine that supported strongly apolitical tenets and banned roots, origins and contexts. The 'scandal' of de Man's Nazi past when it emerged could not, however, be contained by covering statements from high theory and deconstruction. It did provide a most convenient scapegoat for 'French' critical theory elsewhere in the US academy, although ironically Girard's radical theory of the scapegoat complex, already in the public domain in both French and English, was never applied to what may prove a watershed in the unravelling of the hegemony of deconstructive criticism. A future history of how and why certain intellectuals in philosophy, English and critical theory at Yale and other Ivy League institutions were hired during the 1970s and 1980s will perhaps uncover the many neo-Nazi and racist agendas at work much closer to the US, not European, home. The 'high' critical theory that May 1968 is lauded for producing proves also the site on both sides of the Atlantic of a powerful laundering of critical currency to shore up racial and gender inequality.

The four window chapters in this book have in turn and collectively revealed the shadowlands of the cultural and critical fabric, its mechanisms of reaction and fashion, and the deep processes within cultural articulation for regeneration. How these have been suppressed or exercised has been revelatory of critical prejudice against or for certain versions of the cultural story. As the history of cultural production demonstrates, critical counter-reaction works rarely by simple inversion or mockery of what preceded it. Thus, to envisage a future for intertextuality beyond the bounds of its contexts as elucidated above by deconstructing deconstruction, or reprioritizing the world over the world as text, would fail as too mechanistically programmatic. The crisis in the criticism of postmodernism already names impasse *aporia*, and recycling cultural or critical debris cannot be indefinite. It is in the deeper suppressions, however dormant within a longer cultural pattern, that the future lies, because these already have a past. In the previous chapter, the notions of space and the gap were vital, not as metaphors for lack or crisis, but for a sharpened awareness of the potential within threshold experience or national crisis more widely. The highly specialized link devices which span the impossible chasms of plot development when immediate materials dry up, or when there are no ready-made forms to hand, provide intertextuality with its *peripeteia*, its life or death choice. As early as 1969, when contemplating atheism, Ricoeur made the following prophetic statement which so readily applies to intertextuality:

> the process of nihilism has not yet reached its end, perhaps not even its peak: the work of mourning over the dead gods is not finished. The philosopher thinks in this intermediary time [and] stands midway between atheism and faith [. . .] It is the responsibility of the philosopher to delve into the character of the present antimony until he finds the level of questioning which makes possible a mediation between religion and faith through atheism.[10]

Limit experiences, especially shock and impasse, inform all cultural myth-making, religions, philosophies, story situation and criticism. As always prior to language, 'it' must then be expressed as joy or pain, love or agony, to transform emotion into story.[11] It is in this awaiting space as potential for significant cultural revivification or decimation that intertextuality awaits its fifth act, which inevitably follows *peripeteia*, and will always include an element of surprise.

This book therefore offers no decisive conclusions about the definitive future of intertextuality, but contemplates the waiting space at the end of the four-part journey travelled thus far. Four constants present themselves as appropriate candidates for a part in whatever ensues in the fifth act as cultural production continues its referential and anti-referential processes and processing in the twenty-first century. The first, like Dawkins's longevity criterion for the meme, is the running thread within languages themselves for self-illumination and self-perpetuation. This is the ability to form metaphors, particularly root metaphors, which 'assemble subordinate images together and [. . .] scatter concepts at a higher level'.[12] While Ricoeur recalls the similarity between root metaphors and archetypes,[13] it is the constancy yet variation of the image-bearing potential of metaphor that is the more flexible term. Like the exploration of span in the previous chapter, a quality pertaining to all bridging devices regardless of their size, purpose, architecture, engineering simplicity or complexity, metaphors are separate from, but conjoined to, conceptual and psychological fields of reference. There is much in the *metaphoric* language of philosophy, psychology, sacred texts and the sciences to be taken forward by cultural criticism and intertextuality. Tropes of alleged surplus are not merely supplements: metaphor, parable, symbol are figures which give depths to surface meaning and open up possibility for new expression.

The second constant is the power of orality, whether returned to its primary phase or envisaged in its current, digital, forms. Chapter 4 suggested avenues for the rediscovery of oral heritages, so that they can be heard alongside textual cultural productions prioritizing the visual. More work is needed on what makes oral forms *telling*, why proverbs and jokes, for example, are such powerful forces to destabilize fixed positions and to re-empower the disenfranchised.[14] Since aurality is more inherent in cultural persuasion than print or visual cultures might aver, the hidden constant of subliminal control in culture and its ideologies will then become more audible. Mechanisms such as the gramophone, the telephone, the tape-recorder, radio and television are all media for enjoyment or 'communication', yet such devices are also channels of aural manipulation and indoctrination reliant on audiences becoming attuned to certain messages in particular ways.[15] Beyond the 'normal' use of such tactics in advertising, increased exploitation of the subliminal may become more sinister. To know more about how it has been reversed, or can profit from strategic voice-over, will be of benefit to those who have suffered not only prolonged verbal abuse, but also brainwashing by political or religious cults and sects. As mode of survival and protection in the light of print ascendancy, aurality is much more than a redundant echo. The past is an extremely effective echo-sounding for what lies far below the surface of what we 'know', just as auscultation by stethoscope marked a major advance in diagnostic medicine. Revelation may then have as much, if not more, to do with aurality than insight. Epiphany needs to be counterbalanced by experience of logophany.[16]

If intertextuality centred on visual text and its networks sums up Western forms of representation including writing and conveniently forgets Braille, it has also occluded other ways of 'reading', especially in community. On the contrary, Hebrew thought, writing and representation prioritize the aural and intersubjective over the visual and subjective.[17] Lévinas, for example, is acutely aware of the importance of listening before speaking, and an ethics of listening as ground for social change. 'Greek' and 'Jew' as critical positions provide a third constant in this book, for they have been a way to see in the light of perceived differences from the other. As chapter 2 discovered, Bloom and Derrida were found to differ less than they agreed, just as the tenets of Jewish midrash and Western exegesis overlap more than they remain separate from one another. The 'differences' have often been encapsulated in the images of the spider (visible webmaker, solitary Western philosopher) and the bee (social honeymaker in the hidden life of the hive, midrashic interpreter).[18] The invisible and inaudible in these metaphors are none the less important in both cultural traditions as modes of accessing the ineffable. The attempt to reveal this is of equal concern for 'Hebrew' or 'Greek' theology and philosophy through their carefully schooled work of midrash and exegesis (which include reading aloud and oral discussion) to aid interpretation as provisional and cumulative. A sharing of these interpretative traditions may offer ways in which the inaudible and invisible interstices may become more apparent.[19] Understanding and release are heard as much in the still small voice as seen in the earthquake, wind or fire of revolution and social cataclysm.

If intertextuality and the worldwide web take their cue from the 'Greek' image of the spider's web and 'Jewish' textual traditions are likened to bees jealously working and guarding the honeycomb, both have forgotten that both spider and honey bee are female. Montaigne exemplifies male writers who used 'Jewish' bee imagery to validate a policy of appropriation and pollen collection (quotations) from the flowers of others. Images are the property of no one, Jew or Greek, male or female, slave or ruler, yet women have largely been excluded from self-representation and the public domains of all scribal cultures and their book-centred, epistemophilic heritages.[20] Throughout this book, the fourth constant and challenge in each of the windows on intertextuality came through uncovering (the lack of) woman's role, and her place in culture-making and critical response. Spinning, weaving and quilting have all been powerful images for feminist criticism to recuperate the distaff side of cultural storytelling and channels of knowledge.[21] As not only of the head and intellect, or the remit of utilitarian or goal-orientated information technology, knowledge is the distilled wisdom of embodied experience and the spiritual, of prayer, proverb and axiom. As metaphors and in nature, the web and honeycomb offer more than utilitarian or economic structures, although they have use as food stores or as sites for the continuity of

the species. They are also more than models for knowledge processing and encyclopaedic ventures. Rather, it is their very substance,
made out of the stuff of bodies, that makes the work of spider and
bee so redolent of the affirmative powers of quotation in the previous chapter. Superfluously intricate yet life-sustaining structures,
comb and web are co-operations and transubstantiations enabling
new form, creativity, reproduction and community. If feminist critical theories have begun to spearhead vitally important recuperative
work in all these areas, especially informed interdisciplinary work
across the sciences, ethnography and biology, gender and feminist
cultural studies need to keep rebalancing their investigations with a
firmer eye on nature, and an ear to the rituals and expressions that
continue the spiritual impact of humanity in its various environ-
ments, particularly when these are adverse. That the female spider
kills and consumes her mate and that the queen bee is completely
consumed by procreativity *together* rebalance and question gender
itself as category distinct from sex. Perhaps these realities in nature
also encapsulate the psychic fear that feminist study has uncovered
in the history of Western metaphysics and theology, that birthing is
the most overwhelming limit experience for men and the root of a
deeper epistemophobia as the real illness in culture, not male constructions of hysteria. The ethics and politics of spiders and bees for
feminist agendas then suggest ways of truly smashing the 'Grand
Narratives' of Western culture with its claims to global as well as universal truths. The constant of another story about culture from the
womb or the thread from the belly combines the plethora of the bee
with the unprecedented ingenuity and strength of the spider's web.
Procreation and co-creation are the contrary of mass reproduction
and a production line.

The honeycomb and the web return us to the incredible beauty,
intricacy and superfluity of the illumination of a manuscript, its
delight and humour as detail and whole. What is truly superfluous
and integrally harmonious is the rich prodigality of nature, or the
flourish of a final tail of already ornate calligraphy. Curlicues, codi-
cils and codas all defy neat logic, purpose or utility, but are of a piece
with individual style, as afterthought is often more important and
contrary to premeditated scheme. If spinning oral tales or weaving
them as text and illumination has brought intertextuality to face its
networks of ordered grids and links, these speak of bars and chains
on the windows of a prison cell, not exuberance, flair or freedom of
expression. For intertextuality, as for post-postmodern art and
criticism, hypertext is then not the best model for the future. It is
filigree work, manifested in the past by manuscript illustration and
calligraphy, that provides the surprise rediscovery to be outworked.

The forging of matter, experience and craft into an ensemble of the most delicately strong patterns and settings, filigree embodies light and space and the tensile, supportive intricacies of the honeycomb, web and lace. Intertextuality's aspirations are then the jeweller's, not the conservationist's, as has been said before, and in other words, by the Japanese critic Kobayashi Hideo, whose formulations about the nature of art could equally be replaced by that of science or knowledge itself.

Any art of quality possesses a certain reality, like that of someone's glance piercing your heart. If a sign cannot be read as a living structure that moves one toward a passion for reality, then it can be no more than a manual. With a manual, someone can be instructed that by turning right he will reach town. But it cannot make someone who is seated stand up. People do not move because of a manual. They are moved by events. [. . .] Certain centuries possess a myth, a system of belief so alive and animated as to seem almost organic, and to the artist of such a period, 'art for art's sake' is an absurdity beyond comprehension. Still other centuries are so radically fragmented and broken down that they generate no desire or longing, and so art does not exist. [. . .] I cannot tell if our contemporary world possesses a constructive myth or one of decadent ruin. Yet I do not put much faith in Japan's young proletarian writers, whose work is unsustained by the blood of human destiny. And I do not trust either our intellectual epicureans, who embrace one cynical dream after another in such rapid succession as to dizzy themselves. [. . .] It is not for art to reveal a world of truth apart from this world, or again, to depict some other world of beauty. Art is always the place where human passion exists in its clearest symbolic condition.[22]

Critics have always looked for ideas, metaphors or models for ways of working that clarify or counter their own. For this study of intertextuality's debates and contexts by means of its shadowlands and windows, my hope is that it proceeds to renew and stimulate more precise and passionate critical contemplation of the intertextual in particular corpuses and cultural traditions close to and far beyond those covered. More than this, because the frame terms intertextuality, influence, imitation and quotation are not categories but springboards to deeper and wider cultural understanding and dialogue, my hope is that this book enables newcomer critics to see exceptions and alternatives. What is vital in our twenty-first-century global textual economy is that culture is not reduced to the same, but allowed to celebrate its organic plethora. Intertextuality can then be a rich contribution to the filigree of a world of diverse cultures we all share because they are at our fingertips. To the end of both bio- and

intercultural diversity, and knowing better how to put the human
back into humanities and revelation back into re-evaluation, is where
I pass this study to another runner. As Lear invited Cordelia, so the
invitation stands: 'Speak again!'

Notes

Prologue

1 See Moi (1986), pp. 4–7, for a representative and short history of Kristeva in the context of May 1968 and *Tel Quel*. For a view in French of May 1968, see Certeau (1994).
2 Plottel and Charney (1978), p. xiv. Plottel is among the very few critics to see in Humpty Dumpty and Alice in *Alice in Wonderland* a serious challenge to critical theory's reliance on Saussurian linguistics. For a useful study of nonsense as intellectual category, see also Stewart (1978).
3 Among the key examples, see Plottel and Charney (1978), Schmid and Stempel (1983), Broich and Pfister (1985), Worton and Still (1990), Plett (1991), Asholt (1994), Limat-Letellier and Miguet-Ollgnier (1998), Piégay-Gros (1996), Allen (2000) and Samoyault (2001).
4 The term is Siegfried Loewe's translation of Umberto Eco's name for 'postmodern', in Asholt (1994), p. 316. Asholt's collection firmly categorizes intertextuality as synonymous with 'postmodern'.

Introduction

1 For examples of the former, see Worton and Still (1990), Asholt (1994), and Limat-Letellier and Miguet-Ollgnier (1998); and of the latter, see Genette (1982) or Piégay-Gros (1996).
2 For an introduction to *Tel Quel*, see Ffrench (1995).
3 See, for example, Plottel and Charney (1978), Broich and Pfister (1985), Worton and Still (1990), Clayton and Rothstein (1991), Plett

(1991), Asholt (1994), Bruce (1995), Piégay-Gros (1996), Limat-Letellier and Miguet-Ollgnier (1998), Allen (2000) and Samoyault (2001). The exception is the special number of *Poétique* (1976), which pluralizes the term.

4 See Hebel (1989) or Asholt (1994), for example.

5 See, for example, Mai's bibliographical overview in Plett (1991), pp. 237–50.

6 See, for example, Limat-Letellier and Miguet-Ollgnier (1998), p. 22.

7 Examples are Worton and Still (1990), Asholt (1994), Piégay-Gros (1996), Limat-Letellier and Miguet-Ollgnier (1998) and Samoyault (2001).

8 See in particular Lachmann in Lachmann (1982), pp. 51–62, and her later essay in Stierle and Warning (1984), pp. 133–8. These ideas mesh with those of Schmid and Stempel (1983).

9 As the title, 'La Stratégie de la forme', of Jenny (1976) reformulates, as well as acknowledging Lotmann (1976, pp. 257, 264). This is the only essay selected for translation into English from this collection, as 'The strategy of forms' (note the plural!), in Todorov (1982), pp. 34–63.

10 Jenny (1976), pp. 271 and 262 respectively.

11 Dällenbach's work here, pp. 282–96, is integrated into his later monograph of 1977. 'Autotextualité', or references by a work to itself or previous works by the same author, is also known as 'intratextuality'. See Orr (1993), pp. 175–91. For a different view of *mise en abyme* as Chinese boxes, see Bal's term, 'narrative embedding': Bal (1997), pp. 44–52.

12 Perrone-Moisés (1976), p. 374.

13 Brée (1978), p. 4 (my emphasis).

14 Plottel in Plottel and Charney (1978), p. vii.

15 Ibid., pp. xix–xx.

16 The essays in *Poétique* (1976) and Broich and Pfister (1985), and Hebel's overview survey in Hebel (1989), are all illustrations of this.

17 As Allen (2000) did later (he had no knowledge of this prior reader), Piégay-Gros (1996) subdivides her book round issues. Chapter 1 deals with 'les relations de coprésence' (citation, reference, plagiarism, allusion). Chapter 2 looks at 'relations de dérivation' (parody, travesty, burlesque, pastiche) before examining a 'poetics' of intertextuality – first significations (characterization, place, memory, myth, history) – then reader response. The final chapter examines the aesthetics of intertextuality, such as imitation and invention, the palimpsest, the deconstructed fragmented text, collage and bricolage.

18 See Limat-Letellier in Limat-Letellier and Miguet-Ollgnier (1998), p. 15. Samoyault (2001), p. 6, emphasizes 'la mémoire de la littérature', but is largely a reprise of Piégay-Gros (1996).

19 See Hebel (1989), p. 2 for example.

20 Schoek (1991), p. 181.

21 The essays in Asholt (1994) are instructive of this phenomenon as tantamount to Derridean deferral of meaning, underpinned by intertex-

tual narratives of disillusionment and excesses of form, to comprise the 'subversive'. What makes the postmodern new then requires ever-increasing degrees of the extreme, the virtuoso or the utterly banal.

22　Clayton and Rothstein (1991) is among the only critical reappraisals of intertextuality to attempt to retrack influence, but it returns to intertextuality's ragged edges because it finds Bloom's theories wanting.

23　Compagnon (1998), p. 20. Earlier he remarks on the dependency of literary theory on the very terms it seeks to erase (ibid., p. 15).

Chapter 1　Intertextuality

1　See, for example, the opening sentiments of Allen (2000) and Pasco (1994).

2　As Samoyault (2001), for example.

3　See Lachmann (1982) or Broich and Pfister (1985), as discussed in the introduction.

4　See, for example, Bruce (1995), pp. 152–3, who notes how Kristeva eschewed low-cultural example or reception.

5　Lechte (1990), p. 66.

6　Kristeva published the essay as 'Bakhtin, le mot, le dialogue et le roman' in 1967. While Moi (1986) provides some context for Kristeva's fourth essay of *Semeiotikè* as 'Word, dialogue, novel', she reprints the 1980 Roudiez translation, which remains the unchallenged version for English speakers.

7　Moi (1986), p. 37, and Kristeva (1969), p. 85.

8　Kloepfer (1982) takes up the problem of Kristeva's similar terms, 'Polylogues', and intertextuality, as 'einfach viel zu weit gefasst' (p. 92), as monolithic and therefore unusable for specific tasks.

9　See Knight (1997) for a full bibliography of Barthes in translation. While Moi commissioned translations of further excerpts from *Semeiotikè* (Moi, 1986), Kristeva's fifth essay, 'Towards a semiology of paragrams', was translated only in 1998 (Ffrench and Lack, 1998). See Smith (1998) for the fullest list available of translations of Kristeva.

10　A case in point is Allen (2000). In her introduction, Smith (1998), p. 5, touches on the problem of Anglo-American reception of Kristeva's ideas, but not the unreliability of their vehicle. 'There is a certain Anglophone representation of Kristeva, influenced by the feminist readings of Stone, Oliver and Jardine, which tends to characterize her conservatism, religiosity and lack of political edge or de-politisation.'

11　This is Manfred Pfister's term in Broich and Pfister (1985), p. 20.

12　Exceptions include Orr (2000) and (2002).

13　Lechte (1990), for example, has no reference to intertextuality in the index to his study and mentions it only once in a tortuous gloss, p. 104. For an example of a feminist study, see Smith (1998), which is overtly about the Kristeva of psychoanalysis. Although the first section of Moi (1986) looks at 'Linguistics, semiotics, textuality', it focuses more on the issues of the second part, 'Women, psychoanalysis, politics'.

14 Vice (1997) makes small inroads, but reads Kristeva in English translation.

15 Plottel and Charney (1978), p. xiv.

16 See Manfred Pfister's opening essay in Broich and Pfister (1985), p. 1, which considers Kristeva's work as a completion of Bakhtin's.

17 Kristeva (2001), p. 32, takes full credit for disseminating Bakhtin into France and wider critical theory.

18 See for example, Bruce (1995), 132–4.

19 See especially the work in the mid-1980s of German critics such as Lachmann (1982) and Schmid and Stempel (1983), where overt use of the word 'Dialogizität' or 'Dialog' in the titles of their collections clearly indicates their prioritizing of Bakhtin's concept over Kristeva's. Stierle and Warning (1984) again follow Bakhtin by focusing on *Das Gespräch* or *Speech Genres* in other words. For an important discussion of kinds of 'Dialog', see Lachmann in Lachmann (1982), p. 8, and her later essay. Jauss (1982), p. 22, n. 13, calls the Kristevan version a 'Verkürzung' of Bakhtin's dialogism. Preisendanz (1982), p. 28, raises the question whether dialogism and intertextuality are theories of reception or production.

20 Moi (1986), p. 37; Kristeva (1969), pp. 84–5. The French of the first sentence refers not to his works but to Bakhtin as synonymous with them, 'Chez Bakhtine . . .'

21 Moi (1986), p. 37; Kristeva (1969), p. 85.

22 Kristeva (1969), p. 52; my translation.

23 Ibid., p. 53: 'L'idéologème d'un texte est le foyer dans lequel la ratio-nalité connaissante saisit la transformation *des énoncés* (auxquels le texte est irréducible) en un tout (le texte), de même que les insertions de cette totalité dans le texte historique et social.'

24 Manfred Pfister (Broich and Pfister, 1985, p. 6) is among few critics to understand in Kristeva a follower of Bakhtin's socio-critical impact.

25 Kristeva (1969), p. 150: 'A mi-chemin entre le savoir et le non-savoir, le vrai et le non-sens, le vraisemblable est la zone intermédiaire où glisse un savoir déguisé, pour maîtriser une pratique d'investigation translinguistique par le "vouloir-s'entendre-parler absolu." '

26 My translation of Kristeva (1969), p. 9.

27 My paraphrase of ibid., p. 23.

28 See ibid., p. 194: 'Pris dans l'intertextualité, l'énoncé poétique est un sous-ensemble d'un ensemble plus grand qui est l'espace des textes appliqués dans notre ensemble. [. . .] Il est le lieu de croisement de plusieurs codes (au moins deux) qui se trouvent en relation de néga-tion l'un par rapport à l'autre.' This vocabulary is strikingly similar to 'se croisent' and 'se neutralisent' in 'Le Texte clos'.

29 The problem created by this move has been pointed out by Moi (1986), p. 25: 'Insisting as it does on the the heterogeneity of language, semiotics is caught in a paradox: being itself a metalanguage [. . .] it cannot but homologize its object in its own discourse.'

30　See Kristeva (1969), p. 196: '[les textes poétiques de la modernité] se font en absorbant et en détruisant en même temps les autres textes de l'espace intertextuel; ils sont pour ainsi dire des *alter-jonctions* discursives.' Disconjoint does not, however, mean 'barred', that is pure representation or its absence (as is the case with the Lacanian 'symbolic' or 'real').

31　My paraphrase of Kristeva (1969), p. 13.

32　Kristeva (1997), reprinted in *French Studies* 52 (1998), 385–96.

33　Moi (1986), p. 13, offers an intriguing but unexplored questioning of how Kristeva negotiates the subject-in-language between deconstructive and essentialist positions.

34　See, for example, Kristeva (1969), p. 27.

35　Bruce (1995), p. 11, is the only other critic to my knowledge who has hinted in this direction, but he leaves the thought unsubstantiated.

36　My paraphrase of Kristeva (1969), p. 197.

37　Kristeva has not gone on to explore an 'Einsteinian' theory of psychoanalysis as such. Her 'home' is within post-Freudian psychoanalysis and its graft on literature for its paradigms. For a psychoanalytic approach that emerges not from Freud, but from Einstein's view of science, see Zohar (1991).

38　Kristeva (1988), translated by Roudiez (1991).

39　My view counters Friedman's reinsertion of authors for the 'it' or 'psyche' in Clayton and Rothstein (1991), p. 150.

40　See A. Brown (1992), p. 74, who avers that, for Barthes, 'system first, then drift.'

41　Bruce (1995), p. 125, is dismissive of 'Kristevan' intertextuality, but considers it closer to Noam Chomsky's theory of transformative grammar than Saussurian linguistics.

42　Rajan in Clayton and Rothstein (1991), p. 68.

43　My paraphrase of Barthes (1971, pp. 7–8).

44　Barthes (1973a), p. 104. As above, Barthes elides Kristeva's sense of these terms to fill their space with a further theatrical reference in apposition to her terms. See A. Brown (1992), p. 90, for the importance of the art of elliptical citation as 'one of Barthes's most constant tactics' and quotation as 'one of Barthes's many prolepses'.

45　My translation of Barthes (1973a), p. 59.

46　While the mediator-translator function goes some way to challenging Bruce's criticism that Kristeva has no space for the transcoding of text (Bruce, 1995, p. 146), ultimately there is, as he says, no *locus* for the reader in her theorization.

47　For a succinct and searching exploration of theatre in Barthes, see Moriarty (1997).

48　Barthes (1973a), pp. 45–6. This is the famous 'death of the author' passage.

49　Ibid., p. 57, where the writer is 'un jouet [. . .] un joker, un mana, un degré zéro, le mort du bridge.' See also ibid., pp. 88–9, where the writer is a configuration suggested by erotic or fetishistic markers in the text.

50 Ibid., pp. 100–1. This is the famous text as 'tissue' passage, but its concluding remarks, text as 'hyphology' or the gossamer of a spider's web, is rarely cited.

51 Ibid., pp. 24–5.

52 See Pfister's introduction (Broich and Pfister, 1985) for a discussion of reader response theory to these issues, and how Charles Grivel attempts to maintain the terms by reclassifying intertexts as intentional or non-intentional (pp. 22–3).

53 For a more detailed exploration of Barthes's understanding of Freud, epistemophilia and the fetishism of the text, see A. Brown (1992), pp. 86–7.

54 Barthes (1975), p. 148.

55 See A. Brown (1992), pp. 15–17, for a study of the many facets of Barthes's 'dérive', which Brown admits (p. 14) 'is nowhere defined by Barthes: he uses it as a floating signifier'. Barthes (1973a), pp. 32–3, does in fact describe the 'dérive'.

56 Barthes (1973a), p. 105. There is something quite Gothic here. For Leitch (1983) Barthes's intertextuality is a crypt.

57 See A. Brown (1992), pp. 51 and 73.

58 Is it coincidence that Jean-Francois Lyotard's essays called *Dérive à partir de Marx et Freud* appeared also in 1973?

59 Pfister (Broich and Pfister, 1985) distinguishes Barthes's very different theory of the reader to Riffaterre's, pp. 20–2.

60 Riffaterre (1978), p. 195, n. 27.

61 Freund (1987, p. 160) sees it as a 'pedagogically compelling performance', whereas Suleiman (Suleiman and Crosman, 1980, p. 13) merely classifies Riffaterre as 'a structural stylistician'. Although talking about 'grammaticalities' of reading, Gasché (1998) refers to Riffaterre only in passing, while Allen (2000), p. 6, is more deferential.

62 Bruce (1995), p. 158, reads Riffaterre as a contributor to theories of the *phenomenology* of the act of reading and hence textual transmission.

63 Riffaterre (1978), p. 42.

64 Ibid., pp. 168–9, n. 16. Riffaterre fully acknowledges his particular evolution of the term via Starobinski.

65 Broich (Broich and Pfister, 1985), p. 45, names this deciphering the 'Aha-Erlebnis', a mix of recognition and relief.

66 Barthes (1973a), pp. 9–10.

67 See Riffaterre (1980), p. 4.

68 Riffaterre (1978), p. 1. Note the overlap between Riffaterre's 'indirection' and Barthes's 'dérive'. The one is indirection as new direction of the old, as against tangential movement away from the old.

69 Ibid., p. 12.

70 Ibid., p. 164.

71 As, for example, Culler (1981), p. 94, claims.

72 Riffaterre (1978), p. 117.

73 Ibid., p. 124.

74   Worton and Still (1990), pp. 1–2. Tilottama Rajan in Clayton and Rothstein (1991), p. 68, charges Kristeva's theory similarly of not being able to distinguish 'two kinds of texts: those that are "passively" and those that are "actively" intertextual.'

75   Riffaterre includes nonsense as one of the special kinds of hypogrammatic structure, but it is always another form of catechresis, pointing out its status as nonsense because it adheres to a 'grammar'.

76   This might be a way of describing the *in absentia* reader in Kristeva: abundant knowledge in a field does not mean its skilful recounting from the place of understanding.

77   See Bruce (1995), p. 177.

78   As Bruce (ibid.), p. 170, notes.

79   See Rajan in Clayton and Rothstein (1991), especially pp. 69 and 72.

80   A logogriph is a fish basket (net) or riddle: 'A kind of enigma in which a certain word, and other words that can be formed out of all or any of its letters are to be guessed from synonyms of them introduced into a set of verses. Any anagram or puzzle involving anagrams' (*OED*).

81   Riffaterre (1978), p. 39.

82   For Angenot (1983a), pp. 123–4, the nub was lack of a suitable term. He highlights Kristeva's clever repackaging of existing terminology, how her (inter)textual work ('le travail du texte') calques Freud's dreamwork ('Traumarbeit'), while her 'idéologème' is a calque of Bakhtin/Medvedev's 'monème'.

83   Ibid., p. 132.

84   Piégay-Gros (1996), pp. 29–32, is among rare critics, even in France, to address 'interdiscours' as term. However, she links it not to Angenot or his disciple Bruce, but to his analysis within linguistics by Maingueneau (1991). The latter also appears in Bruce's bibliography.

85   In Valdés and Miller (1985), p. 42.

86   See the still seminal work by Pratt (1977).

87   Bruce (1995), especially chapter 1.

88   Ibid., pp. 35–6.

89   Ibid., p. 59. Bruce particularly reviles the 'théorie de la "textualité pure"' as a 'monisme auto-destructeur'.

90   See Pfister in Broich and Pfister (1985), p. 15, for a succinct evaluation of Lachmann's contributions to understanding and expanding 'Dialogizität'.

91   See Eskin (2000), p. 5, for a discussion of utterance's dialogic-existential embeddedness as text.

92   Bruce (1995), p. 57, translates into French Robert Scholes's synopsis of five key semiotic models: Frege's 'expression, meaning, reference'; Carnap's 'expression, intention, extension'; Ogden and Richards's 'symbol, thought, referent'; and Peirce's 'sign, interpreter, object' to contrast Saussure's 'signifier and the signified'.

93   See the introduction to Weingart and Stehr (2000), especially pp. 2 and 41.

94 I distinguish my two orders from those outlined as Mode 1 (hierarchical) and Mode 2 (non-hierarchical) by Julie Thompson Klein in Weingart and Stehr (2000), p. 14.
95 Ibid., p. 7.
96 See Klein in Weingart and Stehr (2000), p. 16.
97 See Weingart in ibid., p. 29.
98 See Bourdieu (1992).
99 Editors' conclusions to Weingart and Stehr (2000), p. 271.
100 See, for example, Armstrong (2001), p. 121.
101 See Yankelovich, Meyrowitz and van Dam (1991), p. 58.
102 Annesley (2001), p. 129.
103 Genette (1982), p. 14.
104 As Bogue (1991), p. 5, in an assessment of Baudrillard, makes plain.
105 See Landow in Delany and Landow (1991), pp. 6–10, for an evaluation of hypertext's transformations of the page. For an interesting Lacanian reading of this as loss, dislocation and the cut, see Harpold (1991), pp. 171–6.
106 Allen (2000), pp. 199–208, has some vague reservations, but is largely non-committal in his conclusions.
107 See Landow in Delany and Landow (1991), p. 19.
108 There has been little work done on the term 'link' (as of chains!), or questioning of it as in fact negative metaphor ('yoked'?). One exception is Harpold (1991), especially pp. 176–8.
109 Black in Bogue (1991), p. 167.
110 See Mey in Weingart and Stehr (2000), pp. 165–7.
111 Landow in Delany and Landow (1991), pp. 20–4, admits that good formulation of questions to contexts is essential for properly critical thinking.
112 See ibid., p. 31.
113 Gaggi (1997), p. 117.
114 See Annesley (2001), p. 227, for an analysis of William Gibson's *Neuromancer* (1984).
115 Feustle (1991), p. 310, rightly distinguishes ideal hypertextual design *work* as 'labor-intensive', not knowledge-extensive.
116 See, for example, Littau (2000), p. 684.
117 See DeRose (1991).
118 Quoted by Slatin (1991), p. 157.
119 See Too (2000), especially pp. 114–15.
120 As Landow in Delany and Landow (1991), p. 85, notes. See also Jacob (2000), pp. 107–8, for an account of the precise reference systems of Hellenistic historians.
121 See Braund and Wilkins (2000) for a fuller discussion of the impact of Athenaeus.
122 Modernism abounds with experiments in writing technical novelties such as cameras to telephones. See Benjamin (1973), which still remains a critical *locus classicus*, and more recently Danius (2001).

123 The contributors in Delany and Landow (1991), including Landow himself, rant against 'scholars' versed in canonical text, but without exploring textuality prior to the printed book.

124 See Samoyault (2001), who signals that the 'memorial' aspect is intertextuality's strength.

125 For important counter-examples and recuperations, see, for example, Smith (1998).

126 Kristeva (1969), p. 316 (my translation). See above for my choice of 'levelling'.

127 Ecclesiastes, 1: 9. See Culler (1981), p. 117, for an alternative convolution.

128 Barthes (1973a), p. 53.

129 Clayton and Rothstein in Clayton and Rothstein (1991), p. 3.

130 To borrow and adapt the title of Kellmann (2000).

131 Friedman (1991), p. 146.

Chapter 2 Influence

1 Newman (1985), p. 35, more scathingly terms this 'sour irrelevance'.

2 Bloom (1973), p. 70.

3 Clayton and Rothstein (1991), pp. 3–5.

4 See Bauerlein (1995), pp. 2–3, for a more specific, 'American', analysis.

5 See Newman (1985), p. 43, who describes this as 'an ideolocracy of discomfiture'.

6 See Brooker (1992) for more on this debate.

7 As de Bolla (1988), pp. 10–11 and 100, has argued strongly.

8 Allen (1994) sets out very clearly these conflictual dynamics.

9 It is Kristeva's later work that has in fact developed this.

10 Ellmann (1994), p. 27. The quotation is from Bloom (1982a), p. 101.

11 For an investigation of antecedents as obstacles, see Newman (1985), pp. 39–42.

12 Lentricchia (1980), p. 326.

13 See, for example, Bloom (1979) and Salusinszky (1987).

14 See Compagnon (1998), p. 10, for a similar but francophone overview.

15 Although Derrida shares with Kristeva a 'foreign' background as French Algerian Jew, he received his lycée and university education in Paris.

16 See Lentricchia (1980), p. 320, who underscores Bloom's antagonism to Northrop Frye.

17 See Docherty (1987), pp. 260–1.

18 Mileur (1985) has attempted to follow Bloom, as Lacour-Labarthe has Derrida. For an insight into this phenomenon in a French critical context, see Compagnon (1988), p. 12.

19 See Peterson (2001).

20 Clayton and Rothstein (1991), p. 120.

21 See, for example, Cabantous (1998) or Brooks (2000).
22 Clayton and Rothstein (1991), p. 8.
23 See respectively Lentricchia (1980), p. 326, Regard (1992), pp. 8–9, and Conte (1986).
24 See the famous response of Kolodny (1985) and, for a 'postcolonial' view, Awkward (1989).
25 Lentricchia (1980), chapter 9, acknowledges the esoteric aspects of Bloom's work, but sees them as evidence of a lack of critical method, while de Bolla (1988), pp. 10–11, openly refuses to countenance Bloom's Kabbalism.
26 In the revised preface (1997), this is its title.
27 Culler (1981), pp. 106–7, sets out but does not pursue this trail.
28 Hand (1990), p. 85. See also Wright (1984), pp. 150–6, for an important study of Bloom's elucidation of Freud's wilful failure to acknowledge Melanie Klein's work on the pre-Oedipal infant.
29 Allen (1994), pp. 26–9, 49–54, helpfully glosses these six 'ratios' in some detail.
30 Bloom (1975a), p. 84, summarizes all three models in an extremely helpful diagram.
31 Jenny (1976), p. 259, interestingly both misses out one of Bloom's six terms and calls them a 'curieux ballet de figures', but without defining this further.
32 See, for example, Bloom (1975a), p. 79. In chapter 3, there is a fine critique of Derrida's 'Primal scene of writing'. Bloom (1975b), pp. 104–5, also targets Foucault's 'archaeologies'.
33 Bloom (1973), pp. 64–5.
34 De Man (1983), p. 271.
35 Bloom (1997), p. xviii, corrects his earlier intoxication with only the high Romantic poets which his more recent books (see Bloom, 1995) endorse.
36 Bloom (1973), p. 25.
37 Bloom (1997), p. xxiv.
38 Bloom (1975a), p. 12.
39 See Bloom (1973), pp. 13–14 and 60–1. Fite (1985), pp. 27 and 32, examines these aspects of Bloom's work.
40 Bloom (1975a), pp. 24 and 52.
41 See Fite (1985), p. 83, and Allen (2000), p. 144, who continues to paraphrase a very Freudian Bloom by 'applying' the theory to the problem of the female poetic voice.
42 Bloom (1973), p. 8.
43 Bloom (1975a), p. 101.
44 Bloom (1973), p. 10.
45 Ibid., pp. 85 and 100.
46 Bloom (1975a), p. 3.
47 See Culler (1981), pp. 109–10.
48 Bloom (1975a), p. 10.
49 Wright (1984), p. 155. So normally sensitive to sexism, Wright fails to see the double alienation of the female critic.

50 Bloom (1973), p. 26, is equally cognizant of these.
51 Ibid., p. 152.
52 Ibid., pp. 29 and 66 respectively, which are explicit about this and the importance of the language of taboo.
53 Bloom (1975b), p. 15.
54 Rudolph in Hazlett (1991), p. 188.
55 See Handelman in Plottel and Charney (1978).
56 Bloom (1975b), p. 20.
57 Bloom (1975a), p. 4.
58 Bloom (1975b), p. 98.
59 Ibid., p. 39.
60 Scholem (1946), p. 21.
61 Scholem (1965), p. 1.
62 Bloom (1975b), p. 47.
63 Bloom (1982a), p. 4.
64 See Fite (1985).
65 Chadwick (1993), pp. 38–9.
66 Young (1991), p. 140.
67 Bloom (1982a), p. 70.
68 Bloom (1975b), p. 20.
69 Bloom (1975a), p. 43.
70 Bloom (1982a), pp. 34–5.
71 This move encapsulated Bloom's 'metalepsis'; Bloom (1975a), p. 103.
72 Bloom (1982a), p. 15.
73 Bloom (1975b), p. 82.
74 Bloom (1975a), pp. 32, 29 and 40 respectively.
75 Ibid., p. 336.
76 Scholem (1946), p. 37.
77 Moynihan (1986), p. 30.
78 O'Hara (1985), p. 111, who contrasts Bloom with Hartmann's 'mastery'.
79 The question posed but never answered by Fite (1985), p. 12.
80 Bloom in Moynihan (1986), p. 30.
81 Paz (1990), p. 207. The quotation in the quotation is from Amable Audin's *Les Fêtes solaires* (1945), but no page reference is given.
82 Fite (1985), p. 196.
83 Rudolph in Hazlett (1991), pp. 186–207.
84 As Mileur (1985), p. 116, indicates.
85 Hassan (1955), especially p. 73.
86 Block (1970), p. 17. This is the argument that Block in fact refutes.
87 See Cixous (1992), p. 14, where she advocates a vocabulary of nurturing, developed as the expression 'faire blé' (pp. 19–20).
88 Baxandall (1985), pp. 58–9. Also quoted partially in Clayton and Rothstein (1991), pp. 6–7.
89 See Hermerén (1975).
90 See Shaw (1971), pp. 91–3, in respect of 'foreign' influences on an author backed up by external evidence.

91   See Newman (1985), p. 13, who calls this 'inflationary culture'.
92   See A. H. Baker (1991) for the complex ways influence can explain multiple and contradictory causes and effects.
93   Ibid., p. 39.
94   Awkward (1989), p. 10.
95   See Wiesel (1994).
96   See Regard (1992), p. 7.
97   See Newman (1985), pp. 96–7, who argues for literature as not 'intrinsically virtuous, neither weapon nor sanctuary', but ultimately as a gift.
98   Knox (1994), pp. 11–12, on the Greek, *opiso*.
99   See Rorty (1982), pp. 151–2.
100   See Eliot (1965), p. 17.
101   See Hu (2000), pp. 112–13.
102   Miner and Brady (1993), p. x.
103   Knox (1994), pp. 164–5.
104   Culler (1981), p. 13.
105   Balakian (1962), p. 25, actually stipulates that influence should only properly be applied in the case of foreign contact.
106   Conte (1986), p. 23. See also Etiemble (1963), who contrasts comparative critical method in France and the USA, and finds the latter wanting on historical frame.
107   Hermerén (1975), p. 201.
108   See Crapanzano (1995), pp. 140–1, who calls for 'a "Third" to whom rhetorical appeal can be made'.
109   Arguably, Said (1978) and (1993) are pivotal models for such cosmopolitan criticism. See also Moura (1998) for criticism of travel and migrations.
110   See also Benjamin (1973).
111   For a study of detective fiction as genre and its anti-generic developments, see Merivale and Sweeney (1999) and Mullen and O'Beirne (2000).
112   Steiner (1975).
113   See Balakian (1962), p. 29, for some of the criteria of such a critical method.
114   Steiner (1975), pp. 452–3. He borrows the term 'interanimation' from John Donne.
115   See Orr (2002).
116   Eliot (1965), p. 16. On p. 12 he also admits that theorizing is often epiphenomenal of personal taste.
117   Ibid., pp. 12–13. His categories are the Professional Critic, the critic 'with Gusto' (advocate of forgotten texts), the Academic and the Theoretical, the Specialist Critic, and the critic as byproduct of creative activity.
118   Ibid., p. 21.
119   See Morson (1995), p. 35. For wider debates, see Adlam et al. (1997).
120   See Mandelker (1995).
121   See Paz (1990).

122 Japanese literary culture as calqued on classical Chinese offers a fascinating alternative perspective for European Renaissance scholarship and gender studies. See Sarra (1999) and Shirane and Suzuki (2000).
123 Eliot (1965), p. 18.

Chapter 3 Imitation

1 D'Haen in d'Haen et al. (1989), p. 184.
2 Allen (2000), p. 215.
3 See Schwarz (1996), p. 72.
4 Borges's *Quixote* playfully challenges such 'plagiarism'.
5 See, for example, Hutcheon (1988 and 1989) for important critical contributions to postmodern meta-fiction and parody and devices such as *mise en abyme* as a narrative 'artifice'.
6 See Jullier (1997), pp. 7–9, on mimicry and postmodern film.
7 See Schwarz (1996), p. 297.
8 Worton and Still (1990), pp. 4–7.
9 For a pithy history of mimesis, see Ijsseling (1997). Auerbach (1946) remains a classic of its Western literary heritages. See also Prendergast (1986) for its anti-mimetic variants. For its treatment in interdisciplinary contexts, see Spariosu (1984) and Bogue (1991).
10 See, for example, Duff (2000), pp. 1–2, on the current negative aura surrounding genre, or Hawcroft (1999), p. 1, for similar charges against rhetoric.
11 Perloff (1988), p. 4.
12 Ibid., p. viii.
13 See O'Donnell and Con Davis (1989), p. x, who discuss multimedia events as 'surfictional cyborgs'. Intertextuality for them does not so much collapse generic distinctions as historicize them (p. xvi).
14 As Dawkins (1998), p. 214, asserts. Gongorism offers a further model of complexity and amalgamation, yet falls short of monstrosity.
15 Dawkins (1989), p. 32.
16 See Schwarz (1996), pp. 331–2.
17 See Waugh (1984) for a general introduction to meta-fiction.
18 This is not a plagiarism of the title of Lakoff and Johnson (1980).
19 Dawkins (1998), pp. 17–18.
20 Dawkins (1989), pp. 6, 10 and 35, respectively.
21 Dawkins (1998), pp. 193 and 217, respectively.
22 I might have chosen the word 'literature' here, but, as Todorov (1978), p. 13, remarks, this is a relatively recent nineteenth-century term.
23 Duff (2000), p. 17.
24 Dawkins (1989), pp. 15–16.
25 Ibid., pp. 18–19.
26 Ibid., pp. 189–94.
27 See Compagnon (1998), p. 37.

28   Dawkins (1998), p. 306.
29   See Hobson (1982), p. 12, on Gombrich and Hamon.
30   This is my term.
31   Bogue in Bogue (1991), pp. 3–4.
32   See also Blackmore (2000) as another revision and expansion of Dawkins.
33   See, for example, Bruce (1995), p. 183.
34   Cusset (1999), p. 9, notes this neglect but offers no explanation.
35   As Montalbetti (1998), p. 121, notes. See also Limat-Letellier in Limat-Letellier and Miguet-Ollgnier (1998), p. 43.
36   G. Prince, p. ix, in the foreword to the English translation of *Palimpsestes* (1997).
37   Allen (2000), p. 100.
38   Exceptions are Allen (2000), pp. 95–115, who summarizes its place in the light of Genette (1979), and Genette (1987) (all in translation). Bruce (1995), pp. 181–2, situates *Palimpsestes* within Genette's *oeuvre* and his structuralist reappraisal of the rhetorical tradition, but without expanding further.
39   Broich and Pfister (1985), p. xi, in their foreword. They also charge him with not engaging with important elements of post-structuralist theory and his exclusive use of only French examples.
40   Morgan (1989), p. 271. Bruce (1995), p. 185, sees it as a '*variante*'.
41   Detweiler and Doty (1990), p. 143, reminds us that myths reveal 'the nature of *liminality*'.
42   Louis Marin's 'Pour une théorie du texte parabolique', in Claude Chabrol, *Le Récit évangélique* (Paris: Aubier-Montaigne, 1974), p. 167ff. In Genette (1979), the author more nastily inserts a footnote about 'his' term and its dissimilarity from that used by Mary-Ann Cawes in 1978 to dismiss hers. Genette reinvests his own reworked 'l'architexte' in *Palimpsestes* (1982).
43   See, for example, Genette et al. (1980), (1983) and (1984) and Genette and Todorov (1986). He co-founded *Poétique* in 1970 with Todorov and Hélène Cixous.
44   Todorov (1971) and Todorov and Ducrot (1982) are mammoth enterprises in 'rhetoric' disguised as genre and discourse theory that predate the collaborative publications with Genette. See also Todorov (1978), which 'informs' Genette (1979).
45   Duff (2000) goes some way to introducing Russian Formalism and the Polish Formalist Ireneusz Opacki to an English audience, yet omits Yuri Lotman's longstanding work on poetry. Further comparative work needs to take forward investigation of European semiotics, including Italian exponents such as Croce, Conte or Eco.
46   As Hawcroft (1999), p. 245, has noted.
47   See Compagnon (1999), p. 1219, and p. 1233 for an explanation why *explication de texte* gained importance. In 1902 rhetoric was dropped from French school syllabuses for the first time, largely instigated by Gustave Lanson.

48 See Bruce (1995), p. 181, who notes these two rhetorical stages in Genette's work.
49 For two excellent studies on parody, see Rose (1993) and Sangsue (1994).
50 Genette (1982), pp. 91–2. Worton and Still (1990), p. 14, also note this distinction.
51 As Jenny (1976), p. 260, noted.
52 Booth (1974) remains a classic but demonstrates the 'muddle' between modes and genres that Genette avoids. Key to Booth's work is the distinction between 'stable' and 'instable' irony. See also Muecke (1970).
53 As Bouillaguet (1996), p. 5, suggests. See also Sangsue (1994), p. 93.
54 See Fumaroli (1999), p. 14.
55 Duff (2000), p. 3.
56 In his foreword to Thaïs Morgan's gallant translation of Mimologics (1995), p. ix, Gerard Prince clearly separates the perceived redundancies of cratylism from Genette's 'purely' aesthetic appreciation of the literariness of such effects.
57 Morgan's preface as translator (1995), p. xxiv.
58 Genette's pun on Ponge's le parti pris des choses as the 'parti pris des mots' sums up the variety of all these positions that he takes at some time or another throughout Mimologiques against 'pure' cratylism.
59 See, for example, Baudonnière (1997), p. 65, and Oughourlian (1982), p. 19, respectively.
60 Hunt (1996), pp. 32–3.
61 Ibid., pp. 146–8, for a full glossary of rhetorical terms, including these.
62 See Schwarz (1996), p. 251.
63 Girard (1978b), p. 203 (reprinted interview with Girard by Diacritics [vol. 8, 1978, pp. 31–54]), charges Lacoue-Labarthe and all poststructural versions of mimesis as undecidability as not radical enough, and that advances as 'cognitive nihilism' (ibid., p. 213) are erroneous.
64 For a study of Girard and deconstruction, see MacKenna (1992). See also Girard (1978b), p. 220, for his appreciation of Derrida's 'deconstruction of sacrificial thought' and 'the impossibility of a consistent theory of mimesis in Plato'.
65 This place appears very similar to the 'vrairéal' of Irigaray.
66 Girard (1978b), p. vii.
67 See his earlier works, Girard (1961), (1972) and (1978a).
68 Girard (1978b), p. xii.
69 Ibid., p. viii.
70 See Girard (1978b), p. 203. Prefigurations are not transfigurations unless one is the fulfilment of one's own prophecy, which Jesus announces in the Gospels several times that he is.
71 Knox (1994), pp. 11–12.
72 Girard (1978b), p. 215.
73 See Williams (1996), p. 22. This is the direct opposite of the copy process itself. See Schwarz (1996), p. 214, on stenography transforming 'the One into the Many'.

74 Girard (1978a), trans., p. 142.
75 See Williams (1996), p. 263.
76 Girard in Girard (1978b), pp. 206–7.
77 Ibid., pp. 220 and 207, respectively.
78 See Williams (1996), p. viii.
79 Ibid., p. 198. From the Greek, to limp, for Girard, the *skandalon* 'designates a very common inability to walk away from mimetic rivalry which turns into addiction.'
80 Girard (1978a), trans., p. 279.
81 Matt.: 21: 42, Mark 12: 10 and Luke 20: 17.
82 As Oughourlian (1982), p. 48, notes.
83 See Girard (1978b), p. 221, on intertextuality and deconstruction as revelatory of mimetic effects, and ibid., p. 214, for endorsement of Michel Serres's observations on dogmatic methodologies (including the sciences).
84 Girard (1978a), trans., p. 100.
85 Ibid., p. 103.
86 See Cabantous (1998) for a study of blasphemy and Brooks (2000) on 'speaking guilt'.
87 See Girard (1978b), p. vii.
88 Girard in Williams (1996), pp. 208–9, also warns of the victimized victim returning as persecutor.
89 This would include liberation theology and feminist theology. Christ's unveiling of the false religious authorities of his times was an act which demonstrated the Real.
90 Girard (1978b), pp. x–xi. He includes here 'art as pure entertainment', 'art for art's sake', and 'critical methodologies that more than ever deny any real investigative power to a literary work'.
91 For a discussion of Marx and Girard, see Orsini (1986) and Dumouchel and Dupuy (1979). The work of post-Marxists such as Butler et al. (2000) or Bourdieu (1992) has not engaged with Girard.
92 See Girard in Williams (1996), p. 57.
93 See the work of Northrop Frye, Carl Jung and Gaston Bachelard.
94 Girard in Williams (1996), p. 273. Girard cites the women round Jesus at the crucifixion and the Amazonian Yanomamö.
95 See, for example, Flax (1990), who allies feminism and post-modernism but admits (p. 221) that the latter is inadequate for the practice of justice.
96 See Hampson (1990 and 1996) for post-Christian feminist theology and Holloway (1992) for recuperations of older goddess religions.
97 Diamond (1997), p. iii (my emphasis). Her excellent fourteen-page introduction is a model of succinctness covering much of the territory that requires a corpus for Genette.
98 Ibid., p. iv.
99 Ibid., pp. 65–6.
100 See also Judith Butler's further theorization of Irigaray, female performance and gender troubling, Butler (1990).

101   Kristeva (1969) devotes a whole essay to the gestural in communication, but no work, feminist of otherwise, has been done on it.

102   Irigaray is a model scapegoat as she was denied access to psycho-analytic practice (performance?) by Lacan, because of her critique of the false mirrors of his, and therefore not 'universal', model.

103   See Warner (1976), Showalter (1985 and 1997), Gilbert and Gubar (1979). The male critic Oughourlian (1982), pp. 41, 93–4, makes a valiant stab at reinterpreting Eve along Girardian lines.

104   Hawcroft (1999), pp. 2 and 79.

105   See T. M. Greene (1982), p. 1.

106   See Schoeck (1984) and Miner and Brady (1993), p. ix. Compagnon (1979) discusses Montaigne's use of quotation without quotation marks.

107   See Maurel-Indart (1999), especially pp. 2 and 94.

108   Quoted in ibid., p. 48, from the *Canard enchaîné* (12 Jan 1983), but not with respect to electronic hypermedia! See also Schneider (1985), p. 30, and West and Woodman (1979), p. 1, on Latin *imitatio* as 'dynamic law' not plagiarism.

109   See Schwarz (1996), p. 218.

110   Arguably, it also instated 'copywrite'.

111   Hobson (1982), pp. 13 and 18, respectively.

112   Ibid., pp. 18 and 15, respectively.

113   Ibid., p. 44.

114   Ibid., p. 20.

115   See Maddox (1984) for a study of the medieval theatre of the double as lie. See also Déguy and Depuy (1982), Dumouchel and Dupuy (1979) and Ricoeur (1986).

116   Bloom reads Milton's Satan as allegory of the supremely 'strong poet'. See Mileur (1985), p. 10, who lauds Bloom for 'the divinatory element in literature' on the critical agenda. See also O'Hara (1985), pp. 140, 169 and 213, respectively, on Derrida's 'allegorical' anti-mimetic, Frye's 'prophetic literary identity' and de Man's 'critical misrepresentation'. See also Eliot (1953), pp. 52–3, on blasphemy.

117   See Spariosu (1984), p. x.

118   See Stewart (1978), pp. 201 and 209, on the fractures within pure games such as nonsense.

119   See Detweiler and Doty (1990), pp. 11–12 and 21.

120   See Hardie (1993), pp. xi and 1–3.

121   Oughourlian (1982), p. 41. For this critic, it is only of the Devil that one may speak of 'original sin' (ibid., p. 98).

122   Ibid., p. 106.

123   Girard in Williams (1996), p. 265.

124   Ibid., pp. 208–10. Girard does not mince his words concerning the refusal of the Church to take the story of Satan seriously.

125   Ibid., p. 199, and the entry for Satan in the glossary of terms, p. 292. See also Heimonet (1991), who argues for two 'Logos', Heidegger's and St John's.

126   Dawkins (1998), p. 122.
127   See Stewart (1978), p. 9, on common sense. On various aspects of cultural memory, see Conte (1986), p. 49; Flax (1990), p. 221; T. M. Greene (1982), p. 9; and Lukacher (1986), p. 12.
128   Schwarz (1996), pp. 378 and 322.
129   See Genette (1979), p. 58. See also Todorov (1978), pp. 16 and 23.
130   See Wiesel (1994), p. 7.
131   See Schneider (1985), p. 124.
132   Newman (1985), p. 52.
133   See Hawcroft (1999), p. 120. See also Maddox (1984), pp. 95–7, for discussion of medieval literature defined against legal modes of thought.
134   See Stewart (1978), p. 16.
135   Campagnon (1990), p. 11 (my translation).

Chapter 4   Quotation

1   Exceptions are Compagnon (1979), Meyer (1968), Sternberg (1982) and Weisgerber (1970).
2   See Arendt's introduction to Benjamin (1973), especially pp. 9, 28–9, 32–3.
3   See Compagnon (1979), pp. 12 and 37.
4   Ibid., p. 38.
5   See Kellett (1933), p. 50.
6   See Gilman (1946), p. 103, on baroque usage.
7   See Meyer (1968), p. 6, and Kellett (1933), p. 15.
8   Sternberg (1982), p. 109.
9   See Weisgerber (1970), p. 42, and T. M. Greene (1982), pp. 15–17.
10   Kellett (1933), p. 14.
11   See Lee (1971), pp. 10–11.
12   See Bauerlein (1995), p. 11.
13   Quotation is what Derrida (1987) would call 'the invention of oneself as other'.
14   Compagnon (1979), p. 11; Kellett (1933), p. 7.
15   Schlicher (1905), p. 69.
16   See Derrida (1984) and Jefferson (1990).
17   My term here is the inverse process of transubstantiation as the central doctrine of Roman Catholicism, whereby in communion the consecrated bread and wine become the substance of the body and blood of Christ.
18   See Isaiah 40: 3 and John 1: 1–14. In John 1: 15–34, the prophet is distinguished from the Christ.
19   See, for, example, Fishbane (1989), p. 34.
20   See, for example, MacIntyre and Ricoeur (1969).
21   See Ong (1982), p. 53, for the distinction of riddle as oral and syllogism as textual in form.
22   See Jenny (1976), p. 266.

23 Lee (1971), p. 3.
24 Most studies see quotation and allusion in terms of visual illustrations, not aural ones. Exceptions are Hollander (1981) and O'Donnell (1992).
25 Kellett (1933), pp. 13–14.
26 See Ricks (1976), pp. 209 and 211.
27 See Weisgerber (1970), p. 43, and Segal's foreword to Conte (1986), pp. 10 and 12.
28 See Hutcheon, Whiteside and Morrisette in Whiteside and Issacharoff (1987), pp. 1–13, 14–32 and 111–21, respectively. For a study of *mise en abyme*, see Dällenbach (1977).
29 See Pasco (1994), p. 6.
30 Ibid., p. 12.
31 Ibid., pp. 15–16.
32 In the medieval period, exact quotation (*ipsisima verba*) was distinguished from reporting.
33 See Doane (1991), p. 77.
34 See Vinaver (1971), p. 4.
35 This applies equally to the medieval, Coleridgean and deconstructive 'allegory' as the ironic pointing to but deferring of meaning. See de Man (1979). Allegory in medieval writing such as *Piers Ploughman* can be smaller scale and merge with allusion.
36 See Ricoeur (1976), p. 56.
37 Ong (1982), pp. 72, 80 and 82.
38 Dronke (1997), pp. 179–81 (with reference to Francesco Colonna's *Hypnerotomachia*).
39 Tuve (1966), pp. 20 and 25–6.
40 See, for example, Finke and Shichtman (1987) and Stern (1991).
41 Ricoeur (1978), p. 239.
42 Ibid., pp. 242–5. See also Vanhoozer (1990), p. 100. In Hebrew, *dabar* means word and 'event', making language a mode of action, not primarily thought.
43 See Stern (1991), p. 93, and as extended study of allegory, parable and mashal.
44 Ibid., pp. 67–8, where the genre is linked with moral allegory, the exemplum and the *roman à thèse*.
45 Ibid., pp. 15 and 69.
46 See Heinemann (1986), pp. 49–52. See also Handelman in Plottel and Charney (1978), pp. 99–112, of which pp. 101–3 explains the midrashic terminology with clear examples.
47 The spelling adopted by Haddawy's translation of *The Arabian Nights* (1990).
48 Ong (1982), p. 136.
49 It may be telling that a radio soap, the BBC's *The Archers*, is among the longest running.
50 For the problem of distinguishing parody from imperfectly executed imitation in Old French, see Cobby (1995).
51 Besamusca et al. (1994), p. 1.

52 Taylor in ibid., p. 62, distinguishes sequential cyclicity from organic cyclicity, series and plenitude.
53 See Baumgartner in ibid., p. 8.
54 See Vinaver (1971), pp. 6 and 32.
55 See Josipovici (1982), p. 70, for a similar view, but of the novel as *roman*.
56 Vinaver (1971), p. 128. He is more circumspect about direct genealogies of the novel from romance in his introduction, pp. vii–viii.
57 See Chase in Besamusca et al. (1994), p. 179.
58 Brownlee and Nichols (1985), editors' preface, p. 2.
59 Minnis (1984), p. 10, and one of the best studies of medieval authority available.
60 See Hanning in Finke and Shichtman (1987), pp. 29–31, for a study of medieval gloss. For an excellent study of the commentary tradition in medieval theory and criticism, see Minnis and Scott (1988).
61 See Heinemann (1986), p. 49, on aggadah as 'popular philosophy' of the rabbinic period.
62 Midrash means searching. See E. Cohen (1996), pp. 2 and 4.
63 Fishbane (1989), p. 126.
64 Ibid., p. 122.
65 See Heinemann (1986), pp. 52–3.
66 See E. Cohen (1996), p. 9.
67 Hartman and Budick (1986), p. xii. The quotation refers to part of the title of Eliot's famous essay, 'Tradition and the individual talent', Eliot (1953), already discussed in chapter 2.
68 See Banon (1987), pp. 33–5 and 72. This is one of the most far-reaching studies of the richness of midrash, which inserts reading in the place the West reserves for writing. See also Lévinas's preface (ibid., pp. 9–10), which foregrounds 'sollicitation' as the ethical constraint of midrash.
69 See Dronke (1997) for an exemplary study of poetic inspiration, yet which is completely gender blind. See also Ong (1982), pp. 159–60, 178 and 182, who glances past the issues of gender and women's education in pre-postmodernity.
70 See work on native women writers, for example, Hoy (2001).
71 Ong (1971), p. 34.
72 See Holloway (1992), pp. 28–9. She calls such creative and imaginative retelling *nigromantia*, a form of incantatory word (ibid., p. 38).
73 See Idel in Hartman and Budick (1986), p. 142, on alternative Jewish mysticism, and A. H. Baker (1991), pp. 38–9, on the primacy of spirituality as counterintelligence.
74 See Ong (1982), pp. 104 and 113.
75 The prominence of flora and fauna in these illuminations is redolent here of such links. The *physiologus* or discourse about nature was perhaps their more amplified form. See Minnis and Scott (1988), p. 17, for its ends of amusement and edification.
76 See Vinaver (1971), p. 41.
77 See Minnis and Scott (1988), p. 7.

78 See Ong (1982), p. 114.
79 Gellrich (1985), p. 18. This critic emphasizes that 'The idea of the Book in the middle ages consists not simply of a definitive content, but rather of specific ways of signifying, organizing, and remembering' (p. 248).
80 See Kelly (1996), p. 5.
81 I am indebted to Ian Johnson for the phrase 'anxiety of authority' here. See also Kelly (1996), pp. 1–3.
82 See the editors' preface in Minnis and Scott (1988), pp. vii–viii, on Dante as 'the great innovator' at the roots of literary criticism.
83 See Minnis (1984), p. 4.
84 See Prickett (1986), whose title I have borrowed in my formulation, Edwards (1990) and Hartman (1975), pp. 16–17, on various kinds of 'lapsed scripture'.
85 The postmodern equivalent is no less Herculean but as extension, the library (Borges, Perec), or the encyclopedia (Flaubert). See Poirier (1998), p. 6, on 'oeuvres–sommes'.
86 Pasco (1994), p. 98 (following Meyer), recognizes allusion as opposition as a rare form distinct from satire, but does not elaborate on the complexity of such 'reversal' or that of *intaglio* – 'a negative surface which must be filled and cast off in order to reveal the true figure at the center of the narration' (p. 79). Both notions can be subsumed in *peripeteia*.
87 See Stern (1986), p. 108, and the glossary to Hartman and Budick (1986).
88 E. Cohen (1996), p. 6.
89 Vinaver (1971), p. 36. See also ibid., pp. 22–3 and 35, where Vinaver sees this term in its reverberations with '*Verbindung* ("connection"), *Vermutung* ("conjecture"), and *Schlussfolgerung* ("chain of reasoning", "argument") [. . .] ("theme")'.
90 See Hunt (1978), as instigator of the term 'bridge work', and Kelly (1996).
91 Kelly (1996), p. 4.
92 Very different approaches to autobiography from those of its canonical critics, such as Lejeune, suggest something of this creative mileage in rethinking the genre. See, for example, Banon (1987), p. 124, and A. H. Baker (1991), pp. 39 and 42.
93 Frow (1986), p. 108.
94 McLuhan (1972), p. 69, names this power tool 'the technique of suspended judgement'.
95 See Overholt (1986), pp. 10–11.
96 See N. O. Brown (1991), pp. 2–3.
97 See Northrop Frye's spectacularly misogynistic re-evaluation of the Muse and male creativity, Frye (1960), pp. 45–8.
98 See Kadir (1992), p. 20, on 'rupture and rapture', and p. 173 for useful distinctions between divination as assuaging and the prophetic discernment as 'eternally fated to be divisionary'.
99 Old Testament prophets were anointed in public. Jonah is a key example of the reluctant prophet.

100　N. O. Brown (1991), p. 98, mistakes dissenters and iconoclasts in the worldly sense with prophets proper who break false idols. In his reading of late capitalism, Brown names the Dionysian as force behind its various media (ibid., p. 191).

101　See Fishbane (1989), p. ix. Serres also chooses this figure as coterminous with elements of his four-part study of postmodernity, communication, interference, translation and distribution (Serres, 1969, 1972, 1974 and 1977, respectively).

102　See J. T. Greene (1989), pp. xvii–xviii, for whom the prophet is more the ambassador, emissary–courier, envoy, herald before being a harbinger.

103　See ibid., p. 151, following James Sanders that 'The Hebrew word for prophet, *nabi*', probably means spokesman.' For Wiesel (1994), p. 930, the prophet is the 'Intercesseur plutôt qu'intermédiaire'.

104　John the Baptist best illustrates this outcome, which concatenates the ends of various Old Testament prophets as reviled, rejected, imprisoned, threatened, harried, assaulted and then killed ignominiously by a Gentile.

105　The model of the prophet as the disobedient servant is Jacob, struggling and wrestling with the angel (stubborness, reluctance to cede). He is defeated only when his hip is touched near the tendon so that he cannot withstand. Only then can he overcome and request a blessing.

106　The *vox clamantis* is often cited, but not the context. The prophet is the word bearer outside the camp in the gap (no place, wilderness) because this is where the Law was originally given to Moses, and where the people of Israel were brought as a place of transition, challenge and change.

107　See Bruggemann (1985), p. 13.

108　See, for example, Allen (2000) and Samoyault (2001). The clearest exceptions remain Hebel (1989) and Broich and Pfister (1985).

109　See Orr (2000) on translation as intertextual generator.

110　Ong (1982), although on orality, is strangely silent on the place of the translator.

111　Copeland (1991), p. 11.

112　Ricoeur (1976), pp. 6–7.

113　Ibid., p. 9. See also Copeland (1991), p. 14, who makes the same point concerning grammar and rhetoric.

114　Steiner (1975), p. xi.

115　Copeland (1991) is a comprehensive and complex study of medieval translation. See especially pp. 3–4.

116　For a comprehensive study of Renaissance translation, see Norton (1984). T. M. Greene (1982), p. 41, speaks of Dante's rewriting as '"modernizing" its aggiornamento'. Arguably the late Middle Ages and early Renaissance are a continuum, caused by momentum, not a break, as Minnis and Scott (1988), p. 374, suggest.

117　See Obaldia (1995) for a study of Montaigne.

118　See Ricoeur (1976), p. 28.

119 Derrida in Hartman and Budick (1986), as 'password' (p. 320), 'the cypher of the cypher' (p. 323) and (pp. 345–6) on circumcision as 'mark of the alliance, it is also an index of exclusion.'

120 See the preface by Arendt, p. 43, in Benjamin's *Illuminations* (1973).

121 See Steiner (1975), p. 25.

122 See Regard (1992), p. 24, for Cixous's positive experience of reading Clarice Lispector in translation.

123 See, for example, Bassnett-McGuire (1980), Lefevere (1992a and 1992b) and Venuti (1992 and 1995).

124 Steiner (1975), pp. 228 and 235, respectively.

125 Ibid., p. 59.

126 See. for example, ibid., pp. 249 and 260, and p. 269: 'Each translation falls short [. . .] From the perception of unending inadequacy stems a particular sadness [. . .] "Wer übersetzt," proclaimed [. . .] Matthias Claudius, "der untersetzt".'

127 Benjamin (1973), pp. 71–2 and p. 77.

128 Ibid., p. 77 (and famously): 'The task of the translator consists in finding that intended effect [*Intention*] upon the language into which he is translating which produces in it an echo of the original. [. . .] The intention of the poet is spontaneous, primary, graphic; that of the translator is derivative, ultimate, ideational.'

129 See Ying (2000).

130 See Ricoeur (1976), p. 84: 'Structuralism and its methods explain, they do not interpret.'

131 See Copeland (1991), p. 7.

132 Steiner (1975), p. 23. Scholarship on the subject is of course immense.

133 Hartman and Budick (1986), p. xi. The shuttle is a rocket, not a weaver's implement.

134 MacIntyre and Ricoeur (1969), p. 65.

135 See Cixous (2001) for a highly informed fictional autobiography of Derrida.

136 See Clément and Kristeva (1998), Irigaray (1983) and Derrida (1996).

137 Thompson (1981b), p. 6, uses this term to characterize the work of Marx, Nietzsche and Freud to distinguish it from Ricoeur's hermeneutics of faith, a revelation of the sacred.

138 Ricoeur (1976), pp. xi–xii. See Thompson (1981a), Kearney (1996) and Valdés (1995).

139 Ricoeur in Thompson (1981b), p. 37. *Oeuvre* seems close in Ricoeur's mind to the verb *ouvrir*. See Ricoeur (1980), p. 18.

140 See Copeland (1991), p. 19.

141 Benjamin (1973), p. 77.

142 See the superb collection of essays on Ricoeur edited by Hahn (1995), including an intellectual autobiography and multilingual bibliography.

143 See Clark (1991), for whom Ricoeur is exemplary by his interdisciplinarity and continuous, modest self-criticism. Van den Hengel (1982), p. xx, describes Ricoeur's method as 'architectonic'.

144 For Ricoeur's concern with intrigue to elucidate the common link between fiction and history, see Ricoeur (1980), pp. 3–4, where he uses the word 'pont'. Thompson (1981b), p. 39, has also suggested the analogy of plot, but it is more strictly linked to its modern form.

145 See Philibirt in Hahn (1995), p. 135.

146 As Kemp in Kearney (1996), p. 41, acknowledges.

147 See MacIntyre and Ricoeur (1969), p. 74, for Ricoeur's 'Lévinasian' awareness of 'autrui' as ethical and philosophical. See also Thompson (1981b), p. 6: '"The symbol gives rise to thought". Hermeneutics [. . .] is animated by faith, by a willingness to listen and it is characterized by a respect for the symbol as a revelation of the sacred.'

148 Ricoeur of course combines reason and revelation dialectically. See Coppieters de Gibson (1977), pp. 15–34 and 51, on revelation, particularly of the 'history–making' nature of foundational events.

149 See Ricoeur's reply to Valdés in Hahn (1995), p. 283: 'the capacity of redescription or refiguration of the world does not occur unless it becomes a "shared meaning": the presumed truth of the redescription of the world can, therefore, only be intersubjective. [. . .] The critic then becomes the arbitrator of the conflict of interpretations.'

150 Ricoeur (1976), p. 46, and Beardsley (1958), p. 134.

151 Among the many studies of metaphor in Ricoeur's work, see Gerhart and Russell (1984) and Klemm (1983).

152 Ricoeur (1976), p. 7.

153 Ibid., p. 16.

154 Ibid., pp. 87–8.

155 See Valdés (1995), p. 279, on how Ricoeur's hermeneutic criticism challenges critical theory.

156 Ricoeur (1976), pp. 94–5.

Conclusions

1 Clayton and Rothstein (1991), p. 172. They see this as the return of the repressed of modernism.

2 O'Donnell and Con Davis (1989), p. xiii.

3 See, for example, Faye (1972 and 1990).

4 Ong (1971), p. 14.

5 See recent work by Butler et al. (2000), Bourdieu (1979 and 1992), and de Certeau (1980 and 1993).

6 Ricoeur (1976), p. 30.

7 See Butler et al. (2000), p. xii.

8 Lategan in Jennings (1990), p. 150.

9 See Bondanella (1997) for a study of Eco and Italian semiotics.

10 Ricoeur in MacIntyre and Ricoeur (1969), p. 70.

11 See Ricoeur in Coppieters de Gibson (1977), p. 27, on limit situations.

12 Ricoeur (1976), pp. 64–5.

13 Ibid. Ricoeur would equate Eliade's symbolic paradigms with Jung's or Bachelard's 'archetypes'. See also Steiner (1975), p. 86, following Cassirer on metaphor as personal 'world-views'.

14 Redfern (1989) is suggestive of ways in which jargon, along with political slogans and rabble-rousing, are aural brainwashing tactics. Rhyming slang is a survival tactic against dominant culture and language.

15 See Ricoeur's throwaway remark in MacIntyre and Ricoeur (1969), p. 72: 'It is not by mere chance that in many of the Western European languages the words for "obedience" are derived from the words for "hearing" or "listening". In Latin, [. . .] *obedientia* [. . .] is related to *obaudire* [to give ear to, to listen].'

16 This is a transliteration of Banon's term, Banon (1995), p. 93.

17 See ibid., pp. 9 and 92.

18 See ibid., pp. 96–7. For further exploration of midrash and intertextuality, see Boyarin (1990).

19 See, for example, Handelman in Plottel and Charney (1978), p. 111.

20 See Cave (1988), p. 495, and his link between knowledge and 'impossible or incomprehensible sexual knowledge'.

21 See LeDoeuff (1989).

22 Hideo (1995), pp. 24–6. Hideo, as Bakhtin and Auerbach, trained first as a medievalist.

References and Bibliography

Adlam, C., Falconer, R., Makhlin, V., and Renfrew, A. (eds) (1997). *Face to Face: Bakhtin in Russia and the West*. Sheffield: Sheffield Academic Press.

Allen, G. (1994). *Harold Bloom: a Poetics of Conflict*. Hemel Hempstead: Harvester Wheatsheaf.

—— (2000). *Intertextuality*. London: Routledge.

Alter, R. (1992). *The World of Biblical Literature*. London: SPCK.

Amossy, R., and Rosen, E. (1982). *Le Discours du cliché*. Paris: CDU/SEDES.

Angenot, M. (1983a). ' "L'Intertextualité": enquête sur l'emergence et la diffusion d'un champ notionnel'. *Revue des Sciences Humaines*, no. 189, pp. 121–35.

—— (1983b). 'Intertextualité, interdiscursivité, discours social'. *Texte*, no. 2 [on 'L'Intertextualité: intertexte, autotexte, intratexte'], pp. 101–12.

Annesley, J. (2001). 'Gibson, globalisation and new media'. *Forum for Modern Language Studies*, 37, pp. 218–29.

Aristotle (1920). *On the Art of Poetry*. Oxford: Clarendon Press.

Armstrong, T. (ed.) (2001). 'Literature and technology'. *Forum for Modern Language Studies*, 37, pp. 121–6.

Asholt, W. (1994). *Intertextualität und Subversität: Studien zur Romanliteratur der achtziger Jahre in Frankreich*. Heidelberg: Universitätsverlag C. Winter.

Auerbach, E. ([1946] 1968). *Mimesis: the Representation of Reality in Western Literature*, trans. W. R. Trask. Princeton, NJ: Princeton University Press.

Awkward, M. (1989). *Inspiriting Influences: Tradition, Revision and Afro-American Women's Novels*. New York: Columbia University Press.

Baker, A. H. (1984). *Blues, Ideology and Afro-American Literature: a Vernacular Theory*. Chicago and London: University of Chicago Press.

—— (1991). *Workings of the Spirit: the Poetics of Afro-American Women's Writing*. Chicago and London: University of Chicago Press.

Baker, M. (ed.) (2000). *The Translation Studies Reader: Lawrence Venuti.* London: Routledge.

Bakhtin, M. M. (1981). *The Dialogic Imagination*, ed. M. Holquist, trans. C. Emerson and M. Holquist. Austin: University of Texas Press.

——(1984). *Problems of Dostoevsky's Poetics*, ed. and trans. C. Emerson, intro. W. C. Booth. Minneapolis and Manchester: University of Minnesota Press.

——(1986). *Speech Genres and other Late Essays*, ed. C. Emerson and M. Holquist, trans. V. W. McGee. Austin: University of Texas Press.

Bakhtin, M. M., and Medvedev, P. N. (1978). *The Formal Method in Literary Scholarship*, trans. A. J. Wehrle. Baltimore: Johns Hopkins University Press.

Bal, M. (1997). *Narratology: Introduction to the Theory of Narrative*, 2nd edn. Toronto: University of Toronto Press.

Balakian A. (1962). 'Influence and literary fortune: the equivocal junction of two methods'. *Yearbook of Comparative and General Literature*, no. 11, pp. 24–31.

Banon, D. (1987). *La Lecture infinie: les voies de l'interprétation midrachique.* Paris: Seuil.

——(1995). *Le Midrach.* Paris: PUF.

Barth J. (1977). 'The literature of exhaustion'. In *The Novel Today: Contemporary Writers on Modern Fiction*, ed. M. Bradbury. London: Fontana, pp. 70–83.

——(1980). 'The literature of replenishment: postmodern fiction'. *The Atlantic*, no. 245, pp. 65–71.

Barthes, R. (1963). *Sur Racine.* Paris: Pierres Vives.

——(1967). *Système de la mode.* Paris: Points Seuil.

——(1970). *S/Z.* Paris: Points Seuil.

——(1971). *Essais critiques.* Paris: Points Seuil.

——(1973a). *Le Plaisir du texte.* Paris: Points Seuil.

——(1973b). 'Texte (théorie du)'. *Encyclopédie universalis.*

——(1975). *Roland Barthes.* Paris: Points Seuil.

Bassnett-McGuire, S. (1980). *Translation Studies.* London: Methuen.

Baudonnière, P.-M. (1997). *Le Mimétisme et l'imitation: un exposé pour comprendre, un essai pour réfléchir.* Paris: Flammarion Dominos.

Bauerlein, M. (ed.) (1995). *Joseph N. Riddel Purloined Letters: Originality and Repetition in American Literature.* Baton Rouge and London: Louisiana State University Press.

Baxandall, M. (1985). *Patterns of Intention: on the Historical Explanation of Pictures.* New Haven, CT, and London: Yale University Press.

Beardsley, M. (1958). *Aesthetics: Problems in the Philosophy of Criticism.* Indianapolis: Hackett.

Benjamin, W. (1973). 'The work of art in the age of mechanical reproduction'. In *Illuminations*, ed. H. Arendt. London: Fontana Press.

Bennington, G., and Derrida, J. (1991). *Jacques Derrida par Geoffrey Bennington and Jacques Derrida.* Paris: Seuil.

Bernard, G., and Poswick, R.-F. (eds) (1990). *Les Chemins du texte: le livre des traces.* Paris and Geneva: Champion-Slatkine.

Besamusca, B., Gerritsen, W. P., Hogetoorn, C., and Lie, O. S. H. (eds) (1994). *Cyclification: the Development of Narrative Cycles in the Chansons de Geste and the Arthurian Romances*. Amsterdam, Oxford, New York and Tokyo: North-Holland.

Bevan, D. (ed.) (1993). *Modern Myths*. Amsterdam and Atlanta: Rodopi.

Björk, E. L. (1993). *Campus Clowns and the Canon: David Lodge's Campus Fiction*. Stockholm and Umeå: University of Umeå Press.

Black, M. (1962). *Models and Metaphors: Studies in Language and Philosophy*. Ithaca, New York and London: Cornell University Press.

Blackmore, S. (2000). *The Meme Machine*. Oxford: OUP.

Block, H. M. (1970). *Nouvelles tendances en littérature comparée*. Paris: Nizet.

Bloom, H. (1962). *The Visionary Company: a Reading of English Romantic Poetry*. London: Faber & Faber.

——(1963). *Blake's Apocalypse: a Study in Poetic Argument*. London: Gollancz.

——([1959] 1969). *Shelley's Mythmaking*. New York: Cornell University Press.

——(1973). *The Anxiety of Influence: a Theory of Poetry*. Oxford: OUP.

——(1975a). *A Map of Misreading*. Oxford: OUP.

——(1975b). *Kabbalah and Criticism*. New York: Continuum.

——(ed.) (1979). *Deconstruction and Criticism*. New York: Seabury Press.

——(1982a). *Agon: Towards a Theory of Revisionism*. Oxford: OUP.

——(1982b). *The Breaking of the Vessels*. Chicago and London: University of Chicago Press.

——(1995). *The Western Canon: the Books and Schools of the Ages*. London: Macmillan.

——(1997). *The Anxiety of Influence*, 2nd edn. Oxford: OUP.

Bogue, R. (ed.) (1991). *Mimesis in Contemporary Theory: an Interdisciplinary Approach*, Vol. 2: *Mimesis, Semiosis and Power*. Philadelphia and Amsterdam: John Benjamins.

Bolla, P. de (1988). *Harold Bloom: Towards Historical Rhetorics*. London and New York: Routledge.

Bolter, J. D. (1984). *Turing's Man: Western Culture in the Computer Age*. Chapel Hill: University of North Carolina Press.

Bonandella, P. (1997). *Umberto Eco and the Open Text: Semiotics, Fiction, Popular Culture*. Cambridge: CUP.

Booth, W. C. (1974). *A Rhetoric of Irony*. Chicago and London: University of Chicago Press.

Boring, M. E. (1982). *Sayings of the Risen Jesus: Christian Prophecy in the Synoptic Tradition*. Cambridge: CUP.

Bouillaguet, A. (1996). *L'Ecriture imitative: pastiche, parodie, collage*. Paris: Nathan.

Bourdieu, P. (1979). *La Distinction critique sociale du jugement*. Paris: Minuit.

——(1992). *Les Règles de l'art: genèse et structure du champ littéraire*. Paris: Seuil.

Boutet, D., and Harf-Lancner, L. (eds) (1993). *Ecriture et modes de pensée au moyen age (VIIe–XVe siècles)*. Paris: Presses de L'Ecole Normale Supérieure.

Boyarin, D. (1990). *Intertextuality and the Reading of Midrash*. Bloomington: Indiana University Press.

Brandt, J. (1997). *Geopolitics: the Politics of Mimesis in Poststructuralist French Poetry and Theory*. Stanford, CA: Stanford University Press.

Braund, D., and Wilkins, J. (eds) (2000). *Athenaeus and his World: Reading Greek Culture in the Roman Empire*. Exeter: University of Exeter Press.

Brée, G. (1978). 'The archaeology of discourse in Malraux's *Anti-memoirs*'. In *Intertextuality: New Perspectives in Criticism*, ed. J. P. Plottel and H. Charney. New York: New York Literary Forum.

Broich, U., and Pfister, M. (eds) (1985). *Intertextualität: Formen, Funktionen, anglistische Fallstudien*. Tübingen: Niemeyer.

Brooker, P. (ed.) (1992). *Modernism/Postmodernism*. London and New York: Longman.

Brooks, P. (2000). *Troubling Confessions: Speaking Guilt in Law and Literature*. Chicago and London: University of Chicago Press.

Brown, A. (1992). *Roland Barthes: the Figures of Writing*. Oxford: Clarendon Press.

Brown, N. O. (1991). *Apocalypse and/or Metamorphosis*. Berkeley and Oxford: University of California Press.

Brownlee, K., and Nichols, S. G. (eds) (1985). 'Images of power: medieval history/discourse/literature'. *Yale French Studies*, no. 70.

Bruce, D. (1995). *De l'intertextualité à l'interdiscursivité: histoire d'une double émergence*. Toronto: Editions Paratexte.

Bruggemann, W. (1985). *The Prophetic Imagination*. Philadephia: Fortress Press.

Butler, J. (1990). *Gender Trouble: Feminism and the Subversion of Identity*. New York and London: Routledge.

Butler, J., Guillory, J., and Thomas, K. (eds) (2000). *What's Left of Theory? New Work on the Politics of Literary Theory*. New York: Routledge.

Cabantous, A. (1998). *Histoire du blasphème en occident: fin XVIe – milieu XIXe siècle*. Paris: Albin Michel.

Cameron, D. (1985). *Feminism and Linguistic Theory*. Basingstoke: Macmillan.

Carpenter, E., and McLuhan, M. (eds) (1960). *Explorations in Communication*. Boston: Beacon Press.

Cave, T. (1979). *The Cornucopian Text*. Oxford: OUP.

——(1988). *Recognitions: a Study in Poetics*. Oxford: OUP.

Certeau, M. de (1969). *L'Etranger ou L'Union dans la différence*. Paris: Desclée de Brouwer.

——(1980). *Le Parasite*. Paris: Hachette Littératures.

——(1993). *La Culture au pluriel*. Paris: Seuil.

——(1994). *La Prise de parole et autres écrits politiques*. Paris: Seuil.

Certeau, M. de, and Domenach, J.-M. (1974). *Le Christianisme éclaté*. Paris: Seuil.

Chadwick, H. (1993). *The Early Church*. Harmondsworth: Penguin.

Cixous, H. (1992). 'Un lieu de l'autre: un entretien avec Hélène Cixous'. In F. Regard, *Logique de traverses*. St Etienne: CIEREC Université Jean Monnet, pp. 11–26.

——(2001). *Portrait de Jacques Derrida en jeune Saint Juif*. Paris: Galilée.

Clark, S. H. (1991). *Paul Ricoeur*. London and New York: Routledge.

Clayton, J., and Rothstein, E. (eds) (1991). *Influence and Intertextuality in Literary History*. Madison: University of Wisconsin Press.

Clément, C., and Kristeva, J. (1998). *Le Féminin et le sacré*. Paris: Stock.

Cobby, A. E. (1995). *Ambivalent Conventions: Formula and Parody in Old French*. Amsterdam and Atlanta: Rodopi.

Cohen, E. (1996). *Poésie et midrash: entretiens avec Fidel Anthelme X*. Marseilles: Cholet.

Cohen, T. (1994). *Anti-Mimesis from Plato to Hitchcock*. Cambridge: CUP.

Compagnon, A. (1979). *La Seconde Main ou Le Travail de la citation*. Paris: Seuil.

——(1990). *Les Cinq Paradoxes de la modernité*. Paris: Seuil.

——(1998). *Le Démon de la théorie: littérature et sens commun*. Paris: Seuil.

——(1999). 'La Rhétorique à la fin du XIXe siècle (1875–1900)'. In *Histoire de la Rhétorique dans L'Europe moderne 1450–1950*, ed. M. Fumaroli. Paris: PUF.

Conte, G. B. (1986). *The Rhetoric of Imitation: Genre and Poetic Memory in Virgil and other Latin Poets*, trans. C. Segal. Ithaca, NY, and London: Cornell University Press.

Contini, G. (1976). 'Dante et la mémoire poétique'. *Poétique*, 27, pp. 297–316.

Copeland, R. (1991). *Rhetoric, Hermeneutics and Translation in the Middle Ages: Academic Traditions and Vernacular Texts*. Cambridge: CUP.

Coppieters de Gibson, D. (ed.) (1977). *La Révélation: Paul Ricoeur, Emmanuel Lévinas, Edgar Haulotte, Etienne Cornélius, Claude Geffré*. Brussels: Facultés Universitaires St-Louis.

Crane, G., and Mylonas, E. (1991). 'Ancient materials, modern media: shaping the study of classics with Hypermedia'. In *Hypermedia and Literary Studies*, ed. P. Delany and G. P. Landow. Cambridge, MA: MIT Press, pp. 205–20.

Crapanzano, V. (1995). 'The postmodern crisis: discourse, parody, memory'. In *Bakhtin in Contexts: Across the Disciplines*, ed. A. Mandelker. Evanston, IL: Northwestern University Press.

Cros, E. (1990). *De l'engendrement des formes: études sociocritiques*. Montpellier: Université Paul Valéry.

Culler, J. (1981). *The Pursuit of Signs: Semiotics, Literature, Deconstruction*. London: Routledge & Kegan Paul.

Curtius, E. R. ([1948] 1953). *European Literature and the Latin Middle Ages*. trans. W. R. Trask. London: Routledge & Kegan Paul.

Cusset, C. (1999). *La Muse dans la bibliothèque: réécriture et intertextualité dans la poésie alexandrine*. Paris: CNRS.

Dällenbach, L. (1976). 'Intertexte et autotexte', *Poétique*, 27, pp. 282–96.

——(1977). *Le Récit spéculaire: essai sur la mise en abyme*. Paris: Seuil.

Danius, S. (2001). 'Orpheus and the machine: Proust as theorist of technological change and the case of Joyce'. *Forum for Modern Language Studies*, 37, pp. 127–40.

Dawkins, R. ([1976] 1989). *The Selfish Gene*. Oxford: OUP.

——(1998). *Unweaving the Rainbow.* Harmondsworth: Penguin.

Déguy, M., and Dupuy, J.-P. (eds) (1982). *René Girard et le problème du mal.* Paris: Bernard Grasset.

Delany, P., and Landow, G. P. (eds) (1991). *Hypermedia and Literary Studies.* Cambridge, MA: MIT Press.

DeRose, S. J. (1991). 'Biblical studies and hypertext'. In *Hypermedia and Literary Studies*, ed. P. Delany and G. P. Landow. Cambridge, MA: MIT Press, pp. 185–204.

Derrida, J. (1962). *Edmund Husserl: l'origine de la géométrie.* Paris: PUF.

——(1967a). *L'Ecriture et la différence.* Paris: Seuil.

——(1967b). *Grammatologie.* Paris: Minuit.

——(1980). *La Carte postale.* Paris: Seuil.

——(1984). *Otobiographies: l'enseignement de Nietzsche et la politique du nom propre.* Paris: Galilée.

——(1987). *Psyche: inventions de l'autre.* Paris: Galilée.

——(1996). 'Foi et savoir: les deux sources de la "religion" aux limites de la simple raison'. In *La Religion: séminaire de Capri*, ed. J. Derrida and G. Vattimo. Paris: Seuil.

Detweiler, R., and Doty, W. G. (eds) (1990). *The Daemonic Imagination: Biblical Text and Secular Story.* Atlanta: Scholars Press.

D'Haen, T., Grübel, R., and Lethen, H. (eds) (1989). *Convention and Innovation in Literature.* Amsterdam and Philadelphia: John Benjamins.

Diamond, E. (1997). *Unmaking Mimesis: Essays on Feminism and Theatre.* London and New York: Routledge.

Dickey, W. (1991). 'Poem descending a staircase: hypertext and the simultaneity of experience'. In *Hypermedia and Literary Studies*, ed. P. Delany and G. P. Landow. Cambridge, MA: MIT Press, pp. 143–52.

Doane, A. (1991). 'Oral texts, intertexts and intratexts: editing Old English'. In *Influence and Intertextuality in Literary History*, ed. J. Clayton and E. Rothstein. Madison: University of Winsconsin Press, pp. 75–113.

Docherty, T. (1987). *On Modern Authority.* Brighton: Harvester Press.

Draisma, S. (1989). *Intertextuality in Biblical Writings: Essays in Honour of Bas van Iersel.* Kampen: J. H. Kok.

Dronke, P. (1997). *Sources of Inspiration: Studies in Literary Transformations, 400–1500.* Rome: Edizioni di Storia e Letteratura.

Duff, D. (2000). *Modern Genre Theory.* Harlow: Pearson Education.

Dumouchel, P., and Dupuy, J.-P. (eds) (1979). *L'Enfer des choses: René Girard et la logique de l'économie* Paris: Seuil.

Dworkin, A. (2000). *Scapegoat, the Jews, Israel and Women's Lib.* London: Virago.

Eagleton, T. (1986). *Against the Grain: Essays 1975–85.* London: Verso.

——(1991). *Ideology: an Introduction.* London: Verso.

——(1996). *The Illusions of the Postmodern.* Oxford: Blackwell.

Eco, U. (1976). *A Theory of Semiotics.* Bloomington: Indiana University Press.

——(1979). *The Role of the Reader: Explorations in the Semiotics of Texts.* Bloomington: Indiana University Press.

——(1984). *Semiotics and the Philosophy of Language.* London: Macmillan.

——(1986). *Faith in Fakes: Essays*, trans. W. Weaver. London: Secker & Warburg.

——(1990). *The Limits of Interpretation*. Bloomington: Indiana University Press.

——(1992). *Interpretation and Overinterpretation*, ed. S. Collini. Cambridge: CUP.

Edwards, M. (1990). *Of Making Many Books*. Basingstoke: Macmillan.

Eliot, T. S. (1945). *What is a Classic*. London: Faber & Faber.

——(1953). 'Tradition and the individual talent'. In *Selected Prose*. Harmondsworth: Penguin.

——(1965). *To Criticise the Critic and other Writings*. London: Faber & Faber.

Ellmann, M. (ed.) (1994). *Psychoanalytic Literary Criticism*. London: Longman.

Eskin, M. (2000). *Ethics and Dialogue in the Works of Levinas, Bakhtin, Mandel'shtam, and Celan*. Oxford: OUP.

Etiemble, R. (1963). *Comparaison n'est pas raison*. Paris: Gallimard.

Falck, C. (1989). *Myth, Truth, Literature: Towards a True Post-Modernism*. Cambridge: CUP.

Faye, J.-P. (1972). *Langages totalitaires: critique de la raison, l'économie narrative*, Vol. 1. Paris: Herman.

——(1990). *La Raison narrative: langages totalitaires, critque de l'économie narrative*, Vol. 2. Paris: Editions Balland.

Felman, S. (1978). *La Folie et la chose littéraire*. Paris: Seuil.

——(1987). *Jacques Lacan and the Adventure of Insight: Psychoanalysis in Contemporary Culture*. Cambridge, MA: Harvard University Press.

Felman, S., and Laub, D. (1992). *Testimony: Crises of Witnessing in Literature, Psychoanalysis and History*. London: Routledge.

Felski, R. (1989). *Beyond Feminist Aesthetics: Feminist Literature and Social Change*. Cambridge, MA: Harvard University Press.

Feustle, J. A., Jr. (1991). 'Hypertext for the PC: the Rubén Darío project'. In *Hypermedia and Literary Studies*, ed. P. Delany and G. P. Landow. Cambridge, MA: MIT Press, pp. 299–313.

Ffrench, P. (1995). *The Time of Theory: a History of* Tel Quel *(1960–83)*. Oxford: Clarendon Press.

Ffrench, P., and Lack, R. (eds) (1998). *The Tel Quel Reader*. London: Routledge.

Finke, L. A., and Shichtman, M. B. (eds) (1987). *Medieval Texts and Contemporary Readers*. Ithaca, NY, and London: Cornell University Press.

Fish, S. (1980). *Is there a Text in the Class? The Authority of Interpretative Communities*. Cambridge, MA: Harvard University Press.

Fishbane, M. (1989). *The Garments of Torah: Essays in Biblical Hermeneutics*. Bloomington and Indianapolis: Indiana University Press.

Fiske, J. (1990). *Introduction to Communication Studies*. London: Routledge.

Fite, D. (1985). *Harold Bloom: the Rhetoric of Romantic Vision*. Amherst: University of Massachusetts Press.

Flax, J. (1990). *Thinking Fragments: Psychoanalysis, Feminism and Postmodernism in the Contemporary West*. Berkeley and Oxford: University of California Press.

Foucault, M. (1963). *La Naissance de la clinique*. Paris: PUF.

——(1966). *Les Mots et les choses*. Paris: Gallimard.

——(1975). *Surveiller et punir: naissance de la prison*. Paris: Gallimard.

Fox Keller, E. (1985). *Reflections on Gender and Science*. New Haven, CT: Yale University Press.

Fraistat, N. (ed.) (1986). *Poems in their Place: the Intertextuality and Order of Poetic Collections*. London and Chapel Hill: University of North Carolina Press.

Freadman, R., and Reinhardt, L. (eds) (1991). *On Literary Theory and Philosophy*. London: Macmillan.

Freud, S. (1985). *La Question de l'analyse profane*. Paris: Gallimard [Folio Essais].

Freund, E. (1987). *The Return of the Reader: Reader-Response Criticism*. London and New York: Methuen.

Friedman, S. Stanford (1991). 'Weavings: intertextuality and the (re)birth of the author'. In *Influence and Intertextuality in Literary History*, ed. J. Clayton and E. Rothstein. Madison: University of Wisconsin Press, pp. 146–80.

Frowe, J. (1986). *Marxism and Literary History*. Cambridge, MA: Harvard University Press.

Frye, N. (1957). *Anatomy of Criticism: Four Essays*. Princeton, NJ: Princeton University Press.

——(1960). 'The language of poetry'. In *Explorations in Communication*, ed. E. Carpenter and M. McLuhan. Boston: Beacon Press, pp. 43–53.

——(1976). *The Secular Scripture: a Study of the Structure of Romance*. Cambridge, MA: Harvard University Press.

——(1982). *The Great Code: the Bible and Literature*. London: Routledge & Kegan Paul.

Fumaroli, M. (ed.) (1999). *Histoire de la rhétorique dans L'Europe moderne 1450–1950*. Paris: PUF.

Fuss, D. (1990). *Essentially Speaking*. London: Routledge.

Gaggi, S. (1997). *From Text to Hypertext: Decentring the Subject in Fiction, Film, the Visual Arts and Electronic Media*. Philadelphia: University of Pennsylvania Press.

Gasché, R. (1998). *The Wild Card of Reading: on Paul de Man*. Cambridge, MA: Harvard University Press.

Gellrich, J. M. (1985). *The Idea of the Book in the Middle Ages: Language Theory, Mythology and Fiction*. Ithaca, NY, and London: Cornell University Press.

Genette, G. (1976). *Mimologiques: voyage en cratyle*. Paris: Seuil; trans. T. Morgan, Lincoln and London: University of Nebraska Press, 1995.

——(1979). *Introduction à l'architexte*. Paris: Seuil; trans. J. E. Lewin as *The Architext: an Introduction*, Berkeley: University of California Press, 1992.

——(1982). *Palimpsestes: la littérature au second degré*. Paris: Seuil; trans. C. Newman and C. Doubinsky as *Palimpsests: Literature in the Second Degree*, Lincoln and London: University of Nebraska Press, 1997.

——(1987). *Seuils*. Paris: Seuil; trans. J. E. Lewin as *Paratexts: Thresholds of Interpretation*, Cambridge: CUP, 1997.

—— (1991). *Fiction et diction*. Paris: Seuil.

—— (1999). *Figures IV*. Paris: Seuil.

Genette, G., with R. Barthes and T. Todorov (1980). *Recherches de Proust*. Paris: Seuil.

Genette, G., with R. Debray-Genette and T. Todorov (1983). *Travail de Flaubert*. Paris: Seuil.

Genette, G., with P. Bénichou and T. Todorov (1984). *Pensée de Rousseau*. Paris: Seuil.

Genette, G., with T. Todorov (1986). *Théorie des genres*. Paris: Seuil.

—— (1992). *Esthétique et poétique*. Paris: Seuil.

Gerhart, M., and Russell, A. (eds) (1984). *Metaphoric Process: the Creation of Scientific and Religious Understanding*. Fort Worth: Texas Christian University Press.

Gilbert, S., and Gubar, S. (1979). *The Madwoman in the Attic: the Woman Writer and the Nineteenth-Century Literary Imagination*. New Haven, CT: Yale University Press.

Gilman, S. (1946). 'An introduction to the ideology of the baroque in Spain'. *Symposium*, 1, pp. 82–107.

Girard, R. (1982). *Le Bouc émissaire*. Paris: Grasset & Fasquelle.

—— (1961). *Mensonge romantique et vérité romanesque*. Paris: Grasset.

—— (1972). *La Violence et le sacré*. Paris: Grasset.

—— (1978a). *Les Choses cachées depuis la fondation du monde* [research undertaken in collaboration with J-M. Oughourlian and G. Lefort]. Paris: Grasset & Fasquelle; trans. S. Bann (Bks II, III) and M. Metteer (Bk I) as *Things Hidden since the Foundation of the World*, London: Athlone Press, 1987.

—— (1978b). *'To Double Business Bound': Essays on Literature, Mimesis, and Anthropology*. Baltimore and London: Johns Hopkins University Press.

Gomez-Géraud, M.-C., and Levillain, H. (eds) (1989). *Les Modèles de la création littéraire*. Paris: Cahiers du Département Français de l'Université de Nanterre.

Greene, J. T. (1989). *The Role of the Messenger and Message in the Ancient Near East*. Altanta: Scholars Press.

Greene, T. M. (1982). *The Light in Troy: Imitation and Discovery in Renaissance Poetry*. New Haven, CT, and London: Yale University Press.

Gresset, M., and Polk, N. (eds) (1985). *Intertext in Faulkner*. Jackson: University of Mississippi Press.

Grivel, C. (1982). 'Thèses préparatoires sur les intertextes'. In *Dialogizität: Theorie und Geschichte der Literatur und der schönen Künste*, ed. R. Lachmann. Munich: Wilhelm Fink, pp. 237–48.

Gunn, G. (1979). *The Interpretation of Otherness*. New York: OUP.

Haddawy, H. (trans.) (1990). *The Arabian Nights*. New York and London: W. W. Norton.

Hahn, L. E. (ed.) (1995). *The Philosophy of Paul Ricoeur*. Chicago and La Salle, IL: Open Court.

Hampson, D. (1990). *Theology and Feminism*. Oxford: Blackwell.

—— (1996). *After Christianity*. London: SCM Press.

Hand, S. (1990), 'Missing you: intertextuality, transference and the language of love'. In *Intertextuality: Theories and Practices*, ed. M. Worton and J. Still. Manchester: MUP.

Hansen-Löve, A. A. (1983). 'Intermedialität und Intertextualität: Probleme der Korrelation von Wort- und Bildkunst – am Beispiel der Russischen Moderne'. In *Dialog des Texte*, ed. W. Schmid and W.-D. Stempel. Vienna: Wiener Slawistischer Almanach, pp. 291–360.

Hardie, P. (1993). *The Epic Successors of Virgil: a Study in the Dynamics of a Tradition*. Cambridge: CUP.

Harpold, T. (1991). 'Threnody: psychoanalytic digressions on the subject of hypertexts'. In *Hypermedia and Literary Studies*, ed. P. Delany and G. P. Landow. Cambridge, MA: MIT Press, pp. 171–8.

Hartman, G. (1975). *The Fate of Reading*. Chicago: University of Chicago Press.

Hartman, G., and Budick, S. (eds) (1986). *Midrash and Literature*. New Haven, CT, and London: Yale University Press.

Hassan, I. H. (1955). 'The problem of influence in literary history: notes towards a definition'. *Journal of Aesthetics and Art Criticism*, no. 14, pp. 66–76.

Hawcroft, M. (1999). *Rhetoric: Readings in French Literature*. Oxford: OUP.

Hazlett, I. (ed.) (1991). *Early Christianity: Origins and Evolution to AD 600*. London: SPCK.

Hebel, U. J. (1989). *Intertextuality, Allusion and Quotation: an International Bibliography of Critical Studies*. New York, Westport, CT, and London: Greenwood Press.

Heimonet, J.-M. (1991). *De la révolte à l'exercice: essai sur l'hédonisme contemporain*. Paris: Éditions du Félin.

Heinemann, J. (1986). 'The nature of aggadah'. In *Midrash and Literature*, ed. G. Hartman and S. Budick. New Haven, CT, and London: Yale University Press, pp. 42–54.

Hennig, J.-L. (1997). *Apologie du plagiat*. Paris: NRF Gallimard.

Hermerén, G. (1975). *Influence in Art and Literature*. Princeton, NJ: Princeton University Press.

Hideo, K. (1995). *Literature of the Lost Home: Literary Criticism 1924–1939*, ed. and trans. P. Anderer. Stanford, CA: Stanford University Press.

Hobson, M. (1982). *The Object of Art: the Theory of Illusion in Eighteenth-Century France*. Cambridge: CUP.

Hollander, J. (1981). *The Figure of Echo: a Mode of Allusion in Milton and After*. Berkeley, Los Angeles and London: University of California Press.

Holloway, K. F. C. (1992). *Moorings and Metaphors: Figures of Culture and Gender in Black Women's Literature*. New Brunswick, NJ: Rutgers University Press.

Hoy, H. (2001). *How Should I Read These? Native American Women Writers in Canada*. Toronto: University of Toronto Press.

Hunt, T. (1978). 'Chrestien and the *Comediae*'. *Medieval Studies*, 40, pp. 120–55.

——(1996). *Villon's Last Will: Language and Authority in the Testament*. Oxford: Clarendon Press.

Hutcheon, L. (1980). *Narcissistic Narrative: the Metafictional Paradox*. London: Methuen.

—— (1988). *A Poetics of Postmodernism*. London: Routledge.

—— (1989). *The Politics of Postmodernism* London: Routledge.

—— (1991). 'The politics of postmodern parody'. In *Intertextuality*, ed. H. E. Plett. Berlin and New York: Walter de Gruyter, pp. 225–36.

Ijsseling, S. (1997). *Mimesis: On Appearing and Being*, trans. H. Ijsseling and J. Bloechl. Kampen: Kok Pharos.

Irigaray, L. (1974). *Speculum de l'autre femme*. Paris: Minuit.

—— (1983). *La Croyance même*. Paris: Galilée.

—— (1999). *Entre orient et occident*. Paris: Grasset.

Iser, W. (1978). *The Act of Reading: a Theory of Aesthetic Response*. London: Routledge & Kegan Paul.

Jacob, C. (2000). 'Athenaeus the librarian'. In *Athenaeus and his World: Reading Greek Culture in the Roman Empire*, ed. D. Braund and J. Wilkins. Exeter: University of Exeter Press, pp. 85–110, 545–53.

Jameson, F. (1972). *The Prison-House of Language*. Princeton, NJ: Princeton University Press.

Jauss, H. R. (1982). 'Zum Problem des dialogischen Verstehens'. In *Dialogizität: Theorie und Geschichte der Literatur und der schönen künste*, ed. R. Lachmann, Munich: Wilhelm Fink, pp. 11–24.

Jefferson, A. (1990). 'Autobiography as intertext: Barthes, Sarraute, Robbe-Grillet'. In *Intertextuality: Theories and Practices*, ed. M. Worton and J. Still. Manchester: MUP, pp. 108–29.

Jennings, T. W., Jr. (1990). *The Humanistic Interpretation of the New Testament*. Atlanta: Scholars Press.

Jenny, L. (1976). 'La Stratégie de la forme', *Poétique*, 27, pp. 257–81; trans. R. Carter as 'The strategy of forms', (1982). *French Literary Theory Today: a Reader*, ed. T. Todorov. Cambridge: CUP, pp. 34–64.

Josipovici, G. (1982). *Writing and the Body*. Brighton: Harvester.

Jullier, L. (1997). *L'Ecran post-moderne: un cinéma de l'allusion et du feu d'artifice*. Paris: L'Harmattan.

Kadir, D. (1992). *Columbus and the Ends of the Earth: Europe's Prophetic Rhetoric as Conquering Ideology*. Berkeley and Oxford: University of California Press.

Karrer, W. (1991). 'Titles and mottoes as intertextual devices'. In *Intertextuality*, ed. H. E. Plett, Berlin and New York: Walter de Gruyter, pp. 122–34.

Kearney, R. (ed.) (1996). *Paul Ricoeur: the Hermeneutics of Action*. London: Sage.

Kellett, E. E. (1933). *Literary Quotation and Allusion*. Cambridge: Heffer.

Kellmann, S. G. (2000). *The Translingual Imagination*. Lincoln and London: University of Nebraska Press.

Kelly, D. (ed.). (1996). *The Medieval Opus: Imitation, Rewriting and Transmission in then French Tradition*. Amsterdam and Atlanta: Rodopi.

Kittay, E. V. (1987). *Metaphor*. Oxford: Clarendon Press.

Klemm, D. E. (1983). *The Hermeneutical Theory of Paul Ricoeur*. Lewisburg,

PA: Bucknell University Press; London and Toronto: Association of University Presses.

Kloepfer, R. (1982). 'Grundlagen des "dialogischen Prinzips" in der Literatur'. In *Dialogizität: Theorie und Geschichte der Literatur und der schönen Künste*, ed. R. Lachmann. Munich: Wilhelm Fink, pp. 85–106.

Knight, D. (1997). *Barthes and the Utopia of Writing*. Oxford: OUP.

Knox, B. (1994). *Backing into the Future: the Classical Tradition and its Renewal*. New York and London: W. W. Norton.

Kolodny, A. (1985). 'A map for rereading: gender and the interpretation of literary texts'. In *The New Feminist Criticism*, ed. E. Showalter. New York: Pantheon Books, pp. 46–62.

Kristeva, J. (1967). 'Bakhtin, le mot, le dialogue et le roman', *Critique*, no. 239, pp. 438–65.

——(1969). *Semeiotikè: recherches pour une sémanalyse*. Paris: Points.

——(1970). *Le Texte du roman: approche sémiologique d'une structure discursive transformationnelle*. The Hague: Mouton.

——(1974). *La Révolution du langage poétique*. Paris: Seuil.

——(1983). *Histoires d'amour*. Paris: Denoël.

——(1988). *Etrangers à nous-mêmes*. Paris: Fayard; trans. L. S. Roudiez as *Julia Kristeva: Strangers to Ourselves*. London: Harvester Wheatsheaf, 1991.

——(1997). 'L'Autre Langue ou traduire le sensible'. *L'Infini*, 53, Spring, pp. 15–28; repr. in *French Studies*, 52 (1998), 385–96.

——(2001). *Au risque de la pensée*. La Tour d'Aigues: Éditions de l'Aube.

Lachmann, R. (ed.) (1982). *Dialogizität: Theorie und Geschichte der Literatur und der schönen Künste*. Munich: Wilhelm Fink.

——(1984). 'Ebenen des Intertextualitätsbegriffs'. In *Das Gespräch*, ed. K. Stierle and R. Warning. Munich: Wilhelm Fink, pp. 133–8.

Lakoff, G., and Johnson, M. (1980). *Metaphors We Live By*. Chicago: University of Chicago Press.

Landow, G. P. (1986). *Elegant Jeremiahs: the Sage from Carlyle to Mailer*. Ithaca, NY, and London: Cornell University Press.

——(1992). *Hypertext: the Convergence of Contemporary Critical Theory and Technology*. Baltimore and London: Johns Hopkins University Press.

Lechte, J. (1990). *Julia Kristeva*. London and New York: Routledge.

LeDoeuff, M. (1989). *L'Etude et le rouet*. Paris: Seuil.

Lee, G. (1971). *Allusion, Parody and Imitation*. Hull: University of Hull Press.

Lefevere, A. (1992a). *Translation/History/Culture: a Sourcebook*. London: Routledge.

——(1992b). *Translation, Rewriting and the Manipulation of Literary Fame*. London: Routledge.

Leitch, V. B. (1983). 'Versions of textuality and intertextuality: contemporary theories of literature and tradition'. In *Deconstructive Criticism: an Advanced Introduction*. London: Hutchinson, pp. 55–164.

Lentricchia, F. (1980). *After the New Criticism*. London: Methuen.

Levinas, E., and Ricoeur, P. (1998). *Emmanuel Levinas: philosophe et pédagogue*. Paris: Éditions du Nadir.

Limat-Letellier, N., and Miguet-Ollgnier, M. (eds) (1998). *Intertextualité*. Besançon: Annales Littéraires de l'Université de Franche-Comté.

Littau, K. (1997). 'Translation in the age of postmodern production: from text to intertext to hypertext'. *Forum for Modern Language Studies,* 33, pp. 81–96.

——(2000). 'Hypertext and translation'. In *The Dictionary of Literary Translation,* ed. O. Classe. London: Fitzroy Dearborn, p. 684.

Livingston, P. (1992). *Models of Desire: René Girard and the Psychology of Mimesis.* Baltimore and London: Johns Hopkins University Press.

Lotman, I. M. (1976). *Analysis of the Poetic Text,* trans. D. B. Johnson. Ann Arbor, MI: Ardis.

Lotman, I. M., Ginsburg, L. I., and Uspenskii, B. A. (1985). *The Semiotics of Russian Cultural History,* ed. and trans. A. D. Nakhumovsky and A. S. Nakhamovsky. Ithaca, NY, and New York: Cornell University Press.

Lukacher, N. (1986). *Primal Scenes: Literature, Philosophy, Psychoanalysis.* Ithaca, NY, and London: Cornell University Press.

Lyotard, J.-F. (1971). *Discours, figure.* Paris: Éditions Klincksieck.

——(1973). *Dérive à partir de Marx et Freud.* Paris: UGE 10/18.

McFague, S. (1983). *Metaphorical Theology: Models of God in Religious Language.* London: SCM.

MacIntyre, A., and Ricoeur, P. (1969). *The Religious Significance of Atheism.* New York and London: Columbia University Press.

MacKenna, A. J. (1992). *Violence and Difference: Girard, Derrida and Deconstruction.* Urbana and Chicago: University of Illinois Press.

McLuhan, M. (1962). *The Gutenberg Galaxy.* London: Routledge & Kegan Paul.

——(1967). *The Mechanical Bride.* London. Routledge & Kegan Paul.

——(1970). *From Cliché to Archetype.* New York: Viking Press.

——(1972). *The Medium is the Massage.* Harmondsworth: Penguin.

Maddox, D. (1984). *The Semiotics of Deceit: the Pathelin Era.* Lewisburg, PA: Bucknell University Press.

Mai, H.-P. (1991). 'Bypassing intertextuality: hermeneutics, textual practice, hypertext'. In *Intertextuality,* ed. H. E. Plett. Berlin and New York: Walter de Gruyter, pp. 30–59.

Maingueneau, D. (1991). *L'Analyse du discours: introduction aux lectures de l'archive.* Paris: Hachette.

Man, P. de (1979). *Allegories of Reading: Figural Language in Rousseau, Nietzsche, Rilke and Proust.* New Haven, CT, and London: Yale University Press.

——(1983). *Blindness and Insight.* London: Methuen.

Mandelker, A. (1995). 'Logosphere and semiosphere: Bakhtin, Russian organicism and the semiotics of culture'. In *Bakhtin in Contexts: Across the Disciplines,* ed. A. Mandelker. Evanston, IL: Northwestern University Press, pp. 177–90.

Maurel-Indart, H. (1999). *Du plagiat.* Paris: PUF.

Megill, A. (1985). *Prophets of Extremity: Nietzsche, Heidegger, Foucault, Derrida.* Berkeley: University of California Press.

Merivale, P., and Sweeney, S. E. (eds) (1999). *Detecting Texts: the Metaphysical Detective Story from Poe to Postmodernism.* Philadelphia: University of Pennsylvania Press.

Meutsch, D., and Viehoff, R. (eds) (1989). *Comprehension of Literary Discourse: Results and Problems of Interdisciplinary Approaches.* Berlin and New York: Walter de Gruyter.

Meyer, H. (1968). *The Poetics of Quotation in the European Novel.* Princeton, NJ: Princeton University Press.

Mileur, J.-P. (1985). *Literary Revisionism and the Burden of Modernity.* Berkeley and London: University of California Press.

Miner, E., and Brady, J. (eds) (1993). *Literary Transmission and Authority: Dryden and other Writers.* Cambridge: CUP.

Minnis, A. J. (1984). *Medieval Theory of Authorship: Scholastic Literary Attitudes in the Later Middle Ages.* London: Scholar Press.

Minnis, A. J., and Scott, A. B. (eds) (1988). *Medieval Literary Theory and Criticism c1100–c1375: the Commentary Tradition.* Oxford: Clarendon Press.

Moi, T. (ed.) (1986). *The Kristeva Reader.* Oxford: Blackwell.

Montalbetti, C. (1998). *Gérard Genette: une poétique ouverte.* Paris: Bertrand-Lacoste.

Morgan, T. (1989). 'The space of intertextuality'. In *Intertextuality and Contemporary American Fiction*, ed. P. O'Donnell and R. Con Davis. Baltimore and London: Johns Hopkins University Press, pp. 239–79.

Moriarty, M. (1997). 'Barthes's theatrical aesthetic'. *Nottingham French Studies*, 36, pp. 3–13. [special number on Roland Barthes, ed. D. Knight].

Morson, G. S. (1995). 'Prosaic Bakhtin: *Landmarks*, anti-intelligentsialism, and the Russian countertradition'. In *Bakhtin in Contexts: Across the Disciplines*, ed. A. Mandelker. Evanston, IL: Northwestern University Press, pp. 33–78.

Moura, J.-M. (1998). *La Littérature des lointains: histoire de l'exotisme européen au XXe siècle.* Paris: Honoré Champion.

Moynihan, R. (1986) *A Recent Imagining.* Hamden, CT: Archon Books.

Muecke, D. C. (1970). *Irony and the Ironic.* London: Methuen.

Mullen, A., and O'Beirne, E. (eds) (2000). *Crime Scenes: Detective Narrative in European Culture since 1945.* Amsterdam and Atlanta: Rodopi.

Newman, C. (1985). *The Post-Modern Aura: the Act of Fiction in an Age of Inflation.* Evanston, IL: Northwestern University Press.

Norton, G. P. (1984). *The Ideology and Language of Translation in Renaissance France and their Humanist Antecedents.* Geneva: Droz.

Obaldia, C. de (1995). *The Essayistic Spirit: Literature, Modern Criticism and the Essay.* Oxford: Clarendon Press.

O'Donnell, P. (1992). *Echo Chambers: Figuring Voice in Modern Narrative.* Iowa City: University of Iowa Press.

O'Donnell, P., and Con Davis, R. (eds) (1989). *Intertextuality and Contemporary American Fiction.* Baltimore and London: Johns Hopkins University Press.

O'Hara, D. T. (1985). *The Romance of Interpretation: Visionary Criticism from Pater to De Man.* New York: Columbia University Press.

Ong, W. J. (1971). *Rhetoric, Romance, and Technology: Studies in the Interaction of Expression and Culture.* Ithaca, NY, and London: Cornell University Press.

——(1982). *Orality and Literacy*. London: Methuen.

Orlinsky, H. M. (1969). Introduction to *Interpreting the Prophetic Tradition*. Cincinnati: Hebrew Union College Press.

Orr, M. (1985). 'Translation as intertextual generator in five novels by Claude Simon'. *New Comparison*, no. 8, pp. 66–74.

——(1993). *Claude Simon: the Intertextual Dimension*. Glasgow: Glasgow University Press.

——(2000). 'Intertextuality'. In *The Dictionary of Literary Translation*, ed. O. Classe. London: Fitzroy Dearborn, pp. 710–11.

——(2002). 'Omissions or missions? Missing ph(r)ases in key translations'. *French Studies Bulletin*, no. 84, pp. 13–15.

Orsini, C. (1986). *La Pensée de René Girard*. Paris: Éditions Retz.

Oughourlian, J.-M. (1982). *Un mime nommé désir: hystérie, transe, possession, adorcisme*. Paris: Bernard Grasset.

Overholt, T. W. (1986). *Prophecy in Cross-Cultural Perspective: a Sourcebook for Biblical Researchers*. Atlanta: Scholars Press.

Oversteegen, J. J. (1989). 'Genre: a modest proposal'. In *Convention and Innovation in Literature*, ed. T. d'Haen et al. Amsterdam and Philadelphia: John Benjamins, pp. 17–35.

Parker, A., Russo, M., Summer, D., and Yaeger, P. (eds) (1992). *Nationalisms and Sexualities*. New York and London: Routledge.

Pasco, A. H. (1994). *Allusion: a Literary Graft*. Toronto: Toronto University Press.

Paz, O. (1990). *The Labyrinth of Solitude*. Harmondsworth: Penguin.

Perloff, M. (ed.) (1988). *Postmodern Genres*. Norman and London: University of Oklahoma Press.

Perrone-Moisés, L. (1976). 'L'intertextualité critique'. *Poétique*, 27, pp. 372–84.

Peterson, N. J. (2001). *Against Amnesia: Contemporary Women Writers and the Crisis of Historical Memory*. Philadelphia: University of Pennsylvania Press.

Pfister, M. (1991). 'How postmodern is intertextality?' In *Intertextuality*, ed. H. E. Plett. Berlin and New York: Walter de Gruyter, pp. 207–24.

Piégay-Gros, N. (1996). *Introduction à l'intertextualité*. Paris: Dunod.

Plett, H. E. (ed.) (1991). *Intertextuality*. Berlin and New York: Walter de Gruyter.

Plottel, J. P., and Charney, H. (eds) (1978). *Intertextuality: New Perspectives in Criticism*. New York: New York Literary Forum.

Poirier, J. (1998). *Sur l'héritage*. Dijon: Centre Régional de Documentation Pédagogique de Bourgogne.

Pratt, M. L. (1977). *Toward a Speech Act Theory of Literary Discourse*. Bloomington: University of Illinois Press.

Preisendanz, W. (1982). 'Zum Beitrag von Renate Lachmann "Dialogizität und poetische Sprache"'. In *Dialogizität: Theorie und Geschichte der Literatur und der schönen Künste*, ed. R. Lachmann. Munich: Wilhelm Fink, pp. 25–8.

Prendergast, C. (1986). *The Order of Mimesis: Balzac, Stendhal, Nerval, Flaubert*. Cambridge: CUP.

Prickett, S. (1986). *Words and the Word*. Cambridge: CUP.

Propp, V. I. (1968). *The Morphology of the Folktale*. Austin: University of Texas Press.

Reagan, C. E., and Stewart, D. (eds) (1978). *The Philosophy of Paul Ricoeur: an Anthology of his Work*. Boston: Beacon Press.

Redfern, W. (1989). *Clichés and Coinages*. Oxford: Blackwell.

Reed, W. L. (1993). *Dialogues of the Word*. Oxford: OUP.

Regard, F. (1992). *Logique de traverses: de l'influence: recherches en histoire des idées*. St Etienne: CIEREC Université Jean Monnet.

Rich, A. (2001). *Arts of the Possible: Essays and Conversations*. New York: W. W. Norton.

Ricks, C. (1976). 'Allusion: the poet as heir'. In *Studies in the Eighteenth Century III: Papers Presented at the Third David Nichol Smith Memorial Seminar, Canberra*, ed. R. F. Brissenden and J. C. Eade. Toronto and Buffalo: University of Toronto Press.

Ricoeur, P. (1975). *La Métaphore vive*, trans. R. Czerny et al. as *The Rule of Metaphor*. London: Routledge & Kegan Paul, 1978.

——(1976). *Interpretation Theory: Discourse and the Surplus of Meaning*. Fort Worth: Texas Christian University Press.

——(1978). 'Listening to the Parables of Jesus'. In *The Philosophy of Paul Ricoeur*, ed. C. E. Reagan and D. Stewart. Boston: Beacon Press.

——(1980). *La Fonction narrative*. Montpellier: Études Théologiques et Religieuses.

——(1981). *Essays on Biblical Interpretation*, ed. L. S. Mudge. London: SPCK.

——(1986). *Le Mal: un défi à la philosophie et à la théologie*. Geneva: Labor et Fides Centre Protestant d'Études.

Riffaterre, M. (1978). *Semiotics of Poetry*. Bloomington: Indiana University Press.

——(1980). 'La trace de l'intertexte'. *La Pensée*, no. 215, pp. 4–18.

Robert, M. (1972). *Roman des origines et origines du roman*. Paris: Gallimard.

Rorty, R. (1982). *Consequences of Pragmatism: Essays 1972–1980*. Minneapolis: University of Minnesota Press.

Rose, M. (1993). *Parody: Ancient, Modern and Post-Modern*. Cambridge: CUP.

Roudiez, L. S. (ed.) (1980). *Desire in Language: a Semiotic Approach to Literature and Art*. New York: Columbia University Press [contains 'Word, dialogue, and novel', trans. A. Jardine, T. Gora and L. S. Roudiez].

Sacks, S. (ed.) (1979). *On Metaphor*. Chicago and London: University of Chicago Press.

Said, E. (1978). *Orientalism*. London: Routledge.

——(1983). *The World, the Text and the Critic*. Cambridge, MA: Harvard University Press.

——(1993). *Culture and Imperialism*. London: Chatto.

Salusinszky, I. (1987). *Criticism in Society: Interviews with Jacques Derrida, Northrop Frye, Harold Bloom, Geoffrey Hartman, Frank Kermode, Edward Said, Barbara Johnson, Frank Lentricchia and J. Hillis Miller/Imre Salusinszky*. London: Methuen.

Samoyault, T. (2001). *L'Intertextualité: mémoire de la littérature*. Paris: Nathan.

Sangsue, D. (1994). *La Parodie*. Paris: Hachette.

Sarra, E. (1999). *Fictions of Femininity: Literary Inventions of Gender in Japanese Court Women's Memoirs*. Stanford, CA: Stanford University Press.

Sawyer, J. F. A. (1987). *Prophecy and the Prophets of the Old Testament*. Oxford: OUP.

Schlicher, J. J. (1905). 'The moods of indirect speech'. *American Journal of Philology*, 12, 1, pp. 36–45.

Schmid, W. (1983). 'Sinnpotentiale der diegetischen Allusion'. In *Dialog des Texte*, ed. W. Schmid and W.-D. Stempel. Vienna: Wiener Slawistischer Almanach, pp. 141–89.

Schmid, W., and Stempel, W.-D. (eds) (1983). *Dialog des Texte: Hamburger Kolloquium zur Intertextualität*. Vienna: Wiener Slawistischer Almanach.

Schneider, M. (1985). *Voleurs de mots: essai sur le plagiat, la psychanalyse et la pensée*. Paris: Gallimard.

——(1993). *La Comédie de la culture*. Paris: Seuil.

Schoek, R. J. (1984). *Intertextuality and Renaissance Texts*. Bamberg: H. Kaiser.

——(1991). 'In loco intertexantur: Erasmus a master of intertextuality'. In *Intertextuality*, ed. H. E. Plett. Berlin and New York: Walter de Gruyter, pp. 181–91.

Scholem, G. G. (1946). *Major Trends in Jewish Mysticism*. New York: Schocken Books.

——(1965). *Jewish Gnosticism, Merkabah Mysticism, and Talmudic Tradition*. New York: Jewish Theological Seminary of America.

——(1984). *Textual Power: Literary Theory and the Teaching of English*. Ithaca, NY: Cornell University Press.

Schwarz, H. (1996). *The Culture of the Copy: Striking Likenesses, Unreasonable Facsimiles*. New York: Zone Books.

Serres, M. (1969). *Hermès I: La Communication*. Paris: Éditions de Minuit.

——(1972). *Hermès II: L'Interférence*. Paris: Éditions de Minuit.

——(1974). *Hermès III: La Traduction*. Paris: Éditions de Minuit.

——(1977). *Hermès IV: La Distribution*. Paris: Éditions de Minuit.

Shaw, J. T. (1971). 'Literary indebtedness and comparative literary studies'. In *Comparative Literature: Method and Perspective*, ed. N. P. Stallknecht and H. Frenz. Carbondale and Edwardsville: South Illinois University Press, pp. 84–97.

Shirane, H., and Suzuki, T. (eds) (2000). *Inventing the Classics: Modernity, National Identity and Japanese Literature*. Stanford, CA: Stanford University Press.

Shklovskii, V. (1973). *Sur la théorie de la prose*, trans. G. Verret. Lausanne: L'Age d'homme.

Showalter, E. (ed.) (1985). *The New Feminist Feminist Criticism: Essays on Women, Literature and Theory*. New York: Pantheon Books.

——(1997). *Hystories: Hysterical Epidemics and Modern Culture*. London: Picador.

Silverman, H. J., and Aylesworth, G. E. (eds) (1990). *The Textual Sublime:*

Deconstruction and its Differences. Albany: State University of New York Press.

Slatin, J. (1991). 'Reading hypertext: order and coherence in a new medium'. In *Hypermedia and Literary Studies*, ed. P. Delany and G. P. Landow. Cambridge, MA: MIT Press, pp. 153–69.

Smirnov, I. P. (1983). 'Das zitierte Zitat'. In *Dialog des Texte*, ed. W. Schmid and W.-D. Stempel. Vienna: Wiener Slawistischer Almanach, pp. 273–90.

Smith, A.-M. (1998). *Julia Kristeva: Speaking the Unspeakable*. London: Pluto Press.

Soskice, J. M. (1985). *Metaphor and Religious Language*. Oxford: OUP.

Spariosu, M. (ed.) (1984). *Mimesis in Contemporary Theory: an Interdisciplinary Approach*, Vol. 1: *The Literary and Philosophical Debate*. Philadelphia and Amsterdam: John Benjamins.

Spivak, G. C. (1987). *In Other Worlds: Essays in Cultural Politics*. New York: Methuen.

——(1999). *A Critique of Postcolonial Reason: Toward a History of the Vanishing Present*. Cambridge, MA: Harvard University Press.

Steiner, G. (1975). *After Babel: Aspects of Language and Translation*. Oxford: OUP.

Stempel, W.-D. (1983). 'Intertextualität und Rezeption'. In *Dialog des Texte*, ed. W. Schmid and W.-D. Stempel. Vienna: Wiener Slawistischer Almanach, pp. 85–109.

Stern, D. (1986). 'Midrash and the language of exegesis: a study of Vayikra Rabbah, Chapter One'. In *Midrash and Literature*, ed. G. Hartman and S. Budick. New Haven, CT, and London: Yale University Press, pp. 101–25.

——(1991). *Parables in Midrash: Narrative and Exegesis in Rabbinic Literature*. Cambridge, MA: Harvard University Press.

Sternberg, M. (1982). 'Proteus in quotation-land'. *Poetics Today*, 3, 2, pp. 107–56.

Stevens, B. (1991). *L'Apprentissage des signes: lecture de Paul Ricoeur*. Dordrecht: Kluwer.

Stewart, S. (1978). *Nonsense: Aspects of Intertextuality in Folklore and Literature*. Baltimore and London: Johns Hopkins University Press.

Stierle, K. (1984). 'Werk und Intertextualität'. In *Das Gespräch*, ed. K. Stierle and R. Warning. Munich: Wilhelm Fink. pp. 139–50.

Stierle, K. and Warning, R. (1984) (eds). *Das Gespräch: Poetik und Hermeneutik*. Munich: Wilhelm Fink.

Stock, B. (1985). 'History, literature and medieval textuality'. In *Yale French Studies*, no. 70, ed. K. Brownlee and S. G. Nichols.

Suleiman, S., and Crossman, I. (eds) (1980). *The Reader in the Text: Essays on Audience and Interpretation*. Princeton, NJ: Princeton University Press.

Thompson, J. B. (1981a). *Critical Hermeneutics: A Study in the Thought of Paul Ricoeur and Jürgen Habermas*. Cambridge: CUP.

——(1981b). *Paul Ricoeur: Hermeneutics and the Human Sciences: Essays on Language, Action and Interpretation*. Cambridge and Paris: CUP/Éditions de la Maison des Sciences de l'Homme.

Todorov, T. (1965). *Théorie de la littérature*. Paris: Seuil.

—— (1971). *La Poétique de la prose*. Paris: Seuil.

—— (1978). *Les Genres du discours*. Paris: Seuil.

—— (1981). *Michail Bakhtine: le principe dialogique suivi de Ecrits du cercle de Bakhtine*. Paris: Seuil; trans. W. Godzich, Manchester: MUP, 1994.

—— (ed.) (1982). *French Literary Theory Today: a Reader*. Cambridge: CUP.

Todorov, T., with O. Ducrot (1982). *Dictionnaire encyclopédique des sciences du langage*. Paris: Seuil.

Too, Y. L. (2000). 'The walking library: the performance of cultural memories'. In *Athenaeus and his world*, ed. D. Braund and J. Wilkins. Exeter: University of Exeter Press, pp. 111–23, 553–4.

Topia, A. (1976). 'Contrepoints joyciens'. *Poétique*, 27, pp. 338–50

Tuve, R. (1966). *Allegorical Imagery: Some Medieval Books and their Posterity*. Princeton, NJ: Princeton University Press.

Tynyanov, I. N., and Eikhenbaum, B. M. (eds) (1985). *Russian Prose*, trans. R. Parrot. Ann Arbor, MI: Ardis.

Valdés, M. J. (1995). 'Paul Ricoeur and literary theory'. In *The Philosophy of Paul Ricoeur*, ed. L. E. Hahn. Chicago and La Salle, IL: Open Court, pp. 259–79.

Valdés, M. J., and Miller, O. (eds) (1985). *Identity and the Literary Text*. Toronto: University of Toronto Press.

Van Den Hengel, J. W. (1982). *The Home of Meaning: the Hermeneutics of the Subject of Paul Ricoeur*. Washington, DC: University Press of America.

Vanhoozer, K. J. (1990). *Biblical Narrative and the Philosophy of Paul Ricoeur*. Cambridge: CUP.

Venuti, L. (ed.) (1992). *Rethinking Translation: Discourse, Subjectivity, Ideology*. London: Routledge.

—— (1995). *The Translator's Invisibility: a History of Translation*. London: Routledge.

Verweyen, T., and Witting, G. (1991). 'The cento: a form of intertextuality from montage to parody'. In *Intertextuality*, ed. H. E. Plett. Berlin and New York: Walter de Gruyter, pp. 165–78.

Vice, S. (1997). 'Bakhtin and Kristeva: grotesque body, abject self'. In *Face to Face: Bakhtin in Russia and the West*, ed. C. Adlam, R. Falconer, V. Makhlin and A. Renfrew. Sheffield: Sheffield Academic Press.

Vinaver, E. (1971). *The Rise of Romance*. Oxford: Clarendon Press.

Von Rad, G. (1968). *The Message of the Prophets*. London: SCM.

Warner, M. (1976). *Alone of all her Sex: the Myth and the Cult of the Virgin Mary*. London: Picador.

Waugh, P. (1984). *Metafiction: the Theory and Practice of Self-Conscious Fiction*. London: Methuen.

Weingart, P., and Stehr, N. (eds) (2000). *Practising Interdisciplinarity*. Toronto: Toronto University Press.

Weisgerber, J. (1970). 'The use of quotations in recent literature'. *Comparative Literature*, 22, pp. 36–45.

West, D., and Woodman, T. (1979). *Creative Imagination and Latin Literature*. Cambridge: CUP.

Westermann, C. (1967). *Basic Forms of Prophetic Speech*. Philadelphia: Westminster.

Whiteside, A., and Issacharoff, M. (eds) (1987). *On Referring in Literature*. Bloomington and Indianapolis: Indiana University Press.

Whitford, M. (1991). *Luce Irigaray: Philosophy in the Feminine*. London: Routledge.

Wiesel, E. (1994). *Célébrations: portraits et légendes*. Paris: Seuil.

Williams, J. G. (1991). *The Bible, Violence and the Sacred*. New York: Harper Collins.

——(ed.) (1996). *The Girard Reader: René Girard*. New York: Crossroad.

Wood, D. (ed.) (1991). *On Paul Ricoeur: Narrative and Interpretation*. London and New York: Routledge.

Worton, M., and Still, J. (eds) (1990). *Intertextuality: Theories and Practices*. Manchester: MUP.

Wright, E. (1984). *Psychoanalytic Criticism: Theory in Practice*. London: Methuen.

Yankelovich, N., Meyrowitz, N., and van Dam, A. (1991). 'Reading and writing the electronic book'. In *Hypermedia and Literary Studies*, ed. P. Delany and G. P. Landow. Cambridge, MA: MIT Press, pp. 53–79.

Ying, H. (2000). *Tales of Translation: Composing the New Woman in China, 1899–1918*. Stanford, CA: Stanford University Press.

Young, F. (1991). 'The Greek fathers'. In *Early Christianity: Origins and Evolution to AD 600*, ed. I. Hazlett. London: SPCK.

Zohar, D. (1991). *The Quantum Self*. London: Flamingo.

Zumthor, P. (1976). 'Le carrefour des rhétoriqueurs: intertextualité et rhétorique'. *Poétique*, 27, pp. 317–37.

Index

Directory of Alternative Terms for 'Intertext', 'Intertextuality'

The following words have been used throughout this book to describe the more precise roles, functions, effects, and previous and more recent forms which 'intertextuality' has embraced. This directory offers not an exhaustive list, but a thesaurus of the many existing vocabularies available to the critic working on 'intertextuality' in its many guises.

abridgement
absolutes
abstraction
abundance
academies/academy
accretion
accumulation
acme
acrostic
actor/actress
acumen
adage
adaptation
addiction
adoption
adversary
advertising
affinity
agency/agent
agenda
aggadah
agglomeration
aide-mémoire

alchemy
Alexandrianism
alienation
alignment
allegory
alliance
allusion
alterity
alternative
amalgam/amalgamation
ambassador
ambiguity
amnesia
amplification
amusement
anachronism
anagram
analogue
analogy
analusis
anaphora
Ancients (and Moderns)
andropology

anecdote
angels
annotation
anomaly
anonymous/anonymity
antagonism/antagonist
antecedent
anthology
anthropomorphism
anticipation
anti-mimesis/anti-
    mimetic
anti-model
antimony
antipathy
antiquarianism
antiquity
antithesis
anxiety (of influence)
aphorism
apocrypha
apologetics
apophthegm

aporia
apotheosis
appearance
apposition
apprentice/
   apprenticeship
appropriateness
appropriation
approximation
aptness
arbitrariness/arbitrary
arbitration
arcania
archaeology
archaism
archetype
architecture
architext(e)
arrangement
art for art's sake
articulation
artifact
artifice
asymmetry
attribute/attribution
audiovisual
augur
aurality
authentication/
   authenticity
authorial intention
authority
autobiography
autotextuality
avant-garde
axiom

babble
Babel
background
backlash
ballad
baroque
belatedness
belief
Bible
bibliographies
big bang
bilingual/bilingualism
binary

biography
blanket term
blason
blasphemy/blasphemous
blind spot
block/blockage/blocking
blueprint
blues
Boolean search
boredom
borrow/borrowing
bowdlerization
braid
brand
bricolage
bridge
burlesque
buzzword
byproduct
Byzantine

cacophony
calligraphy
calque
cameo
camera
camouflage
campus novel
canon
capita rerum
caricature
carnival/carnivalesque
cartel
casuistry
catachresis
catalogue
catchphrase
category
catharsis
cathedral
celebration
censorship
cento
centrifugal
centripetal
ceremonial/ceremony
channel
children's literature
chivalric verse narrative
choreography

chorus
chronicle/chronicler
chronology
chronotope
circulation
circumlocution
circumscribe/circumsc
   ription
citation
clairvoyant
clarification
class(es)
classics
classification
clearinghouse
cliché
clone
closure
cluster
cocktail
coda
code
codex
codicil
cognate
coherence
coinage
collaboration
collage
collation
collection
colonization
combination
comedy
commandment
commemorate
commentary
committed literature
commonplace/
   commonplace books
common sense
comparative
   criticism/literature
comparison
competition/competitor
complexity
composition
comprehension
compromise
conceit

concentration
concentric/concentricity
concordance
condensation
confession
configuration
conflation
conflict
confluence
confrontation
conglomeration
conjointure
consciousness-raising
consensus
construct/constructivism
consumerism
contamination
contemplation
continuity/continuum
contradiction
contrafacture
contrast
contravention
contribution
conundrum
convention/conventions
convergence
copiousness
copula
copy
copying-fidelity
copyright
cornerstone
cornucopia
corollary
corpus
correctio
correlation
correspondence theory
cosmopolitanism
costume
counterbalance
counterculture
counterfeit
counterpoint
counter-position/
     reaction
courier
cratylism
crisis

critical edition
critique
cross-fertilization/
     cross-pollination
crossover
crusade
crypt
crystallization
cultural baggage
cut and paste
cyberfiction
cyborg
cycle
cyclification
cynicism
cypher

daemonization
dance
database
debate
debris
deception
deconstruction
decoration/decorative
defence
deferral
deflation
defraction
degeneration
deletion
delusion
demonic
demystification
denigration
denunciation
derision
dérive
desensitization
destiny
detail
detective fiction
development
diachronic/diachrony
dialect
dialogism
dialogue
Diaspora
dichotomy
dictation

dictionary
didactic/didacticism
différance
difference
diffusion
digitalization
digital media
digression
dilemma
dilution
diplomacy
diptych
disaggregation
disbelief
discernment
disclosure
discomfiture
discontinuity
discourse
discrimination
disengage/
     disengagement
disguise
dislocation
dismantle
disorder/disordering
displacement
dispossession
dissemination
dissimulation
distillation
distinction/
     distinctiveness
distortion
distributio
distribution
divergence
divestment
document
documentary
dogmatism
double
double bind
downgrade
drama
dream
duplicate/duplication
duplicity
dynamic
dystopia/distopian

echo
écriture féminine
edification
elaboration
elect/election
elite/elitism
ellipsis
embedding
emblem
embodiment
émigré
emissary
emphasis
empiricism/empirical
emulate/emulation
enact/enactment
encapsulation
encomium
encyclical
encyclopaedia/
   encyclopaedic
endorsement
enigma
enlargement
enlightenment
enrichment
enterprise
entertain/entertainment
envoy
epic
epigone
epigram
epigraph
epimythium
epiphany
episode/episodic
epitome/epitomize
erasure
eroticism
erudite
esoteric
essay
establishment
estimation/esteem
etiology
etymology
eugenics
evolution
exaggeration
exaltation

example
exception
excerpt
excess
exclusion
excommunication
exegesis
exemplar/exemplification
exemplum
exhaustion
exhibitionism
exhortation
exoticism
expansion
expositio
expositor
extension
extraction

fable
fabrication
facsimile
fairy story/tale
faith
fake
fallacy
falsehood
familiarity
fanatic/fanatical
fantastic tale
fantasy
fashion
fatal flaw
fecund/fecundity
feminist writing
fetish
figure
filigree work
film
filter
flattery
floating signifier
flux
foil
folly/fool
force(s)
forebear/foremother
foreign
foreword
forgery

formalism
formula
founder
fracture
fragment
free indirect speech
fundamentalism
futurism/futuristic

gain
game(s)
gatekeeper
genealogy
generalization
generator
genetic criticism
genetic engineering
genius
genome
géno-texte
genre(s)
genus/genera
geometry
Gesamtkunstwerk
gesture
gestus
ghost-writing
globalism/globalist
gloss
glossary
go-between
gongorism
gothic
graffiti
graft
grammar
gramophone
Grand Narrative/Great
   Tradition
grid
grille
griot
grotesque
guide

halakhah
harbinger
harmonization
hedonism
hegemony

marginalia
marginality/
   marginalization
mashal
mask
masquerade
mass-production
mastery
matrix
maxim
mediation/mediator
medium (channel and
   person)
mélange
melting pot
meme
memorial
memory
merger
message
messenger
meta-commentary
meta-fiction
metaphor
metaphysical poetry
meta-textuality
metonymy
microchip
microcosm
midrash
migration
mime
mimesis
mimicry
miniature
miracle
mirror
mise en abyme
misinterpretation
misogyny
mnemonic
mockery
model
modernism
modification
moebius strip
monolingual(ism)
monolith
monologism
monologue

monstrosity
montage
moral tale
morphology
mosaic
mother tongue
motte (and bailey)
motto
multicultural
multilingual
muses
music
mutation
mystery play
mystery story
mysticism
myth/mythology

narcissism/narcissistic
narrator
nationalism
natural selection
negation
neglect
négritude
neologism
network
newcomer
newscaster/newscasting
newspapers
nexus
nimshal
non-conformity
nonsense verse
norm
novel
novelty
nuance
nucleus
nursery rhyme

objection
obsolescence
obstacle
occlude/occlusion
Oedipal
old-boy networks
omission
open letter
opera

opposition
oracle/oracular
orality/oral heritage
oratory
order/orders
origin
originality
ornament/ornamental
orphan
orthodox/orthodoxy
ossification
outrage
outsider
overdetermination
overlap
overstatement
overturning
overview

painting
palimpsest
palinode
pamphlet
pandemonium
panorama
pantheism
papyri
parable
paradigm
paradigm shift
paradox
parallel
paraphrase
parasite/parasitic
paratextuality
pariah-literary
parody
paronomasia
pars pro toto
particularization
password
pastiche
patent/patenting
patronage
pattern
pejorative
percolate
performance
peripeteia
peristyle

permutation
persecution
perspective
persuasion
petihta
petition
phantasmogoria
phéno-texte
photography
physiologus
picaresque
pithiness
plagiarism
pleasure principle
plethora
plunder
poetics
poetry
polarization
polemic
political allegory
polyphonic/polyphony
popular culture
pornography
portmanteau
postcolonial criticism
postmodernism
powerbook
prayer
precedent
precision
precursor
predestination
preface
prefiguration
prefix
prejudice
pressure point
prestidigitation
probability
proclamation
production/productivity
proem
prohibition
proliferation
prologomena
prologue
pronouncement
propaganda
propagation

property
prophecy
prophet/prophetic
proportion
prose
prose poem
prosody
protest
prototype
proverb
provisional
provocation
pseudonymy
psychedelia
psychoanalytic/
    psychoanalysis
pulsation
puns
purge
purloining
puzzle
pyrotechnics

quest
quilting
quotation

radio
ramification
rationalism
reactivation
reader (as text)
reader response
ready-made
reagent
realist novel
reappraisal
rebellion
rebuke
rebuttal
recapitulation
receptacle
reception
recipe
reciprocal/reciprocity
recitation
recognition
recontextualization
recuperation
recycling

redefinition
redemption
redeployment
reduction
redundancy
reference
refiguration
refinement
reflexivity
reformation
refutation
regeneration
regurgitation
reincarnation
reinstatement
reinvention
reinvestment
reiteration
rejection
rejuvenation
relabel
relativism
relevance
relief
religion
remainder
remembrance
reminiscence
renaissance
renewable energy
renewal
renovation
repackaging
repetition
replacement
replica
replication
replicator
reporting
repository
representation
reprise
reproduction
repulsion
reputation
resemblance
response
restitution
restoration
resume

retrospection
revelation
revenge
reverberation
reversal
revision
revivification
revolution
rhapsody
rhetoric
riddle
ritual
rival
roman à thèse
romance
romantic(s)
running thread
rupture

salons
salvation
sampler
sampling (music)
sarcasm
satire
saw
saying
scandal
scanner
scapegoat
schism
science(s)
scribbling
scribe
scroll
scrolling
search
search engine
secondary orality
sediment/sedimentation
seer
self-criticism
self-fulfilling prophecy
self-quotation
semblance
semiotics
sequel
sequence
serendipity
serial/serialization

series
sexism
shadowland
shaman
shock
shorthand
sign
signature
signpost
simile
simplicity
simulacrum
singularity
slang/rhyming slang
slogan
soap opera
song
soothsayer
sophistication
sophistry
sound byte
source
source-hunting
span
specialization
species
spectator
speculation
speculum
speech
speech marks
spin
spokesman/
  spokesperson
springboard
stagnation
stalking horse
standardization
stasis
stenography
stereotype
stigma/stigmatize
stimulus/stimuli
stock (plot, character,
  image)
story/storytelling
structuralism/
  structuralist
stylization
subdivide/subdivision

sublimation
sublime
subordination
sub-plot
subset
subsidiary
substitution
subsume
subversion
successor
summa
superfluity
superimposition
superlative
supernatural
superstition
supplement
suppression
surfer/surfing
surprise
surrealism/surrealist
surrogate
survey
syllepsis
symbol
symmetry
synaesthesia
synchronic
syncretism
synecdoche
synergy
synonym
synopsis
synthesis

taboo
tag
talking cure
talking head
tangent/tangential
tape
target text
tautology
taxonomy
teachings
technology
telephone/telephonic
television/televisual
template
tendon

testimony
text-messaging
thanksgiving
theatre
theme park
threshold
thriller
tissue
title
token/tokenism
touchstone
trace
tracts
tradition
tragedy
transcendental signifier
transference
transfiguration
transformation
transition
translation
transliteration
transmission
transplantation/
    transplanting

transposition
transtextuality
transubstantiation
travel
travelogue
travesty
treatise
trick/trickster
trilogy
trivia/trivial
trope
tunes
turning point
types

umbrella concept
unconscious
undercurrent
unity
universal
unmask
Ursprache
utilitarian
utopia/utopian
utterance

variant/variation
vector
vehicle
verbatim
verisimilitude
vernacular
version
versioning
vicious circle
virtual reality
virtuoso/virtuosity
vision
visionary
voice
voice off
voice over
vortex

weaving
window
wisdom literature
wit
worldwide web
writing

xia/nüxia